Egalitarianism of the Free Society
and the end of class conflict

This is **Robert Corfe's** introductory volume to his 3-volume work, *Social Capitalism in Theory and Practice*. It sets out to examine in detail the sociological aspects of some of the most urgent questions of our time, viz., the problem of maintaining high culture in an egalitarian society; the psychological nature of property as being essential to the freedom of the individual and the community; the misconceptions and difficulties in establishing a truly democratic society; and the epistemological problems in discussing political science and the role for a New Idealism. The book which is written with crystal clarity, in appealing to the general reader as well as the student of politics, presents an exciting and entirely new way of looking at social issues which cuts through all the ideological dross which has dominated thinking for so long a period. The author brings exceptional qualifications to this introductory study of Social Capitalism, for not only has he been a life-long student of the social sciences, but for many years was a senior executive in manufacturing industry, as well as an activist in political life on both the local and national levels.

By the same author –

Freedom From America
for safeguarding democracy & the economic & cultural integrity of
peoples

Populism Against Progress
and the collapse of aspirational values

Deism & Social Ethics
the role of religion in the third millennium

Social Capitalism in theory and practice

Vol. 1
Emergence of the New Majority

Vol. 2
The People's Capitalism

Vol. 3
Prosperity in a stable world

Egalitarianism of the Free Society

and the end of class conflict

Robert Corfe

Arena Books

First published in 2008 by Arena Books *

Arena Books
6 Southgate Green
Bury St. Edmunds
IP33 2BL

www.arenabooks.co.uk

Corfe, Robert
Egalitarianism of the Free Society and the end of class conflict
1. Equality – Great Britain 2. Liberty 3. Capitalism – Social aspects
- Great Britain 4. Democracy – Great Britain 5. Property – Social aspects
- Great Britain 6. Great Britain – Social conditions – 21st century 7. Great
Britain – Politics and government – 1997-
I. Title
305'.0941

ISBN 078-0-9556055-2-9

BIC categories:- HPGM1, JBMC, JPV

Printed and bound by Lightning Source UK

Cover design
by Jon Baxter

Typeset in
Times New Roman

PREFACE

The reforming politics of the future may only be promoted effectively through the philosophy and practice of Social Capitalism. The latter must formulate a vision for a better world which not only seeks to capture the imagination of those committed to reforming politics, but of more importance, seeks to capture a broader support from the mass of the population across cultural and class divides.

But if Social Capitalism is to be truly convincing and win great numbers of people to its cause as lifelong supporters, it must be based on theoretical foundations which are both attractive and irrefutable. The public are sickened by spin-doctoring and public relations exercises, not merely because they are insulting to their intelligence, but because it is a form of trickery or deceitful manipulation. It is a return to principles which is really needed, for only then can activists (and indeed passive supporters) commit their full sincerity to the cause.

If a political movement is honest with itself, it has no need for guile in its relationship with the public, for straight talking and candid attitudes will eventually ensure trust, support, and finally respect. But no movement can be honest with itself unless it is based in firm theoretical foundations which serve as a dialectic for its growth and direction. The trouble today with the parliamentary parties of the left, is that they are without clearly identifiable belief systems. The vacuity of the "Third way" was always empty rhetoric. The problem of the present Labour party, for example, is two-fold: firstly, it needs to maintain the support of Labour party activists (many of whom still describe themselves as Old Socialists); and secondly, it must continue to maintain the support of so-called "middle England" to remain electable.

The solution, therefore, is to bridge this gap. The Labour party leadership is reluctant to initiate a philosophy for Social Capitalism, possibly because of fear of offending either or both opposing wings for potential support; or possibly because the leadership is too near the field of day-to-day action for the more distant perspective needed in formulating a more holistic view. The present book sets out to bridge this gap. What is clear is the *need* for Social Capitalism if reforming politics is to have any meaning in the future, or to extend its constituency over a much broader spectrum of our population. The call for "Old Socialism" of those on the far left is a recipe for failure.

It is also reactionary and denotes a breakdown of imagination in facing the challenges of the future. The Old Socialists fail to appreciate the huge changes in the transformation of society over the past sixty years, and the sociological consequences of this. They remain backward looking and sentimental rather than forward looking and progressive.

A classless society is essential to any form of Social Capitalism, and such a society needs clear definition. The opening chapters of the present book discusses egalitarianism *vis-à-vis* the values of culture. A truly integrated and classless society can only be achieved by appealing to the goodwill of men and women across the class divides. The ideals of Social Capitalism must form the focal point for such unity.

Old Socialism or Marxism, by contrast, was dependent on promoting class war, and for several generations during epochs when workers were denied rights and extreme poverty divided them from the bourgeoisie, it was a useful tool used with full justification. But in the contemporary world the entire sociology of society has been transformed, and class war has become no less unacceptable to those earning less than the average wage than to those earning above the average wage. Those trying to promote class war in the workplace today are dismissed by their colleagues with disgust as aberrant or eccentric. Their efforts are often counter-productive, and during the Thatcher years, huge numbers of working class people were pushed into the Tory party by what was seen as the unacceptability of Skargillism or Old Socialist thinking and strategy.

Furthermore, the call to class war contributes to class entrenchment (which of course is intentional) rather than to the abolition of the class divide. This is another reason why ordinary working people resent the call to class struggle: i.e. increasingly over the past decades they see the reality of greater economic egalitarianism, and the vision of a classless society emerging as an inevitable consequence. When they anticipate their easy emergence into the middle-middle majority, and the seeming improvement in their social status which this brings, they are filled with repugnance when Old Socialist stalwarts urge on them the necessity of remembering their "class roots" and the need for loyalty to proletarian values.

They feel an attempt is being made to drag them down, and their natural response is to distance themselves even more from the labour movement. This, of course, is the major explanation for the total collapse of attendance figures at monthly Labour party meetings throughout the country over the past three decades - particularly in industrial areas. I have attended a number of meetings in different parts of the country, where fifteen to twenty persons were present, to be told that twenty years before, a hundred or two hundred members would regularly attend. The *only* explanation for such a factor is not that members are failing the Labour party, but that the Labour party is failing its members.

If reforming politics is to be made more widely acceptable amongst *all* sectors of the population, then it must seek to be more all-inclusive. It must appeal to the higher reason and goodwill of all men and women, irrespective of their background, and not to their lower instincts or selfish or vicious feelings. Hence, class consciousness must be *out*, not merely as something which is disreputable, but as something which is irrelevant in solving substantive issues, and the business of politics should be concerned solely with the problem-solving of socio-economic questions from a disinterested standpoint.

Of course problems need to be settled between different sectors of the population, but such sectors are no longer necessarily class-based or economic, but rather based on such divisions which are purely occupational, or structural, in terms of re-allocating resources. For example, the fuel crisis initiated by demonstrators against high taxes on petrol and diesel in September 2000, evoked strange and conflicting responses at the TUC Conference held during the same period. Arguments were put pro and contra, but those interpretations attempted by those on the far left to give the issue a class-based slant failed entirely, as the discussion slid into a maze of contradictory and inane accusations about "present demonstrators" being those who would have "crossed the picket lines of the miners twenty years ago." Class issues can no longer stand up as political issues!

In resolving problems amicably in society, classlessness contributes towards this purpose. Class consciousness, on the other hand, because it is exclusive and inward-looking, or nurtures resentment or selfish aims, makes for conflict in society through arousing all kinds of suspicion and misunderstanding and quarrels, which when examined in the cool light of day, are often found to be spurious.

Classlessness is therefore the opposite of class consciousness. That is, the latter promotes attitudes which *prevent* the emergence of the classless society. It must be the primary purpose of Social

Capitalism to create a classless society by the most practicable means, and a priority must therefore be put on outlawing class discrimination in any form or guise in the same way that racial or gender discrimination is already outlawed. By outlawing class discrimination as socially unacceptable, two purposes would be achieved: firstly, an easier facilitation between differing groups in discussing and settling their differences; and secondly, the gradual integration of all groups towards the status of classlessness. By outlawing class discrimination it is not intended that class issues should be eschewed. Class differences, on the contrary, in all their aspects, should be discussed in greater depth and openness by Social Capitalists than they have at any time been discussed by those in radical politics before.

There has to be an honesty in discussing *cultural* differences between the class divides no less than in the discussion of the economic differences, for it is in the first that most of the visible and irritating divisions are found in causing dislike and conflict between different groups and individuals. In the past the discussion of sensitive (or cultural) class differences have tended to be regarded as tasteless, if not a taboo topic. In the future this can no longer be the case, for if a classless society is to be really achieved, all differences must be discussed in preparation for new modes of behaviour and manners in enabling social ease and freer communication amongst varying sectors of the population. Even the promotion of humour and satire on social foibles and class attitudes are justifiable tools towards a greater understanding of the differences in society - however painful these may be in the shorter term. It is Social Capitalists who must be in the forefront of this discussion in the conscious and intelligent struggle for the achievement of a classless society.

In outlawing class discrimination, there would be this difference between that and legislation against racial or gender discrimination: for whilst the first would openly encourage the discussion of differences, perceived and otherwise; the latter unhappily, are only concerned with the suppression of open debate, and consequently, racial and gender issues are swept under the carpet and feed a simmering discontent in the hearts of many. That is, legislation against racial or gender discrimination lays too much emphasis on the careless insult or the isolated act of injustice, and too little attention on changing the attitudes of men and women to a better frame of mind.

Legislation against class discrimination, on the other hand, should be made more in the recognition of the need for a two-way understanding in interconnecting conflicting cultural forms. That is, in a conflict situation both sides should be perceived as having potential rights and wrongs, out of which suitable mediation should settle their differences with complete satisfaction. Therefore, whilst mediation in cases of class discrimination would always be assumed to be between equals in the last resort; racial or gender discrimination nearly always assumes the fault of a dominating party, i.e., either that of a Caucasian or a male. In this light it may therefore be seen that class differences are more easily and better resolved than those concerned with race or gender.

Nonetheless, in creating a classless and more egalitarian society, class discrimination in terms of the insulting epithet or reference should be made no less unacceptable and no less punishable than racial or gender discrimination in similar circumstances. After all, there are greater numbers of people liable to insult or discrimination on account of their class status than there are those belonging to minority racial groups or a particular gender. Furthermore, the cultural manifestations of class status (which are usually the subject of the spontaneous insult) are hardly less difficult to change from one day to the next than are racial or gender characteristics. All that Social Capitalism advocates is a code of good manners amongst all kinds of people, irrespective of their differences, in ensuring easy and free communication of feelings and ideas.

In summary: whilst Socialism in the old conditions promoted class war as a tool for resolving the eventual victory of a dominant proletariat; Social Capitalism in the new conditions promotes the integration of all sectors of the population into a new class known as the Responsible society. It is aptly named the Responsible society, since it is the purpose of Social Capitalism to disseminate power in terms of both management and wealth to the mass of the population in accordance with the needs of social justice and the demands of a highly technological world.

The present book is concerned with a number of issues which lie at the foundations of Social Capitalism. Part I covers the question of culture and egalitarianism, an issue of immense concern to those who fear the consequences of populism. Part II discusses questions of property and the vital importance of its ownership and control by the individual in the development of the personality, and how property issues need to be resolved in creating a fair society. Part III defines democracy in its various forms and how these may be related to a free and egalitarian Social Capitalist society.   Part IV outlines the epistemology of Social Capitalism, i.e. the methodology or dialectic to be employed in ascertaining the truth of opinions. The reasons for the sterility of modern politics are elaborated in some depth, and the primacy of Ideas are identified as the way ahead for a constructive future.

Robert Corfe
February 2008

Contents

CONTENTS

CONTENTS

CONTENTS

CONTENTS

CHAPTER 17
Domination as Possession

PART III

DEMOCRACY: REAL AND ILLUSORY

CHAPTER 18
The Erosion of Freedom

CHAPTER 19
When Old Prejudices Seem Vindicated

CONTENTS

CHAPTER 23
Democratic Society As a Realisation

1 - Economic egalitarianism cannot be equated with social egalitarianism   2 - The class divide is widening   3 - As representative democracy has failed as an agency for social reform other roads to social freedom must be sought   4 - The value of objectivity in unifying society   5 - When representative government is used as an instrument for social oppression   6 - Continental thought giving rise to the idea of the classless society

CHAPTER 24
Democracy For Tomorrow

1 - Britain cannot survive in a vacuum   2 - The challenge must be met   3 - The democratisation of society is the road to its modernisation   4 - Bankruptcy of the confrontational party system   5 - Imperative need for Socialist radical centrism   6 - Problems of centre parties   7 - Failure of the SDP Liberal Alliance   8 - The vice of political "professionalism"   9 - How it became a vested interest party   10 - Actions not words must be the criterion of a party   11 - Hope for a merging or withering away of parties   12 - Representation through pure political power   13 - As a step towards the achievement of direct democracy

PART IV

THE ROAD TO CONSTRUCTIVE POLITICS

CHAPTER 25
The Unseen Real Issues of Politics

1 - Failure of modern politics to solve substantive issues   2 - Government policies fail to reflect underlying causes of ills   3 - Examples of superficial problems perceived as underlying ills   4 - Demonstration of the false perception of these issues   5 - Deceit behind such false perceptions   6 - Public acceptance and hardening of these false views   7 - This compounded by anxiety of self-justifying to others   8 - Consequently, the truth in political discussion and thought is poisoned   9 - Hence the intellectual paralysis of political life

CHAPTER 26
The Causes For Our Intellectual Disability

1 - Our problems may be blamed on an intellectual disability   2 - The poverty of new ideas   3 - Comparison with the political creativity of the 19th century   4 - The eight causes for our intellectual paralysis   5 - I: The polarisation of political

CONTENTS

CONTENTS

CONTENTS

PART I

Culture and Egalitarianism

"Culture is a bed-rock, the final wall, against which one leans one's back in a god-forsaken chaos."

J. C. Powys, *The Meaning of Culture*, p. 262.

C ulture not only creates the ambience of a society but marks its external appearance, and of most significance, it reflects the attitudes of a people. Mainstream culture describes the ideals of a people, and in this context, it is how a nation would like to see itself.

The following chapters are not primarily concerned with a description of how a Social Capitalist society might emerge in the future. They are instead concerned with the apparent problems of reconciling high culture and egalitarianism in a Social Capitalist society. In the eyes of many the two are irreconcilable, and as will be shown in the opening chapter, there are leading intellectuals who view the advance of democratic socialisation with horror as the frontier leading into an age of barbarism. Old Socialism or Marxism, of course, had its own concept of culture, viz., proletarianism and Socialist Realism as a universal standard for behaviour, art, and thinking in all situations. It is not exactly an ideologically imposed proletarianism which is feared today, so much as a general dumbing down and lowering of standards in the wake of populism.

Some three years after the political victory of 1997, New Labour and Tony Blair were viciously attacked by an eminent novelist as threats to the "idea of civilisation" and as the holder of the "black flag ... the skull and crossbones." At the time I dismissed such an accusation as wild and falsely founded, but with the passing of the years, I now have to admit that I was wrong and the novelist entirely correct in his predictions.

Social Capitalism which is formulated in the light of changing social realities appreciates people as they actually *are*, as opposed to how old-fashioned ideologues would like to view them. That is, a free society is necessarily a fluid society of the upwardly aspiring, and egalitarianism is consequently re-defined in terms of that majority occupying a middle margin within the structure of the community. Classlessness is based on upward and downward fluidity based on merit, but unhurtful to those who lose out in the higher stakes of their ambitions, since minimum material standards are generous, whilst the most affluent are not perceived as exploiting or oppressing those beneath them. The values of such a society, of course, are based on universal educational standards very much higher than those of the present day, where differences of merit or ability are appreciated as natural and inevitable, and so give no rise to envy or conflict.

Such a society is the natural outcome of human will. As will be shown in the opening chapters, class betrayal is the natural behaviour of groups as soon as they reach a certain level of material success relative to those above them. Working class people are no less inclined to class "treason" than are those of the middle or upper-middle classes. This presented Socialists with a terrible dilemma, which doctrinally they were unable to overcome. If class solidarity and class consciousness could not be maintained, what then? Social Capitalism, in recognising this sociological reality, glorifies in the fact! If class loyalties cannot be maintained, then an end to all the old classes! This is the only gateway to the emergence of true classlessness. It is the beginning of what we have described as the Responsible society.

We show in the following chapters that Social Capitalism, far from debasing culture, will on the contrary promote culture, and witness a greater appreciation of culture than in any previous era. Furthermore, culture will be allowed to flourish in a psychologically more healthy environment. This is because as snobbery becomes socially unacceptable as class associations with certain cultural forms fall away, culture will be appreciated in all its purity for its substantive value, and not according to peripheral factors or as mere social events in the calendar.

Nevertheless, there are real threats to high culture in the future and these are examined in some depth in the following six chapters. These threats have nothing to do with the existence of established forms of popular culture. They stem, on the contrary, from a form of vulgar *populism*, and more specifically, from a money-oriented value system and mode of marketing imported from across the North Atlantic. The culture of America (if this is not a contradiction in terms) entails a wave of barbarism threatening to engulf the world. It is because of the enormity of this threat that so much space is given over to the problem of American cultural domination. The question is of vital concern to ourselves (as well as others) for the reason that efforts to raise cultural and educational standards are countered by the constant onslaught of the American mass media which essentially is anti-culture.

The following chapters will convey the impression that American culture is used as a metaphor for everything which threatens to undermine cultural standards in this country (and worldwide) in the struggle to create a classless and democratic society with high aspirations for the future. This is partly true. Having to write the following chapters was not an enjoyable task for it was not my wish to present a diatribe against America, but the facts were too true to be avoided, and there is something very wrong with a value system which allows price to poison the springs of creativity. I believe, nonetheless, that many well-intentioned Americans will appreciate the arguments laid out in the chapters below

America is a country which has both the best and worst in abundance. In science and inventiveness she is unsurpassed and cannot but deserve our respect. Her people are generous, and she has much of the finest high culture to be found anywhere in the world, even though this may not be evident to many. To take one branch of culture, music, and to take a small sector of that, viz., singers of outstanding international merit of serious music, the following may be listed as amongst the greatest of the 20th century: Clarence Whitehill; Geraldine Farrar; Rosa Ponselle; Jan Peerce; Lawrence Tibbett; Leonard Warren; Richard Tucker; Robert Merrill; Risë Stevens; Leontyne Price; Marilyn Horne; James King; Beverly Sills; Cathy Berberian; Anna Moffo; Jess Thomas; James McCracken; Barbara Hendricks; Thomas Hampson; Grace Bumbry; Kathleen Battle; Arleen Augér; Marion Anderson; Samuel Ramey; Neil Schicoff; Sylvia McNair; Jessye Norman; and Sherrill Milnes. A number of other deserving names may doubtless be added to the above list

The above may not be household names, but as recorded voices they will live forever, and in a better future age of high culture, they will be heard and respected long after their pop-singing better-known contemporaries have been consigned to oblivion. And when America comes into its own, it will recognise the genius of its past, and the value of a high culture which was buried under a midden of obscene commercialism.

CHAPTER 1
Culture Versus Populism

"The great law of culture is: let each become all that he was created capable of being."

Thomas Carlyle, *Essays: J.P.F. Richter.*

1 – Fear of democratic socialisation undermining cultural standards

There is a fear amongst many people in both this country and abroad that democratic socialisation is a threat to high culture, and heralds a general lowering of standards as culture is understood in its best and broadest meaning. This fear is perhaps best reflected in the statement of Santayana when he wrote that, "Culture is on the horns of this dilemma: if profound and noble it must remain rare, if common it must become mean."[1] It is thereby implied that socialism reduces everything to the "common" norm.

This fear was recently highlighted by V. S. Naipaul in a bitter attack on what was alleged as the "Cultural vandalism" of Tony Blair's Labour government, and in this he was joined several days later, with equally vituperative remarks by Doris Lessing. In turning exactly to what Naipaul said in his now notorious interview with Geordie Greig,[2] it is difficult to avoid the first impression that his outburst was the result of unfair prejudice. He exclaimed, "Everyday, you hear on the radio some (government) minister ... saying something about things no longer being for the privileged few. This, of course, has destroyed the idea of civilisation in this country. It began with a long process of reform, active socialist legislation. We

---

[1] George Santayana, *The Life of Reason*, ii, iii.

[2] *The Daily Telegraph*, 11th July 2000.

now have a full socialist revolution and the bizarre thing is that it does not mean high culture becomes available to everybody." What does he mean here? In his second sentence, he seems to clearly imply that the "idea of civilisation" is "destroyed" when culture is passed onto the many, but in the last sentence one is led to understand his regret that high culture is not "available to everybody."

2 – The blame of plebeianism

He continues his indignant attack with the condemnation of our "terrible" plebeian culture, "an aggressively plebeian culture that celebrates itself for being plebeian; and he concludes by saying, "There are still people chattering about the need to bring the elites down, long after the elites have been destroyed. It is not only Blair. He comes at the end of a period of destruction going back fifty years. But yes ... he is in command now, holder of the black flag, the skull and crossbones." This emotional outburst is not quoted simply because they are the words of an eminent novelist, but because they reflect ideas so commonly overheard in many circles where the arts and culture are discussed.

But what is really the crux of Naipaul's argument? What does he mean by a "period of destruction going back fifty years," when Tory governments were in power for more than two thirds of that time? Does he blame Labour only whilst exempting Tory governments from any share in the blame for the alleged undermining of standards? And anyway, what exactly does he mean by the reduction of standards to plebeian levels? Those were my feelings, and that was my intellectual response, shortly after the publication of Naipaul's comments. Irrespective of the underlying rightness or wrongness of his remarks, they remained tasteless and tactless, and for those reasons I presented a critical response. Time, however, has proved me wrong, and I now have to acknowledge in hindsight that the warning words did convey something of the incisive prophet.

3 – Threats to culture but not from democratic socialisation

The discussion of cultural values in a society is always a dangerous topic. This is, firstly, because they always excite high emotions, and secondly, because they so often generate much nonsense and muddled thinking. The political criminal who once exclaimed, "When I hear the word culture, I reach for my revolver,"[3] may in this instance have spoken with a certain profundity, in expressing impatience with the woolly arguments used for supporting the cultural values in his particular regime, but it is an exclamation, the validity of which, may equally be applied in many other situations in other societies. The same sentiment was rather more nicely put by the architect and town planner, Lord Esher, on exclaiming, "When politicians and civil servants hear the word 'Culture' they feel for their blue pencils."

The question of culture is nonetheless important, for all the dangers it poses as a topic of controversy, if only because of the allegations made above. There are threats to the cultural values of this country and to most countries of the world. That is true! But it is most unlikely that those threats stem solely from the growth of democratic socialisation.

It is necessary at this point to identify those false perceptions which have led to the idea that the radical left is responsible for debasing cultural values. This is due to the mistaken impression that the contemporary parties of the left, in advanced industrial economies, represent a vast underclass, or proletariat, with its own values and pursuits, which must be made the model for the culture of the future. The impression is therefore created that governments of the left must somehow defer to popular taste, with the result of dragging down the more educated or privileged echelons of society to a lower level, in achieving a greater egalitarianism. This reflects both an unrealistic picture of the present structure of society, and a twisted view of what enlightened governments of the left have been out to achieve.

4 – The threat to taste from mass production

Before attempting to describe the cultural values of Social Capitalism, let us first dissipate the anxieties of those concerned aesthetes of the world, by identifying what are really the threats to cultural standards. These may be brought under four separate headings, and there is a certain overlapping amongst each of the categories.

The first stems from the mass production of design resulting from the outcome of the industrial revolution. This aspect of the lowering

---

[3] The outburst, "Wenn ich Kultur höre ... entsichere ich meinen Browning," derives originally probably from Hanns Johst's 1933 play, *Schlageter*, Act I, Sc. I.

of cultural standards is predominantly seen as a historical factor. It was something which obsessed the minds of the Victorians and reams were written by such thinkers as Carlyle, Ruskin, and William Morris on the desecration or cheapening of taste by the factory methods of the time. In retrospect, however, many of their conclusions today would be seen as highly subjective. Nevertheless, their conclusions were powerful and enduring, and even up until the immediate post-War period, much Victorian building, furniture, and other artefacts, were often judged as absurd, vulgar, tasteless, or of little value.

The vandalism of the 1960s in destroying much of our Victorian heritage would not have been possible without the residue of these attitudes. There has since been a transformation in our perception of the arts and artefacts of the Victorian era. I can still remember the cut-off point when Regency furniture was appreciated for its elegance and simplicity of design, and was antique and hence valuable; whilst Victorian furniture (from the 1830s onwards) was judged over-decorative and pretentious, and so only fit for the scrap yard. Such early Victorian furniture today would, of course, bring very high prices in any sale room. Meanwhile, there are many Victorian artefacts, which although the products of the factory system, would today be judged of great beauty and unique craftsmanship, and cabinet making, a craft of great skill with a long tradition, has now been all but lost to the world. Pre-Raphaelite painting, on the other hand, as a re-discovered art form, is one of the few things which may be said to link up the mind of its contemporary appreciators with that of the high cultural taste of our Victorian forefathers.

Nevertheless, Victorian critics, living at the start of the new industrial age, were right in propounding a principle that mass production must ultimately cheapen taste, and lower standards as to the sense of beauty to things around the home and elsewhere. Today we are forced to live in a society of mass production, but higher educational standards and a greater consciousness of design, has allowed us to escape some of the pitfalls which afflicted many in previous generations. For example, it is no longer necessary (or excusable) that any of us should decorate our homes with mass produced ornaments or cheap prints on our walls. We can instead buy original artefacts from potters or craftsmen, or paintings from Summer exhibitions in place of shoddy reproductions. Although the Victorian era did produce a great deal of ugliness, it should be remembered, that it was a prominent socialist, viz. William Morris, who was in the forefront of fighting against the ugliness of mass production with his return to the ideals of craftsmanship and natural beauty and colour which should be made available to us all.

5 – The threat of proletarian cultural values

The second threat to higher standards stems from the proletarianisation of cultural values. Again, this may be seen as a historical factor, and not really applicable in Western Europe. The imposition of overtly proletarian standards in the Communist East bloc countries wreaked havoc in their respective countries. This was brought about, firstly, unintentionally through the incapacity of the system to develop markets, with the result of standardising products in societies with very limited choice; and secondly, through ensuring that all standards adhered to the perceived values of Socialism. Hence clothing was drab, ill-fitting and badly made - if not comprising an actual uniform - whilst almost all manufactured products were well below the norm of those acceptable in any Western country.

The most notorious example of the imposition of Socialist values was during the Cultural Revolution in China (1966-1976), during one phase of which a conscious attempt was made to destroy the cultural traditions of ancient China on the grounds of their irrelevance to the future. Huge numbers of artefacts of irreplaceable value were destroyed forever. Everywhere in the East bloc the imposition of so-called socialist values entailed not only the distorted re-writing of history, but the enforcing of literature and the visual arts into the straitjacket of Socialist Realism. In this way artistic values were usually sacrificed in the cause of didacticism and insincerity.

6 – The threat of populism

The third threat to cultural standards stems from simplistic cultural forms, or dumbing down, or populism, as a mode of bringing higher forms of culture more easily within the reach of the masses. When this is applied to artefacts it is usually referred to as *Kitsch*, e.g., the kind of products usually found in any tourist shop, which the careless buy for friends to decorate their mantelpieces or set behind glass fronted cabinets. In the sphere of the film or the TV drama, it usually refers to adapting an old classic into a "costume drama" suited to the mentality of a contemporary audience but bearing little resemblance to the original. In the sphere of music, literature, or the other arts, it usually refers to the poor imitation of greater models for the consumption of a wider audience.

7 – The threat of Americanisation

The fourth and final threat to cultural standards stems from the Americanisation of life, or more specifically, the reduction of cultural standards to the principles of marketing, or that price should become the criterion for cultural value. The term the *Americanisation of life* is justified on the grounds that north America presents a threat to cultural standards worldwide on so many fronts, and because American cultural values are quite different from those of any other country on earth. Radio broadcasting matching the level of the BBC, for example, would be impossible in America. This is because commercial pressures are allowed to depress standards to the lowest common denominator. In Britain, fortunately, at least until the present point in time, the ideals of the British Broadcasting Corporation have been allowed to predominate over other factors, and consequently, British radio is highly appreciated throughout the four corners of the globe.

8 – The higher aspirations of the middle-middle majority

Having listed briefly the four real sources of danger to culture everywhere, we shall demonstrate clearly in these opening chapters, that not only will Social Capitalism bring high culture to a greater fruition than in any previous epoch of history, but that high culture will be appreciated with a greater understanding or sincerity than ever heretofore. This may sound a rash claim, but it may only be appreciated by comprehending exactly what is meant by a Social Capitalist society. Social Capitalism means the ascension to power of the upward aspiring middle-middle majority. As explained elsewhere,[4] Social Capitalism has developed as an inevitable consequence in the wake of the complete transformation of society and the sociology of work over the past fifty years.

---

[4] See chapters 7 & 11 of *Reinventing Democratic Socialism.*

The perception of egalitarianism, too, has changed in the wake of this development. Up until the first half of the 20th century socialism was a distinctly proletarian movement. That is, its activities for reform were class-based, and concentrated on a huge cloth-capped proletariat employed in the mines, huge factories, and low-paid manual public sector occupations. The transformation in the world of work due to information technology; the huge demand on brainpower; and the unprecedented expanse of higher education, have changed relationships in the workplace. In addition to this, not only have living standards changed out of all comparison with the pre-War period, but house ownership, and new patterns of leisure, have generated an individualism and sense of responsibility which is at odds with the collectivism of the past.

9 – Their betrayal of proletarian values

An egalitarianism which appeals to those "at the bottom of the pile" no longer has any pull in political electioneering. The worker of the 1930s, or even the 1960s, may have felt himself at the bottom of the pile in a pyramid formed society, but such a society no longer exists. Today we have an egg-shaped society, and the great majority are the new middle-middle class, most of whom once formed the proletariat. The improvement in the living conditions of the majority did not simply entail a change in material well-being. Something far more profound occurred. There came a point in time (due to education, increasing personal responsibilities, etc.) When the proletariat repudiated its past in adopting middle class values.

As far as Old Labour was concerned, this was the point when the working class forgot its origins and betrayed its proletarian past. The victory had been won, but the workers forgot their debt to the labour movement which had fought so hard and so long on their behalf. This was sad indeed! It was ingratitude on a staggering scale. But history had witnessed a similar episode of class betrayal during an earlier epoch. Some hundreds of years before when the emerging middle class found themselves in conflict with a more powerful ruling elite, they too, formulated their own set of values, in strengthening their class values. These were centred around the Protestant work ethic and different forms of religious dissent. As soon, however, as their material status or wealth began to match that of those on a higher social plain, they sought to identify with and absorb themselves with the landed gentry. This, too, was class betrayal!

10 – As human nature aspires towards self-improvement each class eventually betrays its origins

The conclusion to be drawn from these observations is that militant class consciousness is useful during periods of class conflict, but is unattractive as soon as an underclass approaches the economic level of those above, when it imitates, courts the alliance of, and seeks absorption within a higher level of society. As that point is reached, militant class consciousness mutates into snobbish class consciousness, i.e. there is a reversal of attitude from resenting the oppression of those above to despising those below. As an older middle class once pushed itself into a former upper class, so today an older working class has pushed itself into the middle class.

In the same way that a parvenu gentry once turned its back on its middle class origins (as reflected in innumerable English and French novels of the 18th and 19th centuries), so today the new middle-middle majority repudiates the values of its working class forebears. In our time this is expressed through the aggressiveness of Essex man (or woman), and the new membership pattern of the Tory party with its strong ex-working class Thatcherite-like support - even though the Tory party does not really represent the real interests of this emergent sector of the population. But the support of the Tory party by this new middle-middle majority is not so much because of the economic interests represented, but because at last they "have arrived," and wish to distance themselves from what they see as the Socialism of an "underclass."

The decline of trades unionism in manufacturing enterprises, especially in smaller and medium sized companies, is partly explicable on the same grounds. Many factory employees (they often resent the title "workers") feel sickened by what they interpret as the "demeaning" environment of trades unionism, with the call to fight for "rights" of one kind or another, and consequently, they refuse to attend union meetings. Again, trades unionism may have much to offer these and other workers, but it is the style of its message which the new majority find so off-putting.

11 – Class "treason" and the fear of levelling down

The explanation for this class "treason," irrespective of wherever or whenever it is found, is that it is a natural human trait to look upwards for inspiration with regard to the direction of progress. This is the normal attitude of any human being at peace with himself and the world. During episodes of intense struggle, on the other hand, there is class entrenchment. Therefore when Old Socialism enjoyed its full flower, the proletariat was the focus point for political conflict, and egalitarianism meant that all standards should not be *reduced* to proletarian demands, but made to *adhere* to the demands of the working class. Those belonging to the higher levels of society, however, could only interpret this call to egalitarianism as a "levelling down of standards." This false perception arose through the natural fear that the middle and upper classes would somehow be forced to lower their cultural standards to a specified level dictated by the ideology of a socialist regime.

12 – Change in the perception of egalitarianism

Today such a fear need no longer exist. This is because the concept of egalitarianism has changed. In a society which trumpets that its first three priorities are, "Education, education, education," it is inconceivable that government should want a diminution of standards in any sphere of life. Of more significance, however, is the fact that the focus point of Social Capitalism is not a proletariat at the bottom of the pile, but the competitive, individualistic middle-middle majority, constantly concerned with improving its educational lot in keeping a foothold on the employment ladder. Whilst proletarian egalitarianism was passive in the sense that it looked to political and trades union organisation to bring into fruition a set of promised benefits, and so was dependent on the spirit of solidarity and collectivism; the egalitarianism of the middle-middle majority is pro-active in the sense that it is only dependent on government facilitating a series of conditions for equality of opportunity, so allowing the full potential development of the individual.

13 – Definition of Social Capitalist egalitarianism

Hence the egalitarianism of Social Capitalism is overtly upwardly mobile. Does this present a contradiction? No, because the fact it is centred on the majority sets a median or equidistant line in society, acting as a magnetic pull with regard to questions of justice or equity. That is, a mature, well-adjusted middle-middle majority, free of false consciousness, will appreciate the moral justification of its place in society, and will understand the need for downward mobility to balance upward mobility, and the overriding requirement for minimum material standards and rights in protecting those minorities at the base of the community. Downward mobility (which should equal upward mobility in maintaining a properly structured community which ideally should be spherical) is made tolerable by an accepted level of minimum material standards, recognised by the community in total, and the gap between this minimum level and average material standards is the defining margin for the egalitarian society.

Meanwhile, that small minority at the base of the community will comprise those who have fallen by the wayside, e.g., through bankruptcy; or the mentally deficient; single parents; recent immigrants, etc., but under Social Capitalism, the social conscience of a middle-middle majority in a fluid society dependent on achieving and maintaining success through ability alone, will ensure a nice balance in preventing latent conflict.

14 – The Responsible society

This argument is supported by the clear distinction which may be observed between the social consciousness of the bourgeoisie, as described by Marx, and the enlightened attitude of today's middle-middle majority, which cannot in any proper sense be described as bourgeois. For example, the middle class of an earlier era had a pride, self-confidence, and arrogance, quite missing from today's self-effacing and sceptical society. The former class had immense ingenuity and used cruel criteria in differentiating itself from those who failed to reach its own level, and it was callous, unashamedly exploitative, and in its laissez-faire attitude had little thought for the good of the community. Its benevolence was usually reserved for the patriarchal activity of charity.

Today's middle-middle majority, on the other hand, is far more socially aware, sceptical of the untrammelled forces of capitalism, and although not entirely without its selfishness, would be appalled by the mind-set and life style of the middle classes of a hundred years ago. Hence social attitudes have progressed in the intervening period. This new middle-middle majority should not be referred to as a class, but simply given the appellation of the Responsible society.

CHAPTER 2
An Egalitarianism of The Best

"The men of culture are the true apostles of equality."

Matthew Arnold, *Culture and Anarchy*, (1869) ch. 1.

1 – Elitism of the majority

The egalitarianism of Social Capitalism will therefore nurture a cultural elitism for the entire population as a democratic right and in fulfilling the principle of egalitarianism itself. This means that the very best that a civilisation has to offer with regard to high culture, general leisure pursuits, or pleasure, should be made available *de facto*, and not merely in theory, to the entire community.

The only desirable concept for an egalitarian community is not merely one affording equality of opportunity (which too often pertains in theory but rarely in practice) but actually ensures that the best things in life are not only desired by the majority but are available to them. In this lies the essence of a truly democratic society. But the presence of *desire* for the best things in life is no less important as a democratic factor in society, than is the availability of the things desired. Without desire availability is meaningless. Hence sufficient standards of education are necessary to enjoy all the good things of life, irrespective of whether we refer to food, good wines, music, literature, or the appreciation of painting.

If standards of education for the majority are wanting in imparting an appreciation of these things, then the good things in life remain "elitist" in the wrong sense and are unavailable as things of real *value* to that majority. If, however, standards of education are sufficient then the best things in life are no longer elitist or perceived as elitist. I well remember more than fifty years ago at the Christmas dinner of a large company, sitting opposite several elderly working class couples, who were complaining loudly about the "odd" and "disgusting" food served up in front of them. Hors-d'oeuvres of avocado and shrimp in sea food sauce was pushed aside as "foreign muck," and Chablis was spat out as an unacceptable substitute for the usual refreshment of beer. Such an episode would be impossible today when attitudes to food and cooking amongst all classes in Britain have been transformed totally, but even if there is a more egalitarian attitude to cuisine than in an earlier era, the same cannot be said of all spheres of culture.

But it should be understood that this differentiation in the appreciation of cultural forms is not purely a question of class (although it is predominantly), for there are many amongst the so-called upper middle class (who should know better) who sniggeringly refer to certain friends or acquaintances as "wine snobs." In reality there probably exists no such thing as a wine snob, only those who have a more sensitive palate and preference for special wines. It might also be remarked that up until the recent past the English middle classes had the reputation of being the most philistine in Europe. Therefore, the need to educate for an egalitarian society in raising standards, is not a matter of style or class prejudice but of the substantive values of things as they are.

It should be assumed (and research has borne out the fact) that the measure of intelligence or IQ of a population is equally spread out amongst all economic sectors. Hence the stupid and super-intelligent will be found in almost equal proportions amongst rich and poor alike. Therefore, the complexity of cultural forms, i.e. the finest literature, music, etc., should be equally available to all sectors of the population, not according to the factor of complexity but according to the factor of preference for the chosen form. That is, a person with a lowly perceived occupation may choose to enjoy the music of Schoenberg or Hindemith, whilst refraining from appreciating the novels of James Joyce or Proust; whilst a person with the genius level of Bertrand Russell may choose to read detective novels (which he did) rather than fiction of a more complex form.

2 – Democratisation of leisure pursuits

Today leisure pursuits are far more classless than at any time in history. In an earlier age, not so long ago, each sector in society pursued its own separate leisure activities. For example, the less privileged were marked by their interest in dog or pigeon racing; working men's clubs, particular newspapers, etc. In a society where class gradations were sharper than they are today, there was not merely a consciousness throughout society in regard to what cultural values or pursuits belonged to different sectors, but what was *proper* to each. For example, it would have been thought odd for a working person to prefer rugger to soccer, and whilst golf or cricket were predominantly middle class sports, fives or hunting with the hounds were certainly for the upper levels of society. Although the attitude of linking specific pursuits as only *proper* to appropriate sectors of the community clearly reflected social prejudice as to individual choice or proclivity, such prejudice was nonetheless deeply felt and restrictive on the leisure activities of the general population.

Today, however, few such prejudices remain, since, firstly, most such activities are fast losing any association with class; and secondly, the variety of available leisure overall and the exertion of individual choice from purely subjective personal preference, free of inhibiting factors, has become so widespread. In an earlier era the primary determining factor in the differentiation of cultural pursuits was according to the degree of financial well-being; the secondary factor was according to the level of education; and the tertiary factor was dictated by available leisure time and mobility. There were, of course, pursuits which may be labelled as classless, e.g., soccer, horse racing, or vaudeville, but at such events there were usually areas dividing the richer from the less privileged members of the public.

3 – This has not led to a decline of cultural standards

In the age of the middle-middle majority, when affluence, education, as well as mobility and available leisure time, is tending to merge towards a common norm, we are consequently witnessing a situation where cultural activities are taking on an increasingly classless dimension. For example, scuba diving, motor racing, hand-gliding, and yachting, although expensive pursuits, are classless with regard to both their appeal from the viewpoint of spectators, as well as that of participators who invest in the sports. Whilst the greater democratisation of society, following naturally in the wake of the greater affluence of the majority, has led to an expansion in all forms of leisure, it has not in itself led to a decline of cultural standards. If we glance at the status of high culture, it will be found that a far greater proportion of today's population enjoy reading the classics, or attending symphony concerts, or visiting stately homes than fifty years ago, and because huge numbers of people with humbler occupations also enjoy these activities, the latter can no longer be described as elitist in a pejorative sense.

4 – Why high culture is vital for a Social Capitalist society

It may be asked at this stage: of what value is high culture, and why should the question be of such concern to Social Capitalism? If an egalitarian society is to be achieved which looks towards an upwardly aspiring median centred majority as the main focus of its attention, it then becomes the moral obligation of Social Capitalism to ensure that the very best that life has to offer is made available to that majority. This is not argued from the viewpoint of creating a hedonistic society, but firstly as elaborated elsewhere,[5] from that of maximising the individual's potential intellectual and spiritual self-fulfilment, and complete integration as a free agent moving within the community; and secondly, from the viewpoint of eudemonistic principles.

A proper self-consciousness, only available through the best educational system, is necessary for the individual to realise and exploit his full development and abilities as a complete human being. The education of the intellect is necessary for all spheres of life, but for a balanced personality and a deeper and more sympathetic understanding of humanity, it is necessary to educate the spirit. The latter is attained through the benefits of culture, and as Aristotle argued in *The Poetics*, through the catharsis of the soul, i.e. the emotional release we experience through drama, the film, the novel, etc.

5 – Purpose of culture is to increase sensitivity and pleasure

The purpose of all cultural forms - especially higher forms - irrespective of whether it be poetry, music, or the visual arts, is to increase sensitivity; and culture in its broadest meaning includes every aspect of human expression. This includes, of course, language as a mode of communication; the scenic enjoyment of the countryside on a long distance walk; and the ability to derive as much pleasure from drinking finely selected teas as another connoisseur derives from wine; an epicurean appreciation of food; and even the enjoyment of

---

[5] See Chapter 37 of *The People's Capitalism.*

sexual activity as a fine art. None of these things can be enjoyed in their greatest intensity (except in the rarest circumstances) as innate or spontaneous pleasures, but need to be taught or acquired through the learning experience.

6 – But these things need to be taught

The finer pleasures of sexual intercourse, for example, have only been made available to the great majority in the Western world through the publication of literature over the past forty years - of books which would have been banned as obscene in an earlier era. The idea that sexual pleasure was only for men, or women of "depraved morals" is still within the living memory of many, and manuals expressing such prejudice (e.g., by van der Velde) written in the 1930s, were still discreetly available in cellophane wrapping from vendors of "ethical products" in the 1960s.

In poor rural areas, until very recent times, where both men and women laboured from dawn to dusk until exhausted by the waning day, after the first flush of youth, sexual intercourse for many was reserved purely as a procreative activity. The Christian church, of course, has always encouraged such a way of life, or "moral restraint," for traditionally, sex has always been associated with sin, and although the procreative act is permitted as essential to the survival of the species, the church nonetheless regrets the pleasure which it gives. Another Semitic religion, Islam, has gone one step further in preventing pleasure through the sexual act, through the widespread custom of female circumcision entailing the partial or total removal of the clitoris, usually the most erotic zone of a woman's body. Sexual intercourse as a cultivated pleasure in this country only first became widespread amongst the upper and middle classes in the second half of the 17th century with the publication of erotic literature and the manufacture and sale of dildos and other sexual aids, until these too were suppressed through the influence of the church.

7 – Even enjoyment of the countryside is not an intrinsic pleasure

Even the scenic enjoyment of the countryside is an artificial or cultural creation, largely traceable to the imagination and idealism of the Romantic movement, and in this country, especially to Wordsworth. In the 17th century, for example, the prosperous classes sniggered at the idea of walking for leisure in the country as a faintly ridiculous pursuit only resorted to by "country bumpkins," as is made evident by a reading of Restoration drama. Up until the 18th century forests and mountains were regarded as "horrible" places, best avoided as threatening or dangerous, and possibly infested by bandits, or worse still, by witches, hobgoblins, or even dragons. Despite all the efforts of Boswell in taking Dr. Johnson on a tour of the Hebrides in attempting to endear him to his country, the latter still insisted that the best view Scotland had to offer was "the high road leading into England."

8 – Differentiating aesthetics from morality

In closing this chapter something must be said about the distinction between aesthetics and morality, and how the spiritual dimension of the latter may be experienced through high culture. Culture acts as both a stimulant and source of comfort in easing pain, but the pleasure it evokes is morally neutral - or is supposedly so, in maintaining integrity to its differing forms. That is not to deny that cultural forms convey an *implicit* moral message, and that is so for much of the greatest art, but such a message is quite separate from the aesthetic form - or would ruin the latter (through sentimentality, false psychology, vulgarity, etc.) if it so intruded.

That is, there is a clear distinction between aesthetics which is sensual often with connotations of sexuality, and morality which identifies and defines *perceived* gradations of right and wrong. For example, a religious representation may indeed convey a deeply religious feeling to a specific culture, but as a work of art, of integrity to itself, it transcends this dimension on the grounds of aesthetics, and in this light may be appreciated by all educated humanity irrespective of its religious symbolism. The religious feeling evoked by a work of art is therefore separate from its aesthetic component, and the latter is merely used as a medium for creating something which is quite separate from itself.

This essential distinction between aesthetics (to include psychological truth) and morality (or the imposition of rules on the perception of right and wrong) has always been recognised, and the fear of the former as a corrupting influence by religious bodies has often led to the suppression of cultural forms. Hence the Islamic prohibition on the pictorial representation of any living creature by painting, sculpture or other means, known as *aniconism*; or the destruction of religious effigies by the Puritans and other sects on the grounds that aesthetic forms blocked or perverted rather than assisted true religious feeling. Or to go back further in time, the last Book of the *New Testament* has been interpreted as a hymn of hate against the cultural heritage of Romano-Hellenic civilisation.[6]

9 – Cultural implications of this

Until quite recent times, i.e. until the end of the 19th century and beyond, in many rural areas and amongst other sectors of the poorer population, in all parts of Europe, the Bible and other books of an edifying nature, were regarded as the only acceptable reading matter worthy of taking up the time of busy working people. Meanwhile, the spirit of puritanism has looked askance at the novel and other forms of literature which were not overtly didactic or morally improving.

Therefore, the sense that there existed a latent conflict between moral and aesthetic (or cultural) values has never been far from the surface of any society, and perhaps never more so than amongst Anglo-Saxon peoples with their puritanical tendencies - especially those of America. Although the sense of this latent conflict or moral danger is usually repressed within the subconscious, it often comes to the fore in dismissive attitudes to food, or in refraining from expressing pleasure in a variety of situations. Furthermore, the niggling idea that moral values (or the customarily accepted) might possibly be the only worthwhile values, has led to a fear and even a hatred of cultural forms amongst great numbers of people. As Goethe puts into the mouth of Mephistopheles, in the Witch's kitchen scene of *Faust*,

> "Auch die Kultur, die alle Welt beleckt,
> Hat auf den Teufel sich ersteckt."[7]
> (Culture which smooth the whole world licks,
> Also unto the devil sticks.)

When these feelings are experienced by the privileged and leading sectors of society, they may be transmitted into a conservatism which

---

[6] As seen by Ernest Renan in his book, *The Antichrist*, being the fourth volume of his *Origins of Christianity*.

[7] *Faust*, Pt. I, Sc. 6, 1, 160.

wishes to exclude the "lower" orders from the enjoyment of higher cultural forms.

Organised religion, meanwhile, has too often opposed the idea of culture amongst the masses - and the evangelical churches most of all. This is partly because the cerebral or intellectual attractions of higher culture are seen in competition with those of religious faith and the joys of congregational worship. If, as a result of higher educational standards, and increasing scepticism, and a more rational frame of mind, greater numbers of people are discovering spiritual fulfilment in music, literature, and the other arts, as they are today, then this is not only a loss to organised religion but also to a highly-effective mode of centralised social control. There is little the churches can do in the wake of this developing consciousness or progress of the human mind in modern industrial societies.

10 – Why high culture rather than religion will inspire fulfilment in the future

There is also another reason why organised religion is suspicious of secular culture, and its implications are of special significance to Social Capitalism in this discussion of cultural values. The religious or moral (not to be confused with ethical) outlook[8] on the world is essentially and always hierarchical. This is because the gradations of good and bad in the popular imagination take on numberless levels (e.g. Dante's nine levels of wickedness in his description of Hell), and it is only natural that the many ascending steps to ultimate virtue or Sainthood should also find its analogy reflected in the hierarchies of human society. Such a hierarchical perspective is directly contrary to the ideal of egalitarianism - even an upwardly aspiring egalitarianism.

Now cultural or aesthetic values are only concerned with the integrity of things to themselves according to artistic criteria, and comparisons of relative worth are of little significance or interest, since each artefact or cultural creation is of unique value in a specific situation. It is this complexity of judgement in the consideration of aesthetic questions which conflicts with the mind-set of the moralist or the religious leader. But it has to be pointed out that the mind-set of the cultural critic is closer to psychological reality than that of the

---

[8] Whilst morals are only concerned with the subjectivity of accepted custom, ethics is concerned with examining objectively the substantive issues of right and wrong.

latter. This is because organised religion has no firm foundations in truths which may be tested according to demonstrable facts. Religion in general, as well as in particular, may always be explained according to the differing circumstances of psychological motivation giving rise to both right and wrong thinking. For example, the Bible is seen by many as a book of religion, but if it is taken as a purely cultural artefact, the *Old Testament* may be taken as the greatest work of literature in the study of resentment, whilst the *New* may be taken as a study in the need for the renunciation of earthly life for the world of hereafter. There is therefore a natural theological progression from the *Old* to the *New Testament*, from the resentment at the nastiness of earthly existence to the need to renounce that earthly existence for a better life in the world of thereafter.

All this draws us to the conclusion that in a mature and fully conscious society, men and women should derive their spiritual fulfilment as well as moral sense from the greater psychological truths of high cultural forms, rather than from the often unsubstantiated dictates and raw emotion of religious doctrine. True morality is only based in ethics, and the latter, being the most important yet difficult branch of philosophy, is dismissed - often with contempt by churchmen - as irrelevant to the overriding priority of faith. It is this disdain for ethics (ultimately, the only true justification for any religion) which must consign the churches to a role in the twilight for the future. The revival of *true* religion in the future is likely to become dependent on the inspiration and power of Deism.[9]

Spiritual fulfilment (as already for many) and an ethical understanding of the human condition will in the future be derived primarily from the great works of high culture. Furthermore, created as they are within the artistic integrity of their form, they will present a greater truth more powerfully than the overt pronouncements of a religious intermediary.

Recent research overturning the old assumption that old age inclines people more towards organised religion has now demonstrated that - in Europe at least - the elderly today are on the contrary turning away from the churches - often after a lifetime of Christian worship. This should be taken as a sign of greater maturity in the evolution of society, for it does not suggest that the elderly are any less spiritual than before. It may be guessed that they are instead more spiritually fulfilled by the various forms of high culture as

---

9 In this context, see my book, *Deism and Social Ethics*.

anticipated above. If this is a correct conclusion then it offers hope for the future.

CHAPTER 3
Marketing and The Corruption of Culture

"Those who find beautiful meanings in beautiful things are the cultivated. For these there is hope."

Oscar Wilde, *The Picture of Dorian Gray*, Preface.

1 – How culture is poisoned by populism or the principles of marketing

Despite everything we have discussed above, and our optimism with regard to the future of high culture in a Social Capitalist society, there remains the nagging fear that the influences of cultural populism may somehow drag down or depress standards. These fears, it must now be admitted, are not unjustified.

But first we must define cultural populism and how it impacts on society. It usually describes those cultural forms which are produced according to strict marketing criteria. Now marketing, as any business person knows, is not simply a more sophisticated term for selling. It entails research into the basic desire or psychological sales potential for a given product or service, independent of its underlying utility or value as a human need, and it then progresses to devise through ingenious advertising or public relations, a desire for those things so they might be made as widely available as the market allows. But it also works from another direction, i.e. from the perspective of initiating or inventing entirely new products or services which may bring a good financial return. In this role business people will simply sit down and pluck a money-spinning idea out of the sky which is then developed as a purely marketing concept.

Marketing is always devious in the sense that, firstly, it is always dependent on psychological manipulation; secondly, it stimulates an insatiable acquisitiveness through artificial means; and thirdly, in that it often takes no account of underlying human need. It arouses new desires through discontent engendered by a nagging feeling of deprivation. Although the manifestations of marketing techniques are known and accepted by the majority with a cynical compliance as essential to commerce in any advanced industrial state in selling its produce, as soon as these techniques are applied to the world of culture, the latter is poisoned by its influence. Marketing may be fine for the selling of kitchenware or garden tools, but as soon as it lays its cold hand on cultural products, it kills the artistic instinct.

2 – Conditions essential to true art

This is because art, essentially the outcome of the individual imagination, cannot be subordinated to the crudities of the group activity of marketing with its blunt stereotyping tendencies. No cultural form can be made dependent on the criteria of its saleability, and still maintain its integrity. Any cultural form which sets out in advance to assess and maximise its place in the market, and to put a value on such criteria, is doomed in advance to insignificance and annihilation for serious consideration as a work of art.

This is because the spontaneous process of creativity disallows the artist to know the outcome of his work until its completion, and the excitement of all true art lies in the unpredictability of the creative instinct. This is the difference between anticipating the finished product which drops off the end of a conveyor belt, and the commissioned painting completed by an artist. If, however, a cultural form is produced through the collectivity of a marketing project, then its final form may indeed be anticipated to the last detail, but it will no longer be of integrity as a work of art. This is because the conditions laid down in advance constitute a stereotyping of imaginative concepts. Cultural forms which are the outcome of marketing are therefore suffused with artificiality, lack of realism, and false psychology. As they are products out of a common mould, they are dull and hackneyed to the sensitivity of a finer judgement.

3 – Corruption of Hollywood by marketing values

The most notorious example of the cultural form which has been corrupted totally by its reduction to the criteria of marketing values is the Hollywood film. This is not to suggest that every film has been prostituted to marketing standards to the sacrifice of artistic merit, but a sufficient proportion of Hollywood films have been so produced as to ruin the perception of the film as a product of artistic integrity.

Even those films adjudged by serious critics as approaching outstanding quality have usually been spoilt by the Hollywood mark of base coin, and it is the very rare film which has escaped entirely with its artistic merit intact - many of the latter being those of foreign directors who developed their craft in their former or native countries.

The film was the greatest invented art form of the 20th century, and it was the greatest tragedy to civilisation to have been developed on such an industrial scale in Hollywood rather than in some other part of the old world, where true genius may have been given a greater opportunity to develop the cultural form to a higher level of genius. The tragedy lies in the fact that the Hollywood value system was to some extent allowed to influence standards elsewhere, most notably in Britain and India - the latter having developed the worst movie industry in the world, even though they have produced a few outstanding films.

The critique of Hollywood is its resort to stereotypical gestures and modes of expression, whereby the representation of meaning needs always to be explicit with no allowance for the nuances of inference. Such lack of psychological subtlety or realism, or the need to spell out meaning in such a way as to satisfy the understanding of the most obtuse mentality, has made the Hollywood film a very dull and puerile medium of expression. The bluntness and insensitivity of the Hollywood film was possibly in part influenced by the need to cross cultural divides within American itself.

For example, the facial expressions, gestures, and mannerisms of people from Eastern Europe are quite different from those in the Western part of the Continent, as indeed those of Italians are different from Nordic peoples. It is reasonable, therefore, to surmise that Hollywood directors felt obliged to standardise all facial expressions, gestures, and mannerisms in fitting various psychological situations to avoid ambiguity or confusion to cinema audiences. This is because it cannot be credited that the representation of Hollywood actors and actresses on screen really reflect the responses or behaviour of real people. There is an artificiality in Hollywood acting which always seems to defy the natural.

The factor of producing films according to marketing criteria in lowering standards has been further compounded by the imposition of censorship, particularly from the 1930s, in adhering to the strict rules of moral propriety as laid down by the puritanical women's guilds of America. This finally set the seal on the impossibility of great directors expressing with integrity their artistic instinct.

4 – Artistic integrity of the film elsewhere

Consequently, the most interesting and greatest films have usually been produced in the smaller countries of the old world, such as Sweden, France, Japan, and even Soviet Russia. There is a huge irony in the fact that totalitarian Soviet Russia, one of the worst tyrannies of the 20th century, has seen the birth of some of the world's greatest films. This has been due to the fact that Soviet directors were exhorted to produce great works of art, and unlike Hollywood, were not expected to compromise their artistic integrity in pandering to the lowest common denominator. Sergei Eisenstein, the creator of the Soviet cinema, was not only a man with broad cultural interests but widely read in world literature. American directors, on the contrary, although they may have been men of considerable intelligence, were usually philistines with negligible knowledge of any cultural forms. Soviet directors were, of course, expected to work within defined constraints as to politics and ideology, and when they transgressed, their films were withdrawn or cut, but unlimited budgets and artistic freedom did allow them considerable scope for self-expression. The greatest Russian films in the post-Eisenstein era have often been faithful adaptations of the classics, or the presentation of other neutral themes subject only to limited state interference.

Some of the greatest films of the present time are being produced by Nikita Mikhalkov (*Burnt by The Sun*); Pavel Chukrai (*The Thief*); the Vietnamese director, Tran Anh Hung (*The Scent of Green Papaya,* and, *Cyclo*); and the Chinese directors (some of whom have not always met with the approval of their government) Zhang Yimou (*Ju Dou*); Chen Kaige (*Farewell My Concubine*), and Zhou Xiaowen (*Ermo*). This is not only because these directors have total artistic integrity, but of equal significance, they have meaningful stories to tell about the human predicament, and through the power of their communication and the genius of their technique and artistry, they cleanse the soul in the way that Aristotle would have wished.

5 – Exposure to Hollywood is demeaning to our better selves

This has been a long homily on the shortcomings of Hollywood artistic values, but it has not been entirely a digression from our central theme. The reason for this lengthy emphasis is well justified when we realise the ongoing assault on our cultural sensibility through the screening of endless Hollywood movies on our TV channels. The influence of this huge time consumption on millions of lives must leave its baneful mark in coarsening the aesthetic and moral sensibilities of us all, and especially of the rising generation. And neither are we alone in this critique of Hollywood, for at the time of writing (September 2000), during the build-up to the Presidential election in America, both the Republicans and Democrats are vying with one another in attacking the Hollywood film industry for its production of gratuitous violence. In the approaching world of Social Capitalist egalitarianism (as described above) when it is hoped that cultural values will be raised to higher standards than at any time before, is it right we should continue to demean our better selves with all the facile gush and violence of the American cinema?

The situation is not helped, of course, by the subservient adulation of Hollywood by the popular reviewers in our weeklies, and sometimes on screen, with their shallow and inane introductory comments on films to be shown. In raising standards to a more adult level, it might tentatively be suggested that for every American film shown another should be screened from a different country - but even then we would still be swamped by Hollywood guff. In conclusion on this topic, in some future age when humanity has reached a higher level of civilisation, and the film is treated by scholars as a serious art form, it is anticipated there will be a re-ordering in the international appreciation of films worldwide, and it is not improbable that the legacy of Hollywood, after objective consideration, will be consigned to the dustbin of history.

6 – Improvement of British cuisine

In the Anglo-Saxon world it is unusual to associate high culture with cuisine or eating habits, although in Continental Europe - especially in France and Italy - gastronomy is treated as a serious art and certainly as one of the most important components in assessing the culture of any country. Over the past fifty years diet and eating habits in Britain, thanks to foreign travel, better education, and greater affluence, have been transformed for the better out of all recognition. In terms of quality food and variety of national dishes, dining out in London now seriously competes with all that Paris has to offer.

As the source of life itself, cuisine should be of prime importance to us all, and so a consideration of how this particular cultural form is being corrupted by its reduction to the criteria of marketing values is not out of place. If food is to be judged of good quality, interesting, or tasty, it must be submitted to the same criteria of creativity as any other cultural form, irrespective of whether it be a poem, a novel, or a painting, or the way in which a piece of music or a play is performed. That is, it must have the mark of individuality which distinguishes it from the nondescript, the bland, or the downright dull.

7 – How the capitalisation of an economy influences gastronomic standards

The reason that the Continent has traditionally enjoyed a higher standard of cuisine than Britain in the past century is partly accountable to differing capitalistic systems and the mode of funding business. The Productive capitalistic systems of Continental Europe have always been more favourable to the development of small scale private business, as may be witnessed by strolling through the shopping centre of any Continental town. Hence dining places are found in greater abundance and so are forced to meet the competitive challenge of both quality and variety.

The Rentier capitalistic systems of Britain or America, on the other hand, have always been more favourable to the development of impersonal large scale corporate business. Therefore, Britain was at one time dominated by the Lyons cafeterias with their hot and cold meals, or the state run British Restaurants with their gargantuan servings but restricted range, now both happily long gone. In fairness, however, it should be noted that the scale or size of an organisation is more significant in influencing the production of mediocre food than the mode of its capitalisation. For example, the restaurant food of state run organisations in the East bloc (e.g. the HO outlets in East Germany), were consistently poor throughout the post-War period. Or, in the past, the overall quality of food in dining out tended to be better in Norway and Denmark than in Sweden or Finland. This was because the last two countries were dominated by co-operatives and other chains - although it has to be said there was once a time when the cuisine on Swedish State railways was second to none in the world.

8 – These now being undermined by fast food

Having raised our culinary values to a higher level than heretofore, Britain and Europe - and indeed, the world - is now being swamped by a new wave of barbarism which threatens to drive back the march of progress in reducing standards to a new low. These are arriving in the wake of aggressive American marketing methods which try to justify themselves on the spurious grounds of modernity, convenience, speed, and fulfilling popular demand. We justify the epithet *spurious* on the grounds (as we have said before) that marketing artificially *creates* needs rather than *responds* to needs. The arrival of fast food is not only included in this critique. Aimed at a higher marketing level are the Garfunkels and American Steak House which are no less standardised in their boring output than the fast food franchises. But it is the MacDonalds and "finger lickin' good" Kentucky Fried Chickens, polluting our high streets, which need to be confronted as a first priority. This is partly because of the debased nature of their advertising, which not only exploits the innocence of the young (including very small children), but stoops to appealing to the pure animal instinct of hunger as opposed to the sensitivity of a discriminating palate.

It is regrettable that people in a civilised country should be exposed to these fast food outlets, which not only coarsen the appetite of the rising generation, but worse still, put them in a risk situation with regard to their health (especially obesity, for Britain is now the most obese country in the EU), and possibly, even their lives. As Prof. Bob Will, director of the government's CJD surveillance unit in Edinburgh, has recently remarked in alerting the press, it is not improbable that fast food outlets through the offal thrown into their mince meat and pressed into burgers, are contributing to the tragic spread of this killer disease amongst the young.[10] This is not to suggest that such offal is necessarily used by American chains or franchises, but the unhealthy protein and carbohydrates cleverly packaged and deceptively presented in the guise of the eatable by the American fast food outlets should nonetheless be exposed in our schools for exactly what it is. The heroic efforts of Jamie Oliver, in confronting the poor quality of school meals, and their direct threat to our children's health, should therefore be widely applauded.

---

[10] See the report in *The Daily Telegraph* of 17th July 2000.

9 – Marketing and the undermining of publishing standards

The last example of the corruption of a cultural form through its subordination to the criteria of marketing values is possibly the most insidious of all, since it concerns a monopoly in the control of information and the written word by the great international conglomerates. This is in regard to the book trade on two separate fronts: firstly, publishing; and secondly, retailing.

No society can be a democracy in a true sense unless it has a free and vigorous press, and the latter may only be maintained through the competition of many publishers acting as a medium for both free intellectual and artistic expression. It is this which is now being whittled away at an alarming rate. Over the past thirty years the publishing industry in this country and elsewhere has been rapidly transformed. Over the past twenty years most major independent general publishers, many with a long and glorious tradition in having nurtured some of the greatest writers of the recent past, have been bought up and absorbed by approximately five giant conglomerates. Although many specialised and smaller publishers still survive, they cannot compare or compete with the clout of the major conglomerates in dictating the pattern of the retail trade.

The conglomerates, in adhering to the principles of good marketing, have sought to rationalise their product range. That is, in maximising profits they have reduced the number of new titles in concentrating on selling their best seller lists. Worse still is the system of commissioning which limits the dissemination of new ideas, new talent, and new writers. It should be remembered that marketing has no interest in originality, or literature, or the written word as values in themselves, but only in the immediate profits to be derived from printing and selling. The approach is therefore short term in avoiding the expenses of warehousing a large stock.

As marketing is more interested in dictating to rather than responding to the market, and as it has anyway constructed its own detailed vision of what the market really wants, it prefers the pro-active method of commissioning books rather than the passive role of waiting for manuscripts to be sent in by the unknown. Responding to the open market of incoming creativity, or to the talent of anyone who chooses to write in, is regarded as a time-wasting task. Hence the closed market of the commissioned book, applied to all spheres of interest, from the novel to the work of reference, is able to fulfil the specified demands of what is exactly required. This, of course, kills individuality and enforces standardisation, according to the same principles and in the same way that MacDonalds produces a cheeseburger.

As the identity of a writer is of no more interest to a marketeer beyond the profits he or she brings to a corporation, over recent years there has been an increasing interest in books authored by (or more usually ghosted for) prominent personalities from any domain of life: TV presenters, sports people, pop stars, even politicians, etc. This is because it is hoped that the name of a personality will sell a book quite irrespective of its literary merits. Sometimes a book is marketed according to the angle which may be put on the personality of its author: he or she may have been involved in a sensational news event; or be particularly wealthy; or have little other quality than that of being especially photogenic - i.e. if a commercially viable idea for a book can be extracted from this accidental characteristic.

What is certain is that large corporate publishers have little interest in books dependent on intrinsic merit alone, irrespective of whether they be literary or stem from the formulation of new ideas. It is only when a book may be linked to a specific marketable concept that it is judged as a commercial proposition. It is because of this contraction of the publishing industry, resulting from a cosy insiders' exclusivity approach, that it has never been more difficult for worthy new talent to see the light of day. There is a huge cynicism in the British publishing industry today, and professionals jokingly refer to the rare act of creativity which gets into print as a *real book*, in contrast to the *pulp publishing* of the other 90%. Today it is not only more difficult for a new writer to be published, but almost as difficult for a new manuscript to be read or considered by the giant conglomerates controlling the industry.

This is detrimental to the culture of any country and demonstrates clearly the incompatibility between the principles of professional marketing and those of creative values. We now experience the moronic situation when spontaneous creativity is ignored for the consideration of its market potential, and if a projected book fails to fit the matrix of a marketing plan it will simply not be published.

10 – Book retailing and the contraction of free choice

In turning to the retailing of books, it will be found that marketing methods are no less damaging in destroying the range of choice than they are in the realm of publishing. The book trade in Britain is now undergoing its own revolution, and this is threatening the interests of readers everywhere. The turmoil in Waterstone's, for example, was recently featured in the press following the sacking of Robert Topping (described in *The Times* in 1996 as "the best bookseller in the world") from his post as manager of their Deansgate store in Manchester after sixteen years with the company.[11] His sacking followed a dispute with top management during their pressure to centralise buying and contract the number of available titles, as opposed to the current policy of each store being responsible for its own buying policy. Robert Topping lost out in a struggle on behalf of consumers, authors, and the cause of cultural diversity.

Even worse, perhaps, is the aggressive entry into the British book trade of the American corporate giant, Borders, together with the development of their UK subsidiary, Books Etc. This organisation not only already operates a centralised and highly exclusive buying policy, but virtually imposes a censorship of ideas through its narrow buying policy. It has thus set itself on a similar course with W.H. Smith, which only stocks pulp fiction and bland market best sellers. The difference between the two outlets is that whilst Borders and Books Etc project themselves as serious book retailers, W.H. Smith is primarily regarded as a stationers and not really a proper bookshop by the British reading public. In view of the real threat to the freedom of expression in the years ahead, it is a valid proposition to raise the question of legislation to investigate foreign corporations which pursue such undesirable and dangerous activity in hindering the free flow of information.

In summary, therefore, populism manifested through the principles of marketing debases cultural values, since it prostitutes artistic creativity on the altar of an industrial system, and the individualism inherent in cultural activity cannot lend itself to a

---

[11] See *The Times*, 1st July 2000. I was privileged to meet Robert Topping on the day he was protesting with a placard outside Waterstone's in London's Piccadilly when he explained to me at length the internal politics which was damaging his former company.

mechanical process. This is because the sensitivity of good taste is thereby corrupted.

CHAPTER 4
Stripping Culture of its Class Associations

"The purpose of culture is to enhance and intensify one's vision of that synthesis of truth and beauty which is the highest and deepest reality."

J. C. Powys, *The Meaning of Culture*, p. 164.

1 - Function of Social Capitallism to raise aesthetic standards for the majority   2 – How Culture was used as an instrument for social control   3 - How to strip culture of its class associations   4 - Substantive cultural values are classless and hence egalitarian   5 - Why the middle majority will contemn new attempts at class differentiation   6 - The philistinism of class-based culture   7 - Egalitarianism raises rather than diminishes high culture

1 – Function of Social Capitalism to raise aesthetic standards for the majority

In extending the benefits of high culture to all sections of a community it should be noted there is a transitional stage in the development of society when there exists a conflict between cultural and commercial pressures. These will be described below.

By definition mass production is for the masses, and what is cheap in price or quality, or even low in value by some aesthetic criterion (divorced from the element of price), will tend to be taken up by the masses, or imposed upon the masses through necessity, rather than consumed by the more affluent sectors of society. In the sphere of Socialism it was William Morris who first attempted to break down this degrading pattern of consumption through pitting a new school of craftsmanship and design against the established system.

It must be the purpose of Social Capitalism to continue this work through a broader and even more ambitious vision for the future. We have already described how changes are moving in the desired direction through the increasing democratisation of leisure pursuits, and the enjoyment of higher cultural activities by a greater proportion of the population than at any time before. We have also argued how these things are essential in achieving an upwardly aspiring egalitarian society, and that an egalitarianism where the majority do not have access to the very best that life has to offer is worthless and degrading.

2 – How culture was used as an instrument for social control

But we go further than this. There is another quite separate argument we have not touched upon. It should be the function of Social Capitalism to direct society along the tracks towards a higher culture for the benefit of all. Such a stance is not motivated by the "improving" attitude, or the desire to "raise the multitude," but through the necessity of empowering the majority in ending cultural exploitation.

It should be understood that in all societies until the present time culture has been used as an elitist weapon of social control by the wealthy and powerful. There is still a strong resistance by the class conscious in the upper levels of society to deny access to their culture - or the trappings of their culture - to those beneath them. There are some amongst the nobility who resent that the middle or "lower orders" should develop a taste for the finer delicacies of the table as if it were to somehow threaten their own status, and there are many more who seem jealous of the idea that "working people" should show their enjoyment of opera or classical music. It is probable that such prejudice is purely accountable to the class insecurity of such people, and if this is the case, then they should simply be ignored with disdain for the anachronism of their class consciousness.

We have already argued that elitist values should be snatched from the hands of the privileged and handed over to the majority. The influence of culture in its broadest definition means the power of the individual to communicate, impress, and persuade effectively through the benefits of education and experience within a specific community. It is a power which is subtle, quiet, implicit, confident, and even unspoken, and yet it carries a weight with no lesser authority than more direct forms of exerting control. It is the invisible mark which distinguishes the informed and self-fulfilled from the ignorant and impotent. We have elaborated above how leisure pursuits fell into class-based categories until recent times, and how democratisation is now making most activities available to all. This particularly pertains to sporting or outdoor pursuits, but with regard to the higher cultural forms of literature, music, or social conversation, etc., there is still a wide gap between the different sectors of society.

3 – How to strip culture of its class associations

This gap may only be filled through education, and an egalitarianism which rather than seeking to imitate or ape the more privileged members of the community, is concerned rather with adopting their substantive qualities divorced from the style which is used as a mode for class differentiation. For example, the style of Oxford or Queen's English is distinctly class-based, but the best and most correctly spoken English may come from the lips of our BBC news presenters and commentators, which is classless in tone with none of the connotations of style suggesting a sense of superiority or differentiation from the rest of the population. Egalitarianism, therefore, in this desired Social Capitalist sense, means adopting the highest standards within the *essence* of a cultural form, or identifying its *substantive* value, so that such standards are separated entirely from their class associations.

As soon as standards are in this way made classless, they lose their trappings of privilege, and concurrently, all embarrassment falls away, with regard to the aspiration of adopting such standards. All such highest substantive cultural values may then be easily set within the median level of the middle-middle majority for the natural aspiration of all. As soon as standards or values are accepted as classless, they may then correctly be described as egalitarian, i.e. for the enjoyment of all, not simply in theory (which would be meaningless) but *de facto*.

The outcome of stripping cultural forms from their class associations not only makes them egalitarian in themselves, but is a significant step in transforming society itself towards egalitarianism. For example, if speaking the best spoken English; attending Glyndebourne or chamber concerts; reading Descartes or Kant; enjoying the finest wines; horse riding; or punting on the river Cam, etc., become classless pursuits, there may eventually be few (if any) other good things in life, for the rich and privileged to call exclusively their own. They will, as the saying goes, be brought down several pegs through the necessity of having to enjoy pursuits and pleasures which are also indulged in by the wider population. In other words, the process of democratisation will devolve their *exclusive* as opposed to their *real* worth not only in their own eyes but in that of the rest of society.

5 – Why the middle majority will contemn new attempts at class differentiation

The effects of egalitarianism in stripping away all the class associations of cultural forms will help create a far more humane society. In the past, the privileged have always been able to protect their status against democratic changes in society through the invention of new barriers to keep out "upstarts" from below. Nancy Mitford has written much about this with regard to "U" and "Non-U" in differentiating between upper and middle class terminology, but a society comprising the highly educated middle-middle majority is more likely to laugh at such tomfoolery, and not care much one way or the other as to what is "acceptable" or "unacceptable" to a snobbish and pretentious minority intent on safeguarding its worthless exclusivity. This is because society is moving in a direction which increasingly repudiates any kind of vanity or class consciousness wherever it may emerge. It is also much more concerned with the substantive or *real* nature of things as opposed to their *style* or appearance. Such tendencies are wholly beneficial to the cause of culture.

6 – The philistinism of class-based culture

The democratisation of cultural forms and the stripping away of their class associations, is therefore of great benefit to culture itself. Why is this? In an age when high culture was associated as the exclusive preserve of specific elites (and usually only reserved for them), and when it was valued by the vulgar and social climbers for its associations as opposed to its intrinsic worth, snobbish and philistine attitudes predominated. This first occurred when courtiers and other minions failed to understand or appreciate music and other arts for what they were, but only as a way of ingratiating themselves with princes, or for the reflected glory of standing in their presence during a concert or in viewing an exhibition. This led inevitably to the expression of false and hypocritical attitudes, and to an environment which was hateful and pernicious to artists themselves, as is amply reflected in the memoirs and diaries of the latter.

This is illustrated by the fact that the behaviour of a concert audience of two hundred years ago would be unacceptable to today's critical concert goers. In the age of Beethoven, for example, it was often customary for those attending concerts or musical soirées to play cards, talk, drink, laugh, and generally refrain from silence. Even today, there are some cultural pursuits or events attended as social gatherings for the well-to-do, or as hospitality "treats" arranged by corporate bodies, and it is doubtful if the actual performances are appreciated as much as the superficial environment or peripheral benefits before and after the show. That is, the excitement of visiting a famous theatre or other location may be greater than the excitement of the actual performance in which it was held. This is the ignorance and philistinism which too often flourishes in a class-based society.

Or to take another example: one might speculate as to how many owners of our great stately homes have actually read the massive leather bound tomes in their well stocked libraries. This is cultural material, locked up in rooms, going to waste through lack of readers. Or take classical music: this is taken more seriously today than it was fifty years ago, and the depth of appreciation in talks and discussions on Radio 3, or the number and quality of recently published books on music, is evidence of this.

Meanwhile, those who read the voluminous leather bound tomes of Gibbon, Hume, Johnson, or Walpole, probably give greater attention to their content than the more casual readers of an earlier age. This is simply because in an age of greater knowledge of what is available, individual interest combined with aptitude is more easily and sooner matched with what is really sought after. In former times reading enjoyment was too often dependent on serendipity.

7 – Egalitarianism raises rather than diminishes high culture

In stripping away the class associations of culture one is therefore also tearing away the mask of hypocrisy, or false pretensions of those who might be perceived as social climbers, or placing a bar against the well-heeled who might choose to use culture as an instrument for snobbery in putting down those "beneath" them. A society which uses culture for snobbery soon becomes insufferable, and English writers over the past four hundred years have been savage in their satirical depiction of the pretensions of both Snobs and Nobs. Such an undesirable development, which is always an abuse of culture and the worst aspect of philistinism, can only be prevented through an appropriate educational system which generates appreciation for cultural activities within the framework of an upward aspiring egalitarianism.

All this illustrates how an egalitarian society, far from reducing cultural standards, raises them to a higher level than heretofore. In this may be seen the paradox of egalitarianism by our definition. Some sceptics - usually of the older generation - may still ask themselves: but what is the function of high culture in a Social Capitalist society? The answer is that on the collective level it serves as a bonding agent; whilst on the individual level, it confers intellectual and spiritual enlightenment, and ultimately, adds spice to every aspect of life.

But the optimism of the above affords no room for complacency in the future. As cultural standards are raised in most countries of the industrial world, from another direction advances an oncoming wave of barbarism.

CHAPTER 5
The Problem of American Cultural Values

"Culture with us ... ends in a headache ...Do not craze yourself with thinking, but go about your business anywhere. Life is not intellectual or critical; but sturdy."

R. W. Emerson, *Essays: Second Series, Experience.*

1 – The deceptive social egalitarianism of America

The threat of American values swamping across the globe is so great that the effect of this impact must be given more serious consideration in these opening chapters. In promoting the aims of Social Capitalism, there is also another and perhaps more surprising reason for examining the nature of American culture and how it effects the lives of ordinary people.

America, proudly self-proclaimed as the first democracy of the modern world, is in a certain sense the most egalitarian and proletarian country in the world. But this egalitarianism is different from the egalitarianism defined above. America is a country where liberty has been carried to its furthest extreme to the sacrifice of equality, and so its egalitarianism is not material but cultural. This aspect of egalitarianism must in any event be of interest to Socialists, particularly in view of its proletarian characteristics and its appeal to the lowest common denominator as a medium of communication.

Despite all the criticism of American civilisation which may be read into these opening chapters, it remains indubitably true that the American Revolution at the end of the 18th century was more far-reaching in changing the nature of her society, than was any other revolution in modern history in changing theirs. In retrospect, we can now see that the Russian Revolution, for example, was merely a blip in the history of human change: a great outpouring of rhetoric, and development of ideological thought, but finally producing little of permanent value to the future. It could never have been anticipated that after seventy years of Soviet Communism and intensive propaganda, her people might quietly slip back into a mind-set more reminiscent of that of the Tsarist era, with the restoration of the church, a selfish cut-throat attitude to their neighbours, and a general nastiness of life and criminality which might have been taken from the pages of Dostoevsky. The American Revolution, on the other hand, was so far-reaching that it could almost be said to have changed the human nature of her people.

The essence of American democracy lies in the *idea* of equality of opportunity for all, but as this is an illusion, or in the circumstances, an unrealisable ideal, American democracy is only given an appearance of credibility and is only made tolerable as a universal concept, through its cultural egalitarianism.   We have argued elsewhere that America is not a democracy but more correctly a plutocracy.[12] Americans, since before the War of Independence, have always striven consciously for the achievement of a nation of equals, but only via the type of freedom through which each man or woman may selfishly experience self-fulfilment.

The pioneer spirit, enabled through the apparent infinite availability of land and all it had to offer an ingenious and hard-working race, led to the repudiation of the idea of the state as an organising authority guiding people into required spheres of activity, or from a Hobbesian standpoint, protecting them from injuring one another. Concepts from the old world were thought unnecessary for the new. Political thought was concentrated almost entirely on the technicalities of a representative system, but representation is in itself value free and only concerned with balancing conflicting vested interests against each other.

Therefore, in a society which concentrates on the freedom of the individual as opposed to the collective good, or that of the community, the instrument of representation was used ruthlessly to corrupt good intentions and exploit the economically disadvantaged. Whilst representative government, in carrying forward democracy, was always held as inviolable and hence has never been endangered as a system in America, it was nonetheless often used as an instrument of injustice and oppression - quite apart from the more obvious examples in the context of slavery, or the genocide (both unintentional as well as intended) of native American Indians, or the lack of effective measures in alleviating unemployment or poverty.

---

[12] See Chapter 3 sub-section 4 of *The People's Capitalism.*

2 – Why the powerful are invisible

If there was an apparent hypocrisy in American political life, or in the existence of ideals accepted throughout the population which seemed to conflict with the reality of human suffering, this was only made possible through the beautiful image of beneficence, equality, and freedom which the Americans presented as the perception of their own character.

This is most notably marked through the classlessness, and casual attitude to life, the lazy walk and easy swing of the hips, and the over-familiarity when talking with superiors. There is a general attitude that the humblest citizen may talk as an equal with the President of the Union. These things are excellent in so far as they are true, but they reflect rather a *style* than a *reality* to life, and they tend to delude the American citizen no less than the foreigner. The European is filled with conflicting feelings in witnessing the style of American life because of the subjectivity of his own very different environment. For example, the British Army private cannot withhold a sneer when he sees the familiarity of other ranks towards their officers, but there is no reason to believe that the American Army is any less severe towards indiscipline than is the British Army. In summary, the democratic and egalitarian style of American life is highly commendable in so far as it reflects *reality*, but the greater truth is that other factors in their society have made America far less democratic and egalitarian than, for example, the older countries of the EU.

With the achievement of independence the Americans repudiated entirely everything they interpreted as the evils of the old world, viz., aristocratic privilege; the inalienability of land; hierarchical pride; kingship; enforced religious practices; arbitrary political authority; the state regulation of trade; and censorship on any grounds, etc. Their denunciation of these things was sincere and deeply-grounded, but the identification of political ills is not sufficient in creating a benevolent society for the future. When the Americans outlawed these things they felt that only good could fill the void. In this they were wrong. They did not realise that a more constructive vision was necessary in creating the good society.

When social evils began to take root in the growing Republic, there was a blind spot in the collective eye of the American people. This was brought about by the strength of their optimism in the future, their trust in individualism, and confidence in the system, for they could only associate social ills as emanating from the evil conditions of the old world, and from these things they were free. Those who fell by the wayside were responsible for their own fate, since they were nurtured in a nation of freedom and equality of opportunity. As for the high and mighty inflicting these social ills, as instruments of harm to society, they were invisible to both themselves and the rest of the community. This was because they wore no crowns, coronets, or mitres on their heads; had no titles to ensure obeisance to their authority; claimed no special privileges in scaring an underclass; and from the 1760s onwards, the more well-to-do resolved to wear simple homespun clothing which did not differentiate them from the majority. This invisibility of the powerful, in conjunction with shared ideals on the democratic and egalitarian nature of society, more easily facilitated all the injustice and inequity which developed in America. The rich became all-powerful but had none of the *trappings* of power associated with the old world.

3 – America's anti-elitist values

Resulting from the above, from an early stage in her history, America developed a strongly anti-elitist value system which was unique to any society in the modern world. It was this, together with her cultural egalitarianism, which was to differentiate America so sharply from any other nation on earth.

It was the anti-elitist value system of America, or the assertion which seemed to cry from the heart of every individual that "No one is better than me!," which was responsible for a levelling down rather than a levelling up type of egalitarianism. There is a huge irony in the fact that whilst on the one hand Americans have enslaved and oppressed their Afro-American brothers and sisters, on the other hand, they have imitated them. In the words of the famous US jazz saxophonist, Sonny (Theodore Walter) Rollins, "America is deeply rooted in Negro culture: its colloquialisms, its humour, its music." The easy characteristic American walk (which Europeans find difficult to imitate let alone adopt) is that of the Negro tribesman in his native Africa. Levelling down in this context, it should be noted, does not refer to the quality of the characteristics imitated, but only to the fact that they belonged to an enslaved and oppressed people.

The mode of nurturing the child in a pioneer society, so that it might be fit for taking on the responsibilities of adulthood at an early stage in its life; together with the idealisation of youth or the rising generation, in a fast changing but optimistic society, in conjunction with ideas later developed on the theory and practice of education, all led to tendencies on the need to defer to the interests and mentality of childhood. With these needs in mind there was a dumbing down and simplification of cultural forms, and so consequently, standards moved in the same direction, and high culture was pushed aside.

America is essentially a child-centred society, a factor made most evident by the perception in the eyes of the rest of the world of the precociousness and cheekiness of the child, characteristics which irk the European or Asian as charmless effrontery, but are encouraged by Americans as cute and desirable in small people aspiring to adulthood. All this is a reflection of the fact that Americans possibly adore their children more than most peoples, and it certainly contrasts with the north European attitude until recent times when the child was expected to be "seen but not heard."

4 – A Cultural egalitarianism of the lowest common denominator

The toleration and benevolence of Americans towards their children is laudable, and thanks partly to the worldwide dissemination of American ideas on nurture and education, over the past two generations, there has been a transformation in the approach to childhood throughout the industrialised world, in both the home and at school. But this is not to suggest that the American approach to childhood is wholly benign or desirable. The unbalanced personality of so many; the resort of great swathes of the population to "shrinks;" the constant need to boast or create an impression, rather than accept one's personality as it is; the nagging self-consciousness as to psychic health (made evident in almost any Woody Allen film); and the tendency to wreak havoc or violence in a difficult situation, is evidence that the American approach to childhood is far from perfect.

The critique of the American approach to childhood is to be found in the fact that it idealises the latter as somehow a perfect state of nature. In encouraging an imitation of adulthood in the very young, rather than promoting development or precocity in any real sense, it achieves nothing more than exhibitionism. The child may thereby appear "cute" in the eyes of its elders, and furthermore, may encourage a romantic but false view of the nature of childhood; but it should be borne in mind that precocious or inapt behaviour does not normally reflect the underlying mentality or thinking which such behaviour is supposed to represent. In other words, such behaviour is purely artificial, and is liable to confuse the mind of the child, and to retard rather than develop a balanced personality in the future.

The idealisation of childhood, and the exaggerated importance which the child is made to attach to itself, leads eventually to the grown adult yearning subconsciously for the security and adoration it experienced during an earlier stage in life. This results eventually in confusion of identity, and an apprehension and despondency, which needs to be compensated through swagger and pretentiousness. The outcome is that the American is typically left with an immature personality, and this is the exact impression left on the mind of peoples everywhere on the globe.

All the above factors have contributed, therefore to a cultural egalitarianism which looks to the lowest common denominator. An idealisation of childhood which is perverted rather than realistic, in conjunction with a democratic sense which falsely posits that no man or woman is better (or should be better) than another, means that in the light of these perceptions, culture - if it is to be people-friendly - should defer to the simplest mental aptitude. The effect of this has been wide-ranging in influencing American cultural values in raising simplicity on a pedestal in the name of "populism" or serving the "needs of the majority;" whilst condemning complexity as "esoteric" or only fit for "eggheads" or a "snobbish elite." These attitudes, of course, have penetrated every sphere of American life. Consequently, the American has little concept for what in the old world, is described as the "improvement" of society, beyond the idea of what directly touches on his notion of liberty or material well-being.

5 – The emergence of pop culture

The above helps to explain some of the unique characteristics of American popular culture: not unique merely in terms of the simplicity of its technique or appeal, but more significantly, in terms of its acceptance across all levels of society irrespective of economic or educational status. European visitors in American homes, for example, are astonished when they witness adults watching and laughing at cartoons of Donald Duck and Tom and Jerry on their TV screens. There are many situations when the European would be ashamed at the idea of enjoying the childish, naive, or sadistic entertainment so deliciously lapped up by the supposedly educated American adult.

It is no coincidence that populism or pop culture developed specifically as an American phenomenon, and here it is important to differentiate again between populism or pop culture and *popular* culture. Whilst the latter includes high culture which is popular or widely accepted, e.g. Dickens, Verdi, Balzac, or Pushkin, in their respective societies, as well as mediocre works (and so is a value free category); the former defines low (usually marginal) cultural forms which strive to dominate popular taste. Pop culture often stems from the rebellious spirit of minorities, e.g. music from the deep South, or forms which express the discontent of an underclass, and so in inception and development is proletarian in spirit. As soon as such a form becomes widespread in an industrial society it takes on the form of a youth culture, and again, youth culture is a specifically American phenomenon, or develops out of forms from an American pattern. We may hazard the assumption that if America had never existed, then likewise, pop and youth culture would never have come into being.

6 – Pop culture as a foreign import

Whilst the populism of these forms in America has expanded into the mainstream, which is natural in view of its native growth, as soon as it is transferred to a foreign clime, it arrives and usually flourishes within the confines of a youth culture, only rarely penetrating the mainstream culture or values of a people. There are two reasons for this: firstly, because the attractiveness of its proletarian or rebellious spirit, and the simplicity of its form, appeals more to a teenage generation hovering between the uncertainty of childhood and adult status; and secondly, because a foreign culture, imposed as a challenge to the values of a higher civilisation, is bound to be resisted by the mainstream life of a community. American pop culture as a foreign import is therefore something to be "grown out of" by the rising generation - a halfway house - before assimilating the deeper values and greater benefits of mainstream culture.

7 – The consequent debasement of educational standards

Nonetheless, there is a very serious aspect to this American penetration of life on a global scale, and much publicity recently has been given to its undermining educational efforts in this country in raising an underclass - and particularly of male youth. Much has been written about "laddish" attitudes, and the effects of such anti-work and anti-culture youth magazines as *Loaded* and *EHM*. Meanwhile, a prominent academic, Dr. Tony Sewell, a lecturer of Education at Leeds University, who has completed research for the Commission for Racial Equality on the high level of exclusion of black pupils at a London secondary school, and who is himself of African descent, has bemoaned the influence of certain forms of youth culture in hindering the education of teenagers - including Caucasians.

He regretted the idolisation of such pop stars as Puff Daddy, and argued that "while rap music is hailed as the poetry of the ghetto, social scientists and educational experts are increasingly concerned about its more malign influence."[13] He continued, "but that culture is not one that, for example, is interested in being a great chess player, or intellectual activity. It is actually to do with propping up a big commercial culture to do with selling trainers, selling magazines, rap music, and so on. ... These things are not harmful in themselves but what is dangerous is the inability of children to see that they can have this type of culture and still succeed at school. Unfortunately to do good at school is seen as nerdy."

The conclusions of Dr. Sewell follow in the wake of those of Prof. Ronald Ferguson of Harvard, a teacher at the University's John F. Kennedy School of Government, who recently alleged the culture of hip-hop and rap music was damaging the academic progress of American teenagers. He had argued that the phenomenon of rap music as popularised by Lauryn Hill and Puff Daddy was to blame for the declining academic achievements of school and college students.

These concerns must be of importance to Social Capitalism which is naturally obliged to give a high priority to the education of the under-privileged. We see above the evils of American commercialism in its darkest guise in a kind of conspiracy to pull down the cultural and educational standards of the majority. It bears out the thesis we have pursued in these opening chapters.

The fact that American cultural values differ in a quite distinct sense from those of any other country is recognised by peoples throughout the globe, and yet it is a distinction which seems to defy precise definition. It is felt that American culture is anti-elitist and appeals to the lowest common denominator, and these characteristics seem to arouse disdain amongst those on whom its cultural forms are imposed. The conclusion is that somehow American cultural values

---

[13] *The Daily Telegraph*, 21st August 2000.

are demeaning and insulting to our good taste and moral sense. The situation can perhaps best be understood by explaining the idea of values as shared by most peoples throughout the globe as a natural outcome of upbringing.14

---

14 The problem of American culture is pursued in greater depth in my book, *Freedom From America.*

CHAPTER 6
The Value of High Culture

"Culture is the passion for sweetness and light, and (what is more) the passion for making them prevail."

Matthew Arnold, *Literature and Dogma*, Preface.

1 – How price became the criterion for American cultural values

Due to the hierarchical environment of societies in a past age in the non-American civilised world, there developed a consciousness that all things may be graded in an order according to their significance or value, and consequently, that more worthwhile activities (especially in the sphere of culture) should be given the preference of our time.

This sense of value, explicable to its historical origins, is still maintained in the old world irrespective of social or political development. Whilst cultural forms in the old world are deeply ingrained in the ethos of a people, in America their attainment remains superficial and so unsatisfactory to the inner longing for fulfilment. In other words, cultural forms in American, in so far as the majority are concerned, fail to confer that sense of balance and wholeness elsewhere in the world, and it is this factor which elicits the inaccurate accusation everywhere thrown at the nation that "America has no culture!" America has a culture but it is deficient as a medium in developing the maturity and inner self-confidence of her people.

The unique anti-elitist cultural values of America, in conjunction with their appeal to the lowest common denominator, and so to an egalitarianism the reverse of that advocated for a Social Capitalist society, would lead of course to a *reductio ad absurdum*, unless some criterion was used for measuring value. After all, value implies that which may be submitted to a scale of measurement. Something must fill the void of value! When we speak about the anti-elitist cultural values of America we refer to the *intrinsic* value of things which we choose not to put into an order of merit. This is in accordance with the principle of applying egalitarianism to all things, and it arose historically as a response against everything which the old world seemed to represent. The consequence was that all things were levelled down and the good could not be differentiated from the bad or the mediocre.

If the intrinsic value of a thing could not be accepted as a criterion for measuring value, then resort would be had to *extrinsic* qualities. The American did not have far to look - in fact the answer was thrust upon him early in his history. The outcome was inevitable. Price was to be the criterion for measuring the value of all cultural forms!

This easy solution to the problem of culture in a new and rebellious democracy took hold as a logical consequences, since the American colonies had developed in a cultural void. She had no traditions and no past, and her immigrants had made a conscious decision to cut their links with what they perceived was the tyranny of the old world. If later they were to experience a rootlessness, or loss to their human dimension (which they did), then traditions were to be created through immediate invention. But artificial tradition is very different from that which emerges through centuries of growth. When America declared her independence, and founded what was supposedly a classless society, she was not merely reluctant but unable to absorb the European cultural heritage as belonging to her people also, since such a heritage was tainted throughout with associations of elitist privilege.

2 – The egalitarianism of price as value

Hence culture or cultural tradition was not repudiated through explicit intent, but lost through simple default. It was there for the taking but could not be taken up because of the inhibitions of her downward-looking egalitarianism. But some value system was bound to fill the gaping void. In a society advocating freewill and rugged individualism, this was filled immediately by the idea that monetary value superseded all other values, and the democracy and egalitarianism of this concept as perceived in a pubescent or pre-industrial society, seized the imagination of the majority. But price as the criterion of value did not simply emerge as a spontaneous idea. It had its creator and philosopher. The founding father, Benjamin Franklin, had formulated the ideal of monetary accumulation and price as the superseding value in countless books, articles and pamphlets, long before America had gained her independence.[15]

With the brilliant discovery that price was to be the nexus of cultural value, all embarrassment fell away with regard to the elitist associations of art and artefacts. In this way the understanding of culture was to be brought within the ken of all. There is something democratic and egalitarian in measuring the value of an object by its price tag. It subverts the esoteric authority of the aesthetes, who too often bamboozle the majority and speak above their heads. It brings culture within reach of the masses. This is because the simplest person can comprehend monetary value, and relate it to personal experience, and when artefacts are confronted with a price tag of millions, it appeals to the imagination of what could be bought in their stead. To draw an extreme example: when a school party is brought into a gallery, and a price tag is indicated for a Giotto, a Picasso painting, or a sculpture by Canova, a hushed awe is evoked by the figure quoted, and the latter dictates the attention span deserving for each item.

3 – Price as value spelt the death of culture

Price as the criterion for value means the death of culture. The touch of Croesus which turns all to gold, as the legend tells us, transforms the living into the dead. The price factor, in a later epoch was to submit culture to the criteria of marketing values, and as we have seen above, this was to destroy the artistic integrity of major cultural forms. Price as value, in conjunction with professional marketing techniques, was to exacerbate the problem of American culture, for it pushed forward the tendency of populism and low cultural forms.

The promoters of populism justified this on the grounds of responding to demand, and in this they confused demand or free choice with the organised imposition of supply which they designed and created through committees and the power of corporate capital: e.g., through the film industry and music for the mass market. This is quite different from the emergence of the writer, the composer, the musician, or even the film maker as traditionally in the countries of

---

[15] See Peter Baida's biting study, *Poor Richard's Legacy: American Business Values From Benjamin Franklin To Donald Trump* (William Morrow & Co., NY, 1990), which underlines the ultimate emptiness of Franklin's philosophy.

the old world, where talent emerges from the community as a spontaneous process and not through the artificial means of marketing promotion, where hype is made to override aesthetic appreciation.

4 – Religion substituted the spiritual role of culture

The spiritual emptiness of American life through the rejection of high culture in any meaningful sense, and through the glorification of the dollar, or the resort to price as the lone criterion of value for all things, demanded fulfilment from some other source. This was to be found through the consolations of a kind of religion particular to the American people, but it was an unsatisfactory answer to human need. Modern America was to become the most conscientious church-going nation in the world, but it was to reflect a religion which was superficial, hypocritical, corrupt, and fanatical.

The unhealthy religiosity of the Americans, which too seldom works as an influence for good character or towards a more balanced personality, divides naturally into three types of worshippers: firstly, the formal church goers who are intent on showing the label of Christianity and marking out their respectability in the community; secondly, the evangelical and fundamentalist fanatics of the Bible belt with their great faith healing rallies, speaking in tongues, and excitement into a trance-like state or loss of consciousness; and thirdly, the slave morality cults of the closed communities in remote areas, e.g. the Wako community.

The common thread typical of all American religion is a degree of puritanism, and a hatred of high culture and speculative or free thought amongst any sector of the population. Whilst education or training for specific occupations or money-making business or usury is rarely frowned upon by the churches, high culture is regarded as a distraction from religious activity, and speculative thought condemned as a danger to the soul. In these circumstances it is no wonder that high culture was repressed and unable to play a significant role as a civilising influence in American life.

Religion sought and succeeded in substituting the role of high culture as a spiritual factor in the community to such a degree that cultural forms were reduced to the norm of banality and titillation. It is interesting to contrast this situation with that in Europe, where, as we have seen in Chapter 2, high culture as a spiritual influence is displacing the role previously exerted by organised religion.

5 – Why high (or complex) cultural forms are important to peoples in advanced industrial economies

It may be asked at this point: but what is wrong with low culture? There is nothing wrong with low culture *per se*. It has its own values and may be admirable by its own standards, but there are situations when it threatens the civilisation of a people. Culture is more correctly denominated simple or complex, the latter referring to high or more cerebral forms.

If populism or simple cultural forms are allowed to dominate the life of advanced industrial economies, the understanding or consciousness of their peoples will be retarded in failing to keep apace with the *awareness* necessary in wisely directing technological progress. There is then a mismatch between the technological development of a people and its comprehension of new realities and what they mean. This is manifested in all kinds of psychological ills and conflicts.

The value of more complex cultural forms in advanced industrial economies is that they confer both a greater understanding of human nature and a deeper spirituality on the nature of existence. They extend the knowledge and mental powers of the individual, conferring greater cerebral pleasures than could ever be enjoyed by the simpler cultural pursuits which lay greater emphasis on raw emotion. More complex cultural forms are naturally more demanding on the intellect, but the transition from primitive to civilised societies is marked by an increasing use of the intellect in the understanding and enjoyment of life. For example, the cultural enjoyment of a primitive tribe in dancing and singing in a moonlit jungle glade, is so concentrated on the nervous system to the exclusion of cerebral activity that it degenerates into self-induced fits or trances of an ecstatic nature. It results, therefore, in the loss of self-control.

Contrast this with the enjoyment of those attending a symphony concert or a music drama in a modern industrial society where an understanding of leitmotifs and other technical structures adds to the enjoyment of the performance. In this environment, the mind as a thinking mechanism, is never allowed to be disengaged. Whilst the first example is little more than a drugged experience, the second contributes to greater spiritual enlightenment without the individual's need for loss of consciousness. This is an extreme comparison between the mental effects of simple and complex cultural forms, but examples might just as easily be cited from the film or works of fiction. Infinitely more is to be gained by the understanding and moral feelings through the experience of reading a novel like *Crime and Punishment* than the trivia of a pot-boiler; or by watching a mid-period Ingmar Bergman film than a Hollywood second feature.

6 – How low culture corrupts advanced societies

We live in an evolving world where the potential for the improvement of the human race is ever-present. Although the increasing complexity of society, and the broader knowledge and understanding of the individual are not in themselves evidence of goodness or virtue, they undoubtedly increase the potential for these qualities. We could go further and even say that ignorance is evil and that knowledge is good, and build an ethical system on such a contention, even though it might conflict entirely with Judaeo-Christian thought which traditionally has contemned knowledge as a danger to the soul.

The argument pursued in this book, however, and it needs to be upheld by Social Capitalists, is that it is a moral and life-long duty of all to improve their knowledge and intellectual capacity as conscious beings in safeguarding their personal integrity and that of society. An egalitarian society within a framework of justice and freedom cannot exist without the on-going struggle for self-improvement, and in understanding the social environment. The reason for this as a categorical imperative is as a safeguard against exploitation (whether covert or open), or against the development of a false consciousness, and in promoting the co-operative efforts of justice and democracy.

The failure of high (or complex) culture to penetrate the population of modern industrialised America has led to feelings of alienation and rootlessness, perhaps best reflected in the tales of her greatest short story writer, O. Henry, or in the novels of Theodore Dreiser, or in the biting satire of Sinclair Lewis. But worse was to follow with the numbing cult of oncoming waves of differing canons of pop music from the 1950s onwards, and from the start, these were complemented by the post-War American drug culture, which sought to spread its evil tentacles throughout the world, often in the wake of the American armed services. It is no coincidence that pop music should become inextricably linked with the drug culture, since the mindless beat of the former is a reversion to the primitive sounds of the jungle drum, with its concentration on the nervous system and inducement to a trance-like state.

The only difference is that modern pop music fails to engender sufficient intensity for the loss of consciousness towards which it strives, and so drugs become a natural and essential accompaniment in reaching this blessed condition. But another qualifying comparison has to be made: there is a cultural or historical justification for the activity of the primitive tribe in its use of music in reaching a trance-like state, for it is usually linked to a religious or magic ceremony for a specific outcome, e.g., for rain, fertilisation, etc., or to induce an instruction or prophetic advice from the mouth of a tribal sorcerer. No similar justification can be extended to the pop group which strives to lead its audience into a state of semi-consciousness for hedonistic motives alone. This is merely the abuse of a cultural form in debasing those who indulge in its injurious enjoyment.

7 – The good intentions but bad outcome of American cultural domination

The most dangerous aspect of the American value system examined above, is that it is now used increasingly as a ruthless instrument of cultural imperialism, which no one in any part of the world desires apart from those deriving a direct financial profit from its marketing onslaught. It is important to describe exactly what this imperialism in reducing cultural standards to the lowest common denominator means to the peoples of the world. The American does not recognise this process as imperialism, but only as a natural dissemination of American ideas and cultural forms in response to popular demand. He recognises this process with a warm feeling of benevolence and self-satisfaction, under the false impression as if the world was beating a path to his door to enjoy the material benefits of Americanisation. America is filled with goodwill towards the peoples of the world whilst concurrently failing to comprehend their underlying needs or feelings. Her attitude is that of overweening patronage.

The American believes wrongly that all peoples everywhere are the same, and he is only able to hold this belief, since he holds national cultures in disdain as irrelevant to progress or a forward looking approach. He sees national cultures as a barrier of understanding between what his country has to offer and what the world may receive within a universal melting pot. This complacent viewpoint is derived from his own historical past: there was a time when he repudiated the cultural tradition of Europe and all it had to offer, and now he expects the world in its turn to repudiate its past in taking on the material values of *his* civilisation. The American has so much confidence in the superiority of his material civilisation, and puts so much value in materialism itself, that he is unable to see the insolence of this imposition on older and better cultures than his own.

8 – The dangers of American cultural imperialism

The danger to the world through the dissemination of American cultural values is the domination of thought control, or more correctly, the numbing of the mind and the destruction of the capacity for further speculative thought. We have seen something of this in Chapter 3 in the context of marketing applied to book publishing and retailing. Populism cannot simply be accepted on its own grounds as pleasure fulfilment, any more than can the pleasures of opium or cocaine. There comes a point when the mindlessness of pure hedonism destroys the individual and the fabric of society. History itself is a witness to the fact that civilisations fall due to the inner rottenness of their cultures, and the consequent intellectual inability of their peoples to think ahead of events. In the highly technological world of today with its huge demand on brainpower, civilisation cannot be upheld purely through each country maintaining its own tiny controlling elite as may have been the situation in the past.

The majority need to be elevated, not merely intellectually through education, but through a moral will, to a higher level than heretofore, and it is only through culture that this moral will may be promoted. In the industrial countries of the old world there was once a time when conventional religion fulfilled the role of directing this moral will, but as the intellectual development of the churches failed to keep ahead of technological progress and what it meant in changing attitudes, people have increasingly either lost their faith, or turned away from organised religion in disgust at its inability to comprehend the problems of the age and offer a satisfying moral leadership. Hence the vital role of high culture in substituting religion.

But the tide of populism may retard the educational task in elevating the majority. Teachers and other leaders in society are limited in their capacity to change those around them. The threat of populism in this struggle between Ormazd and Ahriman may witness the victory of barbarism, for in the words of Juvenal, the first Satirist, "Anxiously the people desire only two things, bread and circuses."[16]

The self-satisfaction of the common mind in America amongst its own financial-industrial elite, which perceives progress and all serious thinking on the human condition as somehow having reached its completion for all time is mind-boggling in its audacity. Such a book as Francis Fukuyama's, *The End of History*, for example, could only have been written and published in America. The presumption and arrogance of the idea that political thought has come to the end of the road, or that liberal democracy is the ultimate pinnacle of socio-political achievement, is breathtaking in its myopic view of humanity. Such an intellectual perspective, or misinterpretation of reality, could only have come to fruition in a society with a very limited capacity for speculative thought.

9 – The need to resist this

In view of these factors, there is therefore no reason why the non-American world should fight shy of attacking the degradation of populism and low culture wherever it spreads its poisonous tentacles. It is the obligation of educational systems, of schools, parents, and guardians everywhere, not merely to resist but to combat the influence of American cultural values. Such a task is best confronted through the use of shame and ridicule. God or evolution did not intend the human mind to be abused through the ennui of meaningless pursuits to fill in time.

The adult who seeks to stimulate his nervous system whilst numbing his consciousness by spending his leisure hours in amusement arcades or saloon bars feeding fruit machines, or watching Mickey Mouse on TV, or following the pop charts with slavish enthusiasm, is not merely indulging in a form of self-abuse, but demeaning himself and his genetic inheritance as a human being. In the Confucian societies of the Far East it could be argued he was disgracing his ancestors. In the East and West alike it may be pointed out that such an individual sets a bad example to those who are younger or weaker than himself (or herself), and hence is a corrupting influence on society.

All such activities become depraved as soon as they disengage the thinking   mind to become escapist or are a substitute for

---

[16] "Duas tantem res anxius optat, panem et circenses," Juvenal, *Satire* 10, li, 80.

forgetfulness. And all such activities are American not only in the sense that the assisting artefacts or media for such are of American origin or invention, but that the commercial concept and promotion of leisure designed to satisfy the lowest common denominator is specific to that nation and no other. If these pursuits were not designed by the American Rentier financial-industrial establishment for the sole purpose of the mind control of the masses, then they certainly serve that purpose as a "bread and circuses" function in forestalling the discontent of the soul and in nurturing a false consciousness.

In confronting the tide of barbarism from the north American continent it is suggested that Britain enters into a cultural treaty with her EU partners, in addition to the Confucian countries and other Asian and like-minded states, for developing a cultural policy and so increasing cultural exchange with regard to the film, theatre, music, the translation of literature, etc. If such a cultural bloc was sufficiently determined, it might significantly alter the balance of consumption in favour of the more civilised states of the old world. In formulating such a policy, however, and promoting a campaign in attacking barbarism and the ills which it brings in its wake, circumspection would be needed and unanimity amongst states in all decision-making. It would be unwise to implement such a treaty if it risked backfiring, or if it failed to carry the will of the educated majority. What is certain is that such a treaty would be supported with enthusiasm by many millions of highly-educated people from all parts of the world.

10 – Egalitarianism as the aristocracy of the majority

Social Capitalism is deeply concerned with these questions not because of the dignity of the human race, but because of the need for each individual to have a direct controlling power in the management of society. Equality can have no other meaning than this, but in a sophisticated industrial society, it requires that each individual be raised educationally to a much higher level than heretofore, so that as a participating member of society, he or she may be fully aware of the intricacies of governmental power, and so enabled to take on the necessary responsibilities.

But to take on these responsibilities in a meaningful sense, formal knowledge is not in itself sufficient. For an understanding of the spirit, or underlying moral purpose of society, the short cut of organised religion (which too often has its own ulterior motives)[17] is no longer sufficient; and in an increasingly secular and complex world can no longer fulfil the spiritual needs of humankind.   It is the integrity and truth of high culture which is now needed (the natural substitute for the dead and crooked doctrines of organised religion) as expressed through the music, literature and other arts of humankind. It is the assimilation of this which makes every man and woman an equal in an upwardly aspiring egalitarian society.

If Social Capitalism does not seek to create a society of the best - of all and for all - an aristocracy of the majority, then it is failing both the human race and the cause of civilisation.   In our modern society, the middle-middle majority are just not prepared to entertain the idea of a class-based downward looking egalitarianism which glorifies proletarianism as a value in itself.   Such a philosophy as advanced by socialism was doomed to extinction on the day when the bricks of the Berlin Wall were torn to the ground. The future is to be found in the upward aspiring cultural egalitarianism of Social Capitalism, which recognises no classes other than that of the Responsible Society based on the standards of disinterested justice[18] and high culture.

*

---

[17] See Chapter 6 of *The People's Capitalism.*

[18] See Chapter 34 sub-section 7 of *The People's Capitalism.*

PART II

The Politics of Property

"It is the divorce of ownership and control, rather than the democratisation of wealth that has characterised the twentieth century development of capitalist enterprise."

Leslie Hannah, *The Rise of The Corporate Economy*, Methuen, 1976, p. 64.

The most important issues in politics have always concerned property relationships; and nothing has given rise to more conflict and confusion, or to more arguing at corss-purposes.

This is because of the simplistic consideration given to property relationships on the political level. Broadly speaking today, questions of property fall into two schools of thought: those who advocate common ownership and those who advocate private ownership. But whilst "private ownership" or "privatisation" are useless terms because of their breadth and contradiction of interpretation; "common ownership" is also a nonsense, not only because it is unworkable, but because when it allegedly exists, it clearly defies its own definition.

Even those philosophers, who are most commonly referred to on questions of property, have approached the topic from such an emotionally-charged viewpoint, that they have failed to penetrate its sociological reality. They have merely skirted around the issues. Rousseau, Babeuf and Proudhon are chiefly remembered for their several vehement statements on the nature of property – some admittedly, often quoted out of context – all of which have contributed little towards a more realistic understanding. As for Marx and Engels, they have claimed a sociological approach but they uncovered little, and gave a twisted interpretation of the sources used. The sum total of the early writings of Karl Marx on this topic, merely points to the conclusion that the possession and use of private property is de-humanising, and is therefore a bad thing.

Friedrich Engels' much later work, *The Origin of The Family, Private Property and The State*, based on the research of the early American sociologist, Lewis Morgan, comes to the extraordinary conclusion that the common ownership patterns of primitive societies are more virtuous than our own, so implying that they are somehow worthy of emulation. When discussing the family structures of earlier communities, *vis-à-vis* property relationships, he raises a multitude of questions, none of which he attempts to answer in practical terms of relating them to the industrial societies of his time. This kind of naivety hardly takes us a step beyond the romanticism of Rousseau's "noble savage" of more than a century earlier. Whilst the emphasis of earlier writers on property has been a call for more equitable re-distribution; the emphasis of Marx and Engels and their followers up until the very recent past has been a call for the general abolition of private property.

If one turns to the liberal thinkers, from Locke onwards, they defend the principle of freedom implied in the right to private property - even confirming its sacrosanct nature - but they do not begin to formulate a positive general theory defining and justifying the meaning of property as it relates to the totality of the socio-economic mechanisms of society. The nearest they come to this is in the advocacy of laissez-faire, which broadly states that property relationships should be left as they are, since intervention is a breach of liberty. Even if one takes the writings of Ludwig von Mises and F. A. Hayek, who are associated with the right (although they may have repudiated such leanings) - authors very much in vogue during the Thatcherite period in the Anglo-Saxon world - they will be found to have contributed little that is new to the concept of property. All these writers are concerned with freedom, but their concern with justice is deficient because their thinking fails to consider the very real misfortunes that are visited on society through the need to adjust property relationships. Whilst earlier thinkers may have dismissed these misfortunes upon society as merely the "will of God," more contemporary thinkers have simply dismissed them as the "law of nature." Such dismissive attitudes, or such fatalism, clearly reflects a moral callousness.

The enquiry in the following chapters attempts a new approach to the question of property. It unravels the present confusion by creating a synthesis between opposing outlooks, and formulates a radical left or centrist viewpoint. It cuts through the Have and Have-not syndromes of those who have earlier tackled the question from one side or the other, and instead attempts to reach the sociological core of the problem.   If objectivity is the purpose in reaching conclusions that are morally and practically acceptable to the majority, then this approach is necessary.The following eleven chapters set out to formulate a new rationale for property. They are not concerned with the legal or abstract rights of property *per se*, but rather with considering the ownership and use of property as a personal right in developing the full potential of the individual, in the same way that an individual has a personal right to freedom of speech or movement, or the right to an education in developing his or her potential.   This is a positive approach to the concept of property, contrasting sharply with the amoral neutrality of laissez-faire, or the deficiencies of collectivism.   As will become clear, there is a philosophical source to which this idea is indebted. Philosophically, the idea will be found to be in as much conflict with laissez-faire theory as that of common ownership. It is, in a sense, a complete reversal of Marx's early sociological thinking on the nature of private property, for it is now argued that the ownership and control of property by the individual should be so adjusted as to have a humanising influence on society. In the terminology of Social Capitalism it entails a call for the *personalisation* of property relationships.

How is all this to be tied in with the practical reality of our own time? If we study our toughest industrial competitors in the free world, it will be found that they already enjoy societies with property relationships approaching those described in the following chapters. That is, there is a relatively equitable distribution of property, and no highly-significant oppressive sector.   In Britain, we do not yet currently enjoy such a socio-economic situation.

In addition to a deep social divide, we are disadvantaged with unjust property relationships and the inequitable distribution of personal wealth, that is both hindering social progress and the furthering of industrial development. These chapters therefore set out to create a theoretical framework for property relationships inspired by the practical achievement of our European neighbours who are more advanced in this respect.   Such a framework and such comparisons will help us towards solutions of these divisive questions.

CHAPTER 7
Some Popular Misconceptions

"Both the right to property and the rights of property have never been more strongly attacked or more weakly supported. ... property rights on anything more than a domestic scale have come to seem unnecessary if not actually anachronistic."

Daniel Green, *The Politics of Food*, Gordon Cremonese, 1975, p. 150.

1 - Demoralisation in the workplace   2 - Not an intrinsic characteristic   3 - Motivation dependent on the work environment   4 - But most of all on a sense of freewill   5 - Obsolescence of Management theory   6 - The psychological value of possession   7 - Abuses have given rise to false notions on property   8 - Religious leaders on property relationships   9 - Dichotomy between religious and secular values   10 - Political misconceptions on property relationships

1 – Demoralisation in the workplace

It is said that those holding an employed status in Britain - and this includes executives and office staff no less than shop-floor workers - are less motivated, than their counterparts in other advanced countries of the industrialised West.

Research into both attitudes and the productivity of manpower in the industrial sector has confirmed the above assumption, and this factor has to be related as bearing some responsibility for Britain's poor industrial record in the post-War period. But such a conclusion should not be freely interpreted as reflecting the intrinsic characteristics of the British, as is often suggested by the popular press or common opinion, but should rather give rise to a questioning attitude as to why and how this sociological phenomenon may have come about. If our people appear to have lacked a diligence or enthusiasm for work for a long period following World War II, by comparison with what may be perceived amongst our competitors, nothing is achieved by the finality of a fatalistic attitude.[19] Such a stance would explain nothing and gain nothing.

2 – Not an intrinsic characteristic

If attention is turned to the self-employed in Britain - to the small businessman or woman struggling to maintain an export trading firm,

---

19 It should be noted that there has been a reversal of this trend over the past dozen years – certainly in comparison withGermany.

to the proprietor of the corner shop, to the hillside farmer with a limited acreage, to the roofing contractor or carpenter operating from his home - it will be found that these, and many others, work as diligently and as long hours as anyone anywhere in the world. If, on the contrary, one takes the employed electro-technician, or the employed physicist, and transplants him from the urban sprawl of the Midlands to the more salubrious surroundings of a town in Germany or Holland, or elsewhere in the EU, it will soon be found that he works no less diligently and with no less satisfaction to himself and his employers than his new-won colleagues. He becomes a changed man or woman! If, even, one takes the employed brick layer, the crane driver, the general construction worker or the dock workers' foreman, and transplants him from the lately tumble down cities of Liverpool or Newcastle-upon-Tyne to the no-less uncomfortable environments of Riyadh, Doha or Jubail, it will again be found that he works as diligently, willingly and uncomplainingly as anyone can be expected to in the circumstances. Again, he becomes a changed person! It is a nonsense, therefore, to suggest that lack of motivation or reluctance to engage in concerted effort are qualities intrinsic to the British. In fact, over the past fifteen years the British have been transformed into the most hard-working people in Europe in terms of hours worked and the shorter duration of their holidays.

3 – Motivation dependent on the work environment

Work attitudes and work effectiveness are not so much dependent on national or personal characteristics as on the work environment. This, of course, should be obvious merely from a study of differing attitudes and the productivity of manpower found in various spheres of employed work here in Britain. There are certain companies in Britain renowned for having good employee relationships, and in return, this is complemented by higher than average performance standards. The sociology of work is the all-important factor governing attitudes and performance. But when the malaise of Britain is seen in its wider context as a national phenomenon, omnipotent in the world of work and non-work alike, reaching into every cranny of the nation's consciousness, it becomes something that has transcended the capacity of the company alone to counteract. The ailment has become so deep-seated that it is well beyond the ability of the most well-intentioned British-based company to ward off the deleterious influences of de-motivation and underlying suspicion for very long. This is because the company, however large, remains but a microcosm within the infinitely wider influences of society.

4 – But most of all on a sense of freewill

The sociology of work motivation has been well researched, and the conclusions are clear. Work motivation is dependent on such factors as a sufficient wage level for fulfilling material expectations, congenial working conditions, friendly co-operation with peers, and a style of authority which is neither harsh nor oppressive. But the most important factor of all concerns the sense of total control over the functions entailed in the world of work. This is reflected in not merely the ability of the individual to efficiently perform those tasks he is called upon to fulfill, but more significantly, it is also reflected in the discretion or freewill of the individual acting within the sphere of his defined work objectives.

The individual who works free of conscious restraints, voluntarily, as an agent free to exert his own discretion, is, in general terms likely to be more efficient in the execution of his tasks than the individual who is so hemmed-in on all sides by oppressive conditions that he is prevented from using his own good judgement or understanding in applying his labour. This applies to all spheres of employment, not just managerial - but also to repetitive and unskilled work. This is because people, unlike machines, cannot simply be programmed, but are dependent on motivation and feelings of satisfaction by the fact of their humanity. The application of responsibility in the sphere of work, together with commitment to the organisation is ultimately dependent on the power of the individual over the processes of his given tasks. This, of course, is furthered by increasing the employee's power of discretion, by incorporating systems of co-determinational industrial democracy, and most of all, by the final step in granting *ownership*, for this is the ultimate benefit in conferring job responsibility. The owning-employee is actually invested with an element of legal responsibility for ensuring the success of the enterprise - and this he certainly never had before.

5 – Obsolescence of management theory

In advocating the need for co-determination and employee part-ownership, we are thereby implying the obsolescence of American man-management theory and practice as it has developed on the back of the Behaviourist school of psychology. Management as a "science" is possibly America's greatest contribution of the 20th century to the world of business. As a need, it developed out of the intensive industrialism of America, particularly in view of the fact that manufacturing enterprise was conducted on a larger scale, so employing more workers concentrated in one plant than elsewhere. From the closing decades of the 19th century, up until the present time, the literature in terms of books and articles, stemming from America, on the science of Management may be listed in tens of thousands. However, it has to be emphasised that Management is a uniquely American concept, most European languages being without even any equivalent term. Hence the word "Management" has now been adopted into the languages of most countries in the industrialised world. American man-management theories and practices have been accepted world-wide, albeit reluctantly and often with reservations. In Britain especially, because of language and cultural similarities, Management theories have been more readily accepted than elsewhere. In Japan, on the contrary, the influence of such theories and practices have been minimal, or reinterpreted in a quite different manner.

The philosophy of Management theory, it has to be noted, is based on the needs of classical capitalism: i.e. acceptance of the fact of a clear separation between owners and shareholders on the one hand and employees on the other. Hence its object, in the light of this factor, has been to ensure that the psychological needs of employees are fully satisfied within these constraints in lieu of legal or moral rights which need to be sacrificed. This is achieved through applying behaviourist theories in the workplace, but of course this introduces an element of illusion and guile if there is to remain a separation between those who own an enterprise and those who work for it. It also means, of course, that resulting Management practices, even if successful as a carrot-and-stick approach, are devoid of any moral authority.

It is the application of behavioural psychology by one group of humans with a specific set of economic objectives (i.e. maximising the profits of shareholders) to exploit through misleading stimuli, another group of humans with a different set of economic objectives, which makes American man-management practices so grossly immoral. In Britain, from the beginning, because of this whiff of trickery, Management theories were received with dismissive cynicism, but nonetheless, they made their inevitable headway. In the past, British managers and workers alike have been less hypocritical or less "taken-in" than their "simpler" or more optimistic cousins across the Atlantic, preferring instead to openly recognise the divide between capital and labour for what it was.

But these are not factors which have made American Management theories obsolescent. Social changes have achieved that. Management theory and practice possibly achieved its greatest influence as a force in the workplace as a philosophy socially and morally acceptable to the community in general in the decade leading up to the Second World War. This is not to suggest that "scientific" management has not made many advances since then, but it has advanced in a society that has been increasingly sceptical of its purpose. Social changes in the northern hemisphere since the Second World War have seen the development of societies which are very much more conscious of their sociological and economic roles in the community than hitherto. Employees in the contemporary world are illusion-free and can no longer be inveigled into believing themselves to be satisfied workers simply through the ulterior machinations of the behavioural sciences. They demand something more - in America no less than in Europe. They realise that the old system of conventional capitalism by necessity not only fails to satisfy their psychological needs, but more significantly, actually deprives them of rights and privileges to which they feel entitled. And those rights and privileges entail co-determination in the management of the enterprise as well as part-ownership in commitment to its success.

6 – The psychological value of possession

Therefore a free society, and one in which work relationships are best achieved, and where productivity is greatest, is that where the sharing out of private ownership is maximised. This raises the entire question of the theory and practice of possession, not merely with regard to moral or legal rights in society, but more significantly, with regard to its sociological aspects. Only when the latter has been subjected to a full analysis can the concept of property be given an ideal political interpretation. These chapters are therefore concerned with the nature of possession in its widest meaning as it relates to the individual and society, and of all issues in politics, this is possibly the most important yet most misunderstood of all.

7 – Abuses have given rise to false notions on property

For millennia, the nature of ownership as it relates to the individual in society, has given rise to popular misconceptions. These irrational misconceptions have originated from frustration and conflict in society, culminating in the distortion of the true perception of the function of ownership. This tension and conflict has arisen from the inequitable distribution of property and the hardship and injustice for which this has been responsible. Consequently, as a response to this frustration, the following amongst other notions have developed on a recurring basis throughout most societies in the civilised world - notions which if not specifically political have been religious or moral, and have nonetheless for that become ingrained in the consciousness of all classes in communities everywhere. Amongst the most common of these ethical notions with their fallacious bias, pushing their way towards a political solution, may be listed the following:-

1. That the love of property and material possessions is wrong, since it conflicts with the free expression of spiritual needs;

2. That the holding of property is not of paramount importance to the life of the individual, since spiritual needs are foremost;

3. That obsession with property is corrupting, since it diminishes sensibility towards human needs;

4. That all property should be held in common ownership, since only then can distribution be rendered fairly;

5. That money-making is an evil activity, since it encourages an attitude of meanness towards humankind;

6. That a life of ascetic poverty reflects a virtuous existence; and,

7. That the charging of interest is under all circumstances a social evil, since it enriches without labour.

8 – Religious leaders on property relationships

It is not contended that the above seven notions or commands are necessarily the precepts of Christianity or of any other comparable religion. Neither is it to be inferred that each of the above fail to include some aspect of sound sociological truth that may be separated from the purely religious context - however religion may be defined - in satisfying also the agnostic humanist. Whilst not failing to value the contributions to thought of all great religious teachers, it also has to be understood that in the popularising of their ideas, there is a tendency to clouding and so misinterpreting the clarity of those concepts as originally taught. Walter Lippmann has interestingly observed that, "because the teaching of the sages was incomprehensible, the multitude, impressed but also bewildered, ignored them as teachers and worshipped them as gods. In their wisdom the people were not interested, but in the legend of their power, which rumour created, there was something understandable. And thus, the religions which have been organised around the names of great spiritual teachers have been popular in proportion, one might also say, to the degree in which the original insight into the necessity for conviction and self-discipline has been reduced to a system of commands and promises which the common man can understand."[20]

In addition, religious precepts when they are not specific to particular societies at particular points in time, are more usually general commands to be understood in a special context, i.e. not in the sense of universal dogmas, but rather, as general guides to conduct and conscience. This may be particularly applied to those commands on hygiene as found in the Jewish and Islamic faiths. Therefore such precepts have arisen within a historical setting, and because of that and the nature of progress, their validity (as objectively understood) is necessarily limited by the constraints of time and space. The relativity of moral precepts as universal standards has been pointed out by Dr. Rashdell in his book, *The Theory of Good And Evil*, when he observed that, "there is hardly a vice or a crime (according to our own moral

---

[20] Walter Lippmann, *A Preface To Morals*, Allen & Unwin, 1931 ed., pp. 200-201.

standard) which has not at some time or other in some circumstances been looked upon as a moral and religious duty."[21]

The point now being made with regard to the concept of possession as reflected through popular moral or religious opinion, is that the true functions of property as a sociological need in society, have been of little interest to the great religious teachers of the past, and have consequently played an insignificant role in their systems of thought. The attitude of the great religious teachers to property has been dismissive. This is partly because the question of property is political and religious teachers have been predominantly a-political. Hence they have tended to regard the question of property as irrelevant when put beside issues of supposedly "greater" significance. Their message has always been that property is of "no importance" to the essence of humanity, or the individual in his pursuit of salvation or perfection. The first purpose of the great religious teachers has been to persuade the individual to throw aside all feelings of attachment to property, so that he might better devote his mind and soul to a "higher" world, or to cultivating an improved inner self. But on the other hand, it would be entirely false to infer from this that the founders of the great religions and their disciples were "against property" or "against the ownership of property," *per se*. They have always distinguished what belonged to Caesar and what to God. They were only against the different evils to which property gave rise in their own particular societies as they interpreted it, and in this we concur.

9 – Dichotomy between religious and secular values

Nevertheless, for several reasons, viz. because of the separation in the Western world of spiritual values as falling within the realm of religion, from material values (including property) falling within the secular world of political power; and because of the clear separation between church and state in the modern era, there has occurred in society a strange dichotomy between the perception of those matters pertaining to the private conscience of the individual, and those matters pertaining to obligations enforced by secular authority. Consequently, it is only to be expected that there should be in society a confusion and conflict with regard to right and wrong,

---

[21] Quoted in Prof. C.E.M. Joad's, *Decadence*, Faber & Faber, 1948, p. 159.

justice and injustice, *vis-à-vis* the individual and society in relation to the concept of ownership.

The confusion is, of course, compounded by the fact that the privileged and conventional, and the not-so-privileged, concur entirely on the Seventh day of the week - or more commonly, in our contemporary secular society, with their innermost private feelings - with those popular notions in their fallacious guise on the nature of property. If "love of property" or "material values" may be perceived as reprehensible (so these people think) then such principles may always be applied as grounds for moral criticism (however wrongly) of those in opposition to the economic class to which they naturally belong. That is, whilst the proletariat, the poor, or the employed classes - and these include the majority of our population - may look askance at the privileged and wealthy because of their possessions, so too may the latter in our modern affluent society look askance at the greed or "unjustified" demands of the former. None are exempt today from the accusation (however wrongly applied) of pushing their materialistic ends too far. It is then that the fallacious bias (as objective sociological truths) of religious precepts, are used as hypocritical or false excuses by one sector of society to criticise another, or rather, by several sectors of society to engage in mutual recrimination. It is in the interests of the well-to-do to pontificate on "spiritual values" and the rewards of "self-sacrifice" or the need for "deferred benefits," etc., as against the "crass materialism" of our age; as it is of the less fortunate to hide their envy behind such moral platitudes as the impossibility of the camel passing through the eye of a needle.

Such moral values, as we have cited, since they are separated from the values of the secular world, therefore leave at best much room for intellectual self-delusion, or at worst much room for hypocrisy. These chapters, in considering the essential sociological function of possession in society will aim at a synthesis of the moral and political in achieving the ultimate reality on this question of greatest significance in human relationships. That is, there must be a point where the four elements of Acquisitiveness, Expediency, Fairness and Morality, may be found to converge in contributing to the best needs of a democratic, just, contented and Social Capitalist society.

10 – Political misconceptions on property relationships

The deeply held moral or religious notions on the concept of possession, as they have been falsely perceived in the popular mind, have been carried over to the sphere of political thought, where notions of even greater falsity have been allowed to mushroom on an intellectual plane.   These notions, in recent times, have most commonly sprung from Old Socialist patterns of thought.   The following may be listed amongst their number:-

1.   That all property is theft, and that its ownership by the individual is therefore regrettable;

2.   That property should be in common ownership if it is to serve the benefit of all;

3.   That the state should take upon itself the ownership of property in the name of the people, if common ownership is to be achieved in practice;

4.   That the problems of property merely entail the need for its more equal re-distribution;

5.   That the acquisitive instinct, giving rise to the accumulation of property, is a social evil that needs to be crushed through changing the nature of men and women;

6.   That profits are not merely a social evil, but are wrong and unnecessary in the attempt to create an affluent egalitarian society; and,

7.   That the abolition of money would lead to the creation of a benevolent society, freed from all the temptations of greed and want.

As with those seven notions listed in the religious sphere, it is not contended that the above accurately reflect the given precepts or principles of innovative or other political thinkers. They may indeed stem from misquotations or popular misinterpretations of popular texts - but for all their wrong-headedness, they are falsities which remain in the popular consciousness, and to that extent are influential. There is, therefore, all the greater need for identifying the sociological reality of possession as it truly exists. And in any case, we repudiate all the claims and interpretations both implied and explicit, of the above fourteen listed points. They are mischievous and confused - mere mental aberrations arising from the painfully conflicting cultural chaos of the past two millennia. It is now our purpose to discover some sense and order where none has existed hitherto.

CHAPTER 8
Political Conflict and Property

"The fiscal policies adopted this century have led to the destruction of private property on a large scale, to a strengthening of the executive powers of government and to the enthronement of big business."

James Coffield, *A Popular History of Taxation*, Longmans, 1970, p. 49.

1 - Man's unique acquisitiveness   2 - Utopianism is linked to oppression   3 - Oppression stems from the monopoly of power and possession   4 - The solution is to maximise the number of possessors   5 - This is not achieved through Nationalisation   6 - Nor through the misnomer of "Privatisation"   7 - Extending ownership and control increases productivity   8 - Examples of this in rural areas   9 - And in manufacturing industry

1 – Man's unique acquisitiveness

Any discussion of the political problems of property as they occur in society must begin with a consideration of the conflict arising through the struggle for power over resources and people, and the nature of the acquisitive instinct. The apparently unresolvable nature of this conflict stems from the fact that *homo sapiens* is the sole animal in creation whose acquisitive instinct is infinite or never satisfied. The term Acquisitive is meant here in its broadest sense, i.e. not merely as a striving for material possessions, but for knowledge in all its aspects and for the satisfaction and rewards which follow in its wake. Moralists have often deplored this acquisitive instinct by adversely comparing man as the fallen being corrupted by original sin, by contrast with that innocence of the lesser creatures whose lusts are quelled through the satisfaction of immediate need.

Homo sapiens, by contrast, is depicted as greedy, vicious and destructive by the fact of his infinite acquisitiveness alone. The pessimism of Schopenhauer's philosophy, for example, is to be found in his perceiving man as subject to insatiable wants; as an unsatisfied Will based ethically in evil; and a spirit that can know no peace. This, however, is a false perception of the nature of humanity. Without this infinite acquisitiveness, the human race would have remained in the trees alongside the jungle apes. The acquisitiveness of man - unique to him alone - should not be seen as a reprehensible characteristic to be crushed and cursed as an unnatural instinct, but rather as the essence of his creative being in the struggle towards a higher consciousness and fulfilment. The acquisitive instinct, therefore, should not be crushed and condemned but rather sublimated to fulfil a socially useful function. If the natural aggressiveness, which is part of this acquisitiveness, is lacking in a community then there is cause for concern for the future of such a society. In the words of a contributor to the Hudson Report on Britain's economic future, "the very kindliness or lack of aggression, which characterises British social relations may not be entirely unconnected with the country's poor economic performance. If, as is certainly the case, it produces a relaxed environment and figures as one of the characteristics of British society most attractive to foreigners, it is doubtful if this advantage is sufficient to counterbalance the negative consequences."[22] When the acquisitive instinct is missing in a society, then that people has entered on the path of decline and degeneracy - moral as well as physical. The loss of spirit or will to progress, grow or expand, only points towards the direction of debilitating age or death.

2 – Utopianism is linked to oppression

Those throughout the ages, who have rebelled against oppression - and they include nearly all who promote the Socialist ethos - have been obsessed with deprecating man's acquisitiveness in a call for a basic change in human nature. They have adopted this attitude since it is the easiest option for those who are helpless and without power. It needs no effort to invent a system based on moral indignation, i.e. a rationale for justifying hatred of those placed in a stronger position than ourselves. Psychologically, it is often a totally satisfactory recompense for those who are crushed by tyranny. Friedrich Nietzsche, whose philosophy led to existentialism, wrote many volumes explaining just this tendency. The oppressed, in their state of wretchedness, have placed their trust entirely in the hope that man will opt to sacrifice the individuality of his will for the sake of the common welfare. This, of course, is an impossibility. It is as absurd as that expectation that waits for the lion or the wolf to forego their hunting instincts in peacefully lying down with their prey. This unrealistic view for the hope of a change in humankind's nature has led inevitably to two results: firstly, to the creation of societies more

---

[22] *The UK in 1980*, Hudson Report, Associated Business Programmes Ltd., 1974, p. 66.

oppressive or tyrannical than heretofore; and secondly, to a regression towards utopian religiosity and a hope for the achievement of millennial ideals. This is why tyranny and religion in its most superstitious forms are so often found in the same societies. Those throughout the ages who have supported the conservative ethos, whilst upholding the *status quo* in the secular realm - however horrid in its manifestations - have always gained a solace in religion with all its fatalism, in passively accepting the imperfectibility of the world. Both throughout history and within societies there has been a pendulum-like swing, and a complementary reaction, between a passive acceptance of pain and injustice on the one hand, and an empty millennial hope for a better future, either in this world or the next.

The acquisitive or aggressive instinct of man has always in most societies needed an outlet for its expression. In the past, this has always been expressed through tribal or national conflict, and such conflict (however malevolent in its direct consequences) has usually strengthened the customs and cultural bonds of the separate communities, so contributing to what is subjectively referred to as the "moral fibre" of a people. Consequently, in a community not exposed to psychological pressure (irrespective as to whether or not these are of an inter-tribal or inter-national nature) there soon occurs a malaise and a breaking down of traditional relationships - including those of the family - and there develops an ennui and the characteristics of what are commonly described as "decadence." This particularly occurs in a dependent or "welfare" society. This is not an apology for the virtues of war (as might have been made in an earlier era), for in our contemporary age war must be regarded as in every respect an evil, but it is an apology for the need for state-directed economic competition within the community, as a mode for ensuring the expression of freedom in its most realistic form. If the individual is to act as a free and independent individual then this must be in the economic sphere, to which all other freedoms must then become subsidiary. The primary role of the state must be to ensure that this economic freedom is granted to those at the base of society no less than to those at its apex.

3 – Oppression stems from the monopoly of power and possession

The tragedy of reforming politics is that its starting base has always and inevitably been from the stymied viewpoint of the community deviating from its ideal type, i.e. from that of the underprivileged and oppressed. The psychological results of this have been unfortunate. Inescapably, from such a viewpoint, models for the future have been constructed that are unsuitable for humankind in the best or most normal state for its existence. It is the spirit of resentment and measures to enforce uniformity and crush the aspirations of the individual that have so often discredited the aims of reforming movements. But concurrently, political Conservatism has been no less damaging to the community, through blocking avenues to progress, than have reforming movements in producing wrong cures for all the ills of society.

A realistic synthesis between these two opposites can only be achieved by eschewing the vested interests of all social groups, as well as by eschewing abstract morality, in place of a proper understanding of man's genuine nature. Once this fact is grasped, then attempts should be made to ensure that natural desires are channelled into socially beneficial activities so that they are no longer sources for injury or oppression. Social oppression, whether economic or political, individual or institutional, results from the accumulation of excessive power in few hands, whereby a labouring majority with few resources are obliged to work for a leisured minority with excess resources.

In this context the labourers are the wealth producers, i.e. the growers and makers of the material needs for livelihood and comfort, whilst the leisured are the parasites dependent on the wealth created by the majority. Wealth by this definition is meant in its broadest or universal sense, i.e. not necessarily entailing the creation of capital (as is always the case in a capitalist society) but rather in the creation of goods, and services that in certain circumstances, e.g., in a slave community, may be independent of capital formation to any significant degree. This is the most basic yet universal description of the nature of ownership as it both advantageously and disadvantageously effects the different sectors of the community at all times and in all places.

4 – The solution is to maximise the number of possessors

The problem of counteracting the domination of majorities by minorities through the accumulation of property in the hands of the few, can only be achieved by maximising the number of property holders in such a way that competition destroys privileged monopoly. But this can only be achieved successfully by encouraging a spirit of acquisitiveness in the majority, as otherwise that majority would only sink into apathy under the domination of ambitious minority elites. It is the absence of this acquisitive instinct in the majority (and it is a cultural and educational factor) that is most responsible for inequality in society. It is only the apathy of the majority - an apathy encouraged by minority elites, and in earlier times by the anodyne influence of religion, and in more recent times by the titillations of an omnipresent media - that makes possible the domination of the majority by tiny minorities. It is "bread and circuses" that enslave and degrade humanity, for they are given in lieu - and are gratefully accepted - in place of *real* possessions and *real* power in managing the affairs of the community. Therefore monopoly must be destroyed in all its manifestations.

By destroying monopoly and stimulating acquisitiveness not only is property more fairly distributed, but a more universal and democratic ethos is instilled into society. America may be cited as a society with such an ethos where in theory, at least, property ownership is understood to be within the reach of all. Where serious attempts are made to extend the reality of property ownership, and the reality of this lies in direct control over property and not merely in the ownership of an empty "title deed," the majority are thereby raised to the status of the most "powerful and privileged," - or at least, equal to them. This should be the aim and the achievement of every free society. Unfortunately, it is not, for modern governments in the West - and especially in Britain - are more concerned with meaningless abstract interpretations of the definition of property.

5 – This is not achieved through nationalisation

Thus the British left until the recent past were concerned with Nationalisation as the panacea to the question of property. The theory of this is public ownership - ownership by the community in total - but the reality is quite different. The experience of Nationalisation during the post-War period amply demonstrated that its practice only entailed a vast accumulation of power into the hands of a small, highly-privileged bureaucratic elite. Whilst these vast organisations, whether government departments or public utilities, increasingly consolidated their power over the realm as closed and secretive bodies protected by the strength of the law, internally they were governed as authoritarian hierarchical structures. The nature of their authoritarianism did not make them bodies of efficiency in performing the functions they were called upon to undertake, but on the contrary, engendered a spirit of suspicion, resentment and stubborn resistance towards change or innovation of any kind.

6 – Nor through the misnomer of "privatisation"

The British right, in the realm of work, were and remain likewise uninterested in the private or individual ownership of property. When they speak of "privatisation," then the transfer of ownership or the control of organisations or enterprises into the hands of those employing them, is the last thing they have in mind. They are rather only concerned with the public sale of stocks and shares - a very abstract form of ownership - that in fact usually entails the increasing concentration of capital and resources into fewer hands. This is because ultimate control and ownership remains in the hands of a small shareholding elite of board members who through the public sale of stocks and shares are able to further enrich themselves, so promoting their own interests, particularly with the enhanced prospect of additional mergers or acquisitions in view. This is the very reverse of "privatisation" if the word is to be used in a proper sense as equating with individual control.   It might also be added that "privatisation" has admirably served the vested interests of those who have directed the public sector when this has meant - as it often has - the doubling or trebling of their salaries following a transfer of ownership. There is nothing "private" in the concept of "privatisation," and it is a wonderful example of the transformation and deceit in the misuse of the English language.

7 – Extending ownership and control increases productivity

An appreciation of property in its real sense, in terms of its use *and* control, as a right properly belonging to the majority, is therefore not something that in fact has been promoted by either of the two great parties of the left or right. Both have in their different ways reduced the concept of property to a meaningless abstraction. But the ownership and use of property as a social right is possibly an argument that has to be subordinated to its utility as a social dynamic in creating a wealth productive society. If a comparison is made with our toughest industrial competitors it will be found that property, in all its forms, is everywhere more equally distributed.   There is no coincidence in this. The individual's relationship with property in a fully capitalised society is in itself a dynamic, inevitably entailing, use, responsibility and profit, unless extraordinary circumstances prevail to the contrary.

8 – Examples of this in rural areas

For example, 10,000 rural acres in the ownership of one person may indeed be put to good productive use with the aid of automated machinery and chemical fertiliser, even though the balanced ecology of the soil might be damaged and the water-bed poisoned with nitrates.   This, however, would be the fate of good soil in a rich agricultural area, even though that soil would be depleted or raped through over-production. In areas where the soil might be poorer or the terrain more difficult, that 10,000 acres is more often put to wasteful or extravagant use by its single owner.   It might lie uncultivated, fallow or useless, or be used as grouse moor for a very different kind of profitability.

If, on the contrary, those 10,000 acres of good or poor soil were to be divided into 40 250-acre freehold family farming units - and by Continental standards they would remain substantial holdings - far more wealth would be created. This would result from the following factors:-

1. Through the creation of what recent research has confirmed would be a plateau of greater efficiency in the size of farmholding (100 - 300 acres);

2. Through the employment and maintenance of a greater number of people;

3. Through the absolute necessity to maintain a commercially viable business;

4. Through the intensive but balanced cultivation of the land;

5. Through eschewing its wasteful or extravagant use;

6. Through facilitating both greater diversity and flexibility in the productive use of land; and,

7. Through raising the value of land as a source for taxation, so ensuring that its productive use would be sensibly linked to its profitability.

Plots would not thereby be equally divided into 250 acreages. Rich soil on flat terrain might be divided into plots as small as 50 acres, for the use of organically produced vegetables or market gardens, whilst mountainous terrain in the north might be divided into estates of 500 acres for forestry development, cultivating traditional broad-leafed trees for hard timber, as well as faster growing conifers for a quicker profitable return. We shall return to this topic in greater detail in Chapter 13.

In contemporary Britain, rural land is everywhere under-taxed, and this has been the sole reason for the preservation of the huge feudal estates still existing throughout our country. Urban areas, on the contrary, are over-taxed, so oppressing industry and commerce and often affording huge rental profits to undeserving landlords. The transfer of urban land freehold ownership to those who utilise it for productive or residential purposes would therefore be a social benefit, since the first would be enabled to operate more competitively, whilst the second would be afforded savings for greater consumer expenditure – not to mention lower house prices.

9 – And in manufacturing industry

If one turns to the large enterprise or corporation, the general economic disadvantages of such business structures may be listed as under:-
1. High prices resulting from the strength of a monopolistic situation;
2. Lack of flexibility in responding to, a) The competition, and, b) consumer demand;
3. A tendency to dictate the pattern of consumption rather than react to the pattern of demand;
4. Bureaucratisation (or the undermining of the dynamic) of the business process;
5. Over-employment in ratio to profitability;
6. The tendency to channel profits into diversified rentier activities rather than re-investment into greater or more efficient productivity; and,
7. An excess expenditure on buildings and land in relation to modernising manufacturing plant.

It is sometimes imagined that our great conglomerates act as some kind of benevolent institutions, as their advertising agencies would have the public believe. An eminent American thinker has cautioned that "children and economists may think that the men at the head of our great corporations spend their time thinking about new ways to please the customers or improve the efficiency of their factories and offices. What they actually concentrate on is enlisting their government to protect their foreign and domestic interests. ... As economists have long ago argued, the consequences of oligopoly are higher prices, smaller outputs, larger expenditures for advertising, and more trivial changes and miscellaneous product differentiation than would occur in more competitive industries."[23] It is no coincidence that Britain's industrial decline has run a parallel course with the increase in the size of firms representing a higher proportion of total manufacturing output. Thirty years ago the same facts were used to demonstrate the opposite argument, i.e. that to survive firms must merge to compete effectively in the international markets of the world. Since then, much has happened, and it has been amply demonstrated that the bloated size of bureaucratic corporations are far outweighed by the greater productivity of smaller sized concerns. The following figures are of interest:-

In 1900 the 100 largest firms represented 15% of total output
In 1976 the 100 largest firms represented 50% of total output
In 1935 the 136,000 firms employing 200 or less represented
        35% of manufacturing output
In 1976 the 66,000 firms employing 200 or less represented 16% of
        manufacturing output

As long ago as 1926, the top industrialist, Sir Alfred Mond, declared in the House of Commons that, "the essentials of the matter is 'management.' I have come to the conclusion that it is impossible for any human being efficiently to control any industry beyond a certain magnitude. At a certain point they begin to show the paralysis of red tape. In my view it is impossible to organise industries on a national basis and keep them efficient."

The problems of existing property relationships, and the false and prejudiced values pertaining to property still cherished today, are therefore major factors directly responsible for Britain's social malaise and economic decline.

---

[23] Robert Leckachman, *Economists At Bay*, McGraw Hill, NY, 1976, pp. 171 & 174.

CHAPTER 9
Sociology of Possession

"A social order must co-ordinate varying desires if it is to be stable, and the price of stability must be morally justifiable if the social order itself is to be justifiable."

Lawrence C. Becker, *Property Rights*, Routledge & Kegan Paul, 1977, p. 1.

1 - All relationships of the individual with the external world are concerned with possession   2 - Acquisitiveness is vital to survival   3 - "opting out" is not a viable solution   4 - Artificial means needed to adjust property relationships   5 - Anthropology demonstrates that there is no natural form of human society   6 - The instinct for possession and power is one and the same   7 - Property relationships in the primitive society   8 - Complexity of property relationships in modern society   9 - Private property emerged with the differentiation of the social classes   10 - But these are not grounds for reverting to an ideal of "Common ownership"   11 - Meaninglessness of the political term "Private property" as now used   12 - Little to distinguish private from public monopoly

1 – All relationships of the individual with the external world are concerned with possession

All relationships of the individual with the external world are concerned with the nature of possession, and there is nothing that can be excluded from this reality.   That profoundest of thinkers, Hegel, identified the sociological reality of possession when he wrote that, "the rationale of property is to be found not in the satisfaction of needs, but in the supersession of the pure subjectivity of personality.   In his property a person exists for the first time as reason."[24]   No philosopher has come closer to analysing the nature of possession as a sociological reality than has Hegel in his *Philosophy of Right*, and in his examination of the concept of property, may be found the key to unlocking the most difficult issues of our time.

The nature of possession, as it relates to the individual, precedes the concept of legal ownership or the existence of such abstract ideas as custom or contract.   The consciousness of possession begins almost from the moment of birth, when the child is put to the breast after the first moments of life.   But the consciousness of possession is not merely a characteristic of humanity.   It is a biological phenomenon universal throughout the world of animal creation.   All those who live

---

[24]   G.W.F. Hegel, *Philosophy of Right*, trans. By T.M. Knox, OUP, 1942, Addition pp.235-236.

in the country are not awoken every day by the joyous song which greets a new dawn, as our poets would falsely have us believe, but by the entire feathered kingdom proclaiming and defending its threatened territory. In a similar way humans are obliged to be on a constant alert in defending their possessions against a universal enmity which surrounds them, as otherwise their pockets would be emptied of the last penny. Robert Moss has remarked that, "territory for animals, like property for human beings, satisfies three universal psychological needs: the need for security, for stimulation, and for *identity* with something bigger than the animal itself."[25] Property in the sense of both power relationships and territorial ownership is therefore no less real in the animal or insect kingdom than amongst humankind. Even a tame rabbit will attack a dog which tentatively approaches its food bowl.

This is not to suggest that examples from the animal kingdom may be used to justify property relationships in the human world. The consciousness of possession amongst animals has only been cited to demonstrate the reality of property as a basic need to the very existence of all living creatures. So, the child's grasping for the mother's breast is the first manifestation of the instinct of possession. The possessive instinct is thus essential to survival. Its absence would mean death. To condemn the instinct as a manifestation of greed - however violently the child may seem to sate its thirst - would clearly be an absurdity. As the infant grows to adulthood, matures to middle age, or progresses towards the twilight of material existence, the principle of its instinctive possessive relationship with the external world remains unaltered.

2 – Acquisitiveness is vital to survival

Everything outside the individual may be a threat to existence - to be possessed or repulsed - and what does not concern him does not directly matter to him. Money as the medium of exchange for possessions, soon becomes the most important asset of all for the individual, in defending his existence in a hostile world intent on his destruction through dispossession. If his acquisitive instinct is relaxed for a week, he may be doomed to perish. Without the wherewithal for the purchase of food, he will surely starve. Without resources for the

---

[25] Robert Moss, *The Collapse of Democracy*, Temple Smith, 1975, p. 136.

payment of rent or mortgage, bailiffs armed with cudgels and dogs, will surely break down his door and dispossess him of the very shirt on his back. The struggle for existence from birth until death is dependent on the healthy stimulation of the acquisitive instinct in relation to all material phenomena, for everything external to the self - even the closest personal relationships - threaten to swallow us unless we are prepared to exert our identity as a positive force. Mere passivity is the denial of life: it is what distinguishes the brick wall from the amoeba, and possession alone is what distinguishes the self from the external world. Even the mollusc is in possession of its own few square millimetres of rock.

3 – "Opting out" is not a viable solution

In the hard contemporary society, much is spoken about "opting out of the rat race," as if there was the possibility for some kind of satisfactory escape from society itself whilst remaining *within it*, but of course, in reality there is no such alternative. To "opt out of society," if that is what is implied, is only practicable through living off the produce of the land (preferably by a nomadic existence), on the assumption or the fact that the produce of that land is neither in the ownership of individuals nor an authority, and that therefore that produce is for the free taking. However, what is usually meant by "opting out of the rate race," is more often one of the three following alternatives: 1. Retirement; 2. The running of one's own "small business;" or, 3. Joining a commune.

Since all these alternatives usually entail a diminution of earning power, they usually also entail a drop in material living standards. Whilst alternatives 1 and 2 are accompanied by the sweet benefits of independence, they nonetheless require substantial savings for their satisfactory realisation. Alternative 3, however, almost inevitably brings a decrease in independence rather than the contrary, whilst its capacity to give satisfaction in other respects is also questionable. This is because it relies on the illusory ideal projected by the collective, for in a very short while, a pecking order and power relationships are established as in all animal societies. Opting out of the so-called "rat race" is induced by those uncomfortable characteristics of conventional society, but the only really satisfactory, fair and unselfish release from those uncomfortable pressures is not by resorting to an inner escapism within society (unless emigration is what is meant by that) but rather by seeking to *change* society itself. Therefore, "opting out" fails to offer an escape from the ties of possession as we are defining them.

4 – Artificial means needed to adjust property relationships

The nature of possession in the human world, in anything more advanced than the most primitive communities, is infinitely more subtle and complex than that to be found amongst the lower creatures, and consequently, artificial means are needed to adjust these multiple relationships between the individual and his environment. It is then that injustice is seen as something that rises up and acts against nature, or that humankind within the context of society somehow loses its "natural" balance and contradicts what is assumed to be the real sociological needs of humanity. Such perceptions, unfortunately, lead to naivety, and again to a false misunderstanding of the basic needs of the individual in society. What is natural in human society? What form of society most leads to happiness or the diminution of discontent?

5 – Anthropology demonstrates that there is no natural form of human society

Anthropology, which is the only study we have to go on in any approach towards a scientific understanding of society, clearly demonstrates through the great diversity in the structures of different communities, that there is no natural form of human society - no paradigm on which to model the ideal society. There never was any "Golden age" or "Original contract" as so many of our philosophers have falsely assumed in their vain attempts to justify the modelling of an ideal society. What we know of the forms of all societies have merely stemmed from cultural tradition, and this in turn has originated from the artificial imposition of habit, custom and law of dominant groups and individuals.

Even the institution of marriage and the family unit, as we experience it in our Western civilisation, is the result of the subjectivity of cultural development, and should certainly not be understood as some objective process necessarily reflecting the "progress" of humankind, if by such an interpretation we mean the achievement of the ideal, the best, or the happiest state for humanity.

The scale of unhappiness and divorce in the Western world and increasingly in the prosperous Far East, would seem to indicate that the institution of marriage in its present form is hardly a suitable basis for child rearing or successful human relationships. As H.G. Wells has observed, "for husband and wife in most cases monogamic life marriage involves an element of sacrifice, it is an institution of late appearance in the history of mankind, and it does not completely fit the psychology or physiology of any but very exceptional characters in either sex."[26] Progress might well entail the development of new institutions, introducing new legal relationships, for a sharing of children, husbands and wives, and if such relationships led to a more stable society, then such relationships and such a society would be based on more moral foundations.   This would not mean the destruction of the family and family unit, but on the contrary, its *re-construction* on a sounder basis.

6 – The instinct for possession and power is one and the same

Possession begins with that sense of power in controlling phenomena in our environment that we influence for our own satisfaction. Familiarity with that desired phenomena soon engenders a sense of possession, i.e. a sense of natural right to dominate or control those desired objects in the environment. Habitual contiguity alone with that which pleases is sufficient to engender a sense of exclusive possession as a natural right. This covers every object from a loved human being to the paper clips and writing paper of an employer that are used illicitly for a private purpose. Turning to one who would never dispossess another of his property, there was no favour for which Diogenes would exchange his own few square feet of sunlight - not even that of a king.   Possession is therefore instinctive, and as with all instincts, its satisfaction is stimulated by the sense of pleasure, in the same way as hunger, thirst or copulation.

7 – Property relationships in the primitive society

As society advances from a so-called primitive to an allegedly more   civilised   existence,   so   property   relationships   become increasingly complex.   The most primitive societies of all have the

---

[26] H.G. Wells, *Anticipations*, Chapman & Hall, 7th ed., 1902, p. 126.

most rudimentary property relationships, since nearly all property is held in common ownership. There are no fences or strips of land held in individual or family ownership, for amongst nomadic peoples all land is held in the common possession of the tribe, and amongst the most primitive peoples, even dwellings and artefacts for hunting and domestic use are held in common usage and ownership. But the development of peoples, and their settlement into fixed places of abode for the cultivation of the soil, does not lead simply to the acquisition of absolute property rights into the hands of individuals or families or village communities. In fact the acquisition of absolute property rights seldom occurs in any society, and those absolute rights we now enjoy in contemporary Western civilisation are only something which have emerged since the Reformation in conjunction with the break-up of the old feudal order.

Many theories have been held as to the justification for rights in property. Whilst Aristotle argued that property should belong to those who could use it properly; the Christian theory has always been that property should belong to the righteous. The Reformation divines, who were influenced by medieval Schoolmen, justified property on the grounds of experience and expediency whilst insisting that its use be limited at every turn by the rights of the community and the obligations of charity. They saw its practical application as an idealised version of the feudal order which was vanishing before the advance of more businesslike and impersonal forms of ownership. The possession of property in its full or liberal sense has been most clearly defined by A.M. Honoré, who posits the following eleven essential conditions:-

1. *The right to possess* - that is, to exclusive physical control of the thing owned. Where the thing cannot be possessed physically, due, for example, to its "non-corporeal" nature, "possession" may be understood metaphorically or simply as the right to exclude others from the use or other benefits of the thing.

2. *The right to use* - that is, to personal enjoyment and use of the thing as distinct from 3) and 4) below.

3. *The right to manage* - that is, to decide how and by whom a thing shall be used.

4. *The right to the income* - that is, to the benefits derived from foregoing personal use of a thing and allowing others to use it.

5. *The right to the capital* - that is, the power to alienate the thing and to consume, waste, modify, or destroy it.

6. *The right to security* - that is immunity from expropriation.

7. *The power of transmissibility* - that is, the power to devise or bequeath the thing.

8. *The absence of term* - that is, the indeterminate length of one's ownership rights.

9. *The prohibition of harmful use* - that is, one's duty to forbear from using the thing in certain ways harmful to others.

10. *Liability to execution* - that is, liability to having the thing taken away for payment of a debt.

11. *Residuary character* - that is, the existence of rules governing the reversion of lapsed ownership rights.[27]

Turning from theory to practice, it may be noted that the concept of freehold was unknown in barbarian Europe and only imperfectly developed in Imperial Rome and Byzantium. It was only in the medieval period that the church, in securing the permanence of its own properties, came to write the law of freehold into the codes it processed. Meanwhile, for some centuries, secular property was very far from being held in absolute ownership. In the words of the historian, H.J. Perkin, "in feudal societies, property, especially in land, was something more and something less than ownership ... it was also contingent, conditional and circumscribed by the claims of God, the church, the king, the inferior tenants and occupiers, and the poor."[28] As Ayn Rand has pointed out, "the institution of private property, in the full legal meaning of the term, was brought into existence only by capitalism. In pre-capitalist eras, private property existed *de facto*, but not *due jure*."[29]

8 – Complexity of property relationships in modern society

In the contemporary West it is hard to envisage privately held property under any other context than its possession as an absolute right. The emergence of property as things for the ownership, use and responsibility of individuals, families or groups, however, is something that has occurred entailing a complex relationship between

---

[27] See, A.M. Honoré's essay on "Ownership" published in the *Oxford Essays In Jurisprudence*.

[28] H.J. Perkin, *The Social Causes of The British Industrial Revolution*, 1968, p. 163.

[29] Ayn Rand, *Capitalism: The Unknown Ideal*, Signet Books, NY, 1967, pp. 12-13.

owners and owned. Property rights have only developed and been maintained under the most stringent and complex conditions as formed by the custom or law of society. The concept of property and its practical application has always been a reflection of the soul and thinking of society, and hence property relationships have been regarded and defended with the utmost passion. All wars are basically concerned with the question of possession, and leading anthropologists have demonstrated that the first clear distinctions of individual ownership only emerged after tribal warfare resulting in the crushing victory and consequent domination of one tribe over another.

9 – Private property emerged with the differentiation of the social classes

It is also true that the extension of property ownership and its increasing complexity within the legalistic-type framework of society, has developed in conjunction with the emergence of social classes and their increasing differentiation.[30] This unquestionable factor has been no minor influence in persuading Socialist thinkers from Marx and Engels onwards - not to mention philosophers of an earlier period - that the private ownership of property is corrupting, leading inevitably to the injustice of an oppressive society and its division into rich and poor. Everyone knows Rousseau's famous contention that, "the first man who, having enclosed a piece of ground, bethought himself of saying *This is mine*, and found people simple enough to believe him, was the real found of civil society."[31] This is a simplistic interpretation of the origin of property.

10 – But these are not grounds for reverting to an ideal of "Common ownership"

The implied outcome of such a diagnosis, however, viz. that property should be transferred into common ownership is even more naive. Furthermore, the common ownership of the primitive tribe (if that may be considered an ideal existence) cannot be compared to the

---

[30] See Gunnar Landtman's anthropological work, *The Origins of The Social Classes* Kegan Paul, Trench Trubner & Co. Ltd., 1938.

[31] Rousseau's *Discourse on Inequality*, opening words of Part II.

so-called common ownership as found in the highly developed industrialised society. The one cannot possibly be held up as an example for the other because of the wide variations in practice between property relationships.

Such simplistic notions and cures fail to take into consideration both the complex nature of property in the modern society and its sociological reality. For a start, property does not simply entail a division between public and private. Both these terms have widely different meanings as they directly effect the individual and society, but our vocabulary has never been extended to define these meanings. It is necessary to define the different sorts of property before any serious discussion can be entered into on property rights or the best uses of property.

11 – Meaninglessness of the political term "Private property" as now used

The politically charged phrase, "Private property," has possibly caused more confusion and more mischievous conflict in society than any other political term. The all-embracing concept of private property rights has been used by those on the right for justifying the brute force of the well-to-do to oppress the weak and deserving, but by the same token, it has been used by those on the left to dispossess the hard-working from their well-earned labours. The broad term "Private property" is meaningless since it includes everything from the shirt on a man's back to a giant conglomerate which may be owned by a single individual. Even the division between domestic and business ownership is not sufficient to distinguish private property from other kinds of property. For example, it is a nonsense to include the business property of the independent self-employed window cleaner alongside that of the multi-millionaire with his private limited business property; and yet, in political ideology, the two are considered under the same heading as representing the principle of free private enterprise as contrasted with common ownership or Nationalisation. The absurdity is clear, and yet the Tory party is dependent on a large working class vote of independent property owners who are falsely led to believe that their interests must somehow coincide with those of the very rich. The limitations of our political vocabulary and phraseology are alone responsible for this, in conjunction with the falsities and simplifications of Old Socialist thinking.

12 – Little to distinguish private from public monopoly

If there is a world of difference between the concept of private property in terms of the shirt on a man's back and the possessions of the multi-millionaire, so conversely, there may be a negligible difference between the privatised public monopoly and the Nationalised public monopoly as far as the interests of the consumer or ordinary citizen is concerned. Both remain giant megaliths that the ordinary person is equally impotent to influence. If the public monopoly offers a share-ownership to the people, the value of those individual shares, so widely distributed, are valueless *vis-à-vis* the possibility of the individual actually influencing the policies of the concern. The argument can be made that the individual has as much or greater power over the monopoly concern under state ownership through pure political influence. In reality, his influence over the monopoly is negligible, if not nil, irrespective of whether it is state owned or "privatised."

Whilst the nationalised monopoly is managed by an exclusive elite of middle class bureaucrats, cosseted in their activities by the Official Secrets Act, in conjunction with intervention by Treasury and other officials and powerful bankers; the privatised monopoly is managed by financiers in a kind of clandestine relationship with government officials, the latter having a vested interest in ensuring that it remains a source for a sufficiently high level of taxation. To present the nationalised industry as against the "privatised" monopoly, as two politically contrasting modes of ownership, and two conflicting political principles, affecting the ordinary citizen, as is done today by the parties of the left and right - and centre too - is clearly a confidence trick of a high order.

These, then, are some of the political problems of property relationships to be found in the world today.

CHAPTER 10
Property: Its Psychological Function

"The capitalist process, by substituting a mere parcel of shares for the walls of and the machines in a factory, takes the life out of the idea of property. ... The holder of the title loses the will to fight, economically, physically, politically, for 'his' factory and his control over it, to die if necessary on its steps. ... Dematerialised, defunctionalised, and absentee ownership does not impress and call forth moral allegiance. Eventually there will be *nobody* left who really cares to stand up for it - nobody within and nobody without the precincts of the big concern."

Joseph A. Schumpeter, *Capitalism, Socialism & Democracy*, Allen & Unwin, 1943, p. 142.

1 - Decentralised state franchises a realistic alternative to the solutions of left and right   2 - Hiving off the DHSS   3 - The NHS not a sacred cow   4 - True possession entails not merely legal ownership but control, but not necessarily absolute rights   5 - Why property rights should be circumscribed   6 - The first function of property is to give emotional fulfilment   7 - And to extend the personality and human potential   8 - How to achieve this politically

1 – Decentralised state franchises a realistic alternative to the solutions of left and right

There is, however, a realistic alternative to the current theories and policies of "Privatisation" versus "Nationalisation." There is a third alternative that could genuinely benefit society and the ordinary citizen. It would entail breaking up nationalised monopolies into a number of smaller decentralised units as privatised franchises under the *dirigiste* observation and ultimate authority of the state.

Such a policy of state and local authority franchising could be applied to all utilities as gas, electricity, water, telecommunications and refuse collection, and even to the multifarious services of the NHS. The essential utilities could be divided into units as small as those of town boroughs; shares could be offered to the public; a wide discretion could be given with regard to management policies in promoting efficiency and reducing costs; and the overall authority of the state or local council would ensure that charges to the consumer were kept down to a minimum. Competition policies would be introduced through state pressure relaying comparison information on the performance of different franchises and enforce improved standards. Meanwhile, the restricted size of the franchises, working within their limited geographical areas, and their full exposure to public view, would ensure that the ordinary citizen not merely had a more direct control through shareholdership, but also through the exertion of town hall or parliamentary lobbying.

2 – Hiving off the DHSS

With regard to hiving off the DHSS, the resultant franchises would be exposed to even greater competitive pressures. There is a sound argument for this, especially if we accept Harris and Seldon's contention that, "the welfare state has gradually changed from the expression of compassion to an instrument of political repression unequalled in British history and in other Western industrialised societies."[32] Whilst hospitals and clinics would be sold off to partnerships of medical professionals - to nursing staff as well as doctors - the state pension and sickness schemes would be abolished, as they were transferred to a variety of competing insurance associations.

The newly formed insurance and pension funds would operate varying types of policies suiting different sectors of the population. Hence there would be associations for rural employees; associations for factory operatives; for public employees; for the self-employed, etc. Again, the state would have an overall *dirigiste* authority over these independently owned and managed hospitals, clinics and insurance associations, and meanwhile, the entire population would be compulsorily insured for sickness and retirement pensions. Under such a system no service would be lacking which had not previously been offered by the NHS during the best years of its existence.

These ideas have not been plucked out of the air. They reflect the pattern of policies actually in force in Germany and elsewhere, and their success has been long-proven. It is true that such a "privatised" health service and such "privatised" national pension schemes would be more costly than our own NHS, but then they would not be a direct burden on the exchequer (as now in Britain) and then the benefits would be correspondingly greater. The efficiency and diagnostic skills of Continental medicine, and the flexibility and breadth of treatment offered by the German medical profession (for example) puts our own narrow bureaucratic service to shame.

---

[32] Ralph Harris & Arthur Seldon, *Overruled On Welfare*, Institute of Economic Affairs, 1979, p. 204.

3 – The NHS not a sacred cow

All this helps to demonstrate the meaninglessness of those concepts of property that are commonly held, together with their politically misleading emotional attachments. Legal definitions of property are no more helpful than those of political prejudice. The fact that the institution of the NHS has become a sacred cow - and the reality is that those best served by the NHS are not its over-charged "customers," the patients, but the bureaucrats who have a vested interest in maintaining the system - is a shameful reflection of misguided political views. The value of the institution in itself is valueless: it only takes on value through the utility of its purpose. It is therefore absurd to imagine that the abolition of the NHS would mean the abolition of all those values it is meant to represent but doesn't, i.e. modern, efficient, free and comfortable health services open to all British nationals - and to others by arrangement. The problem in contemporary Britain is that the NHS has become a symbol of what it now fails to be. The popular perception of an institution and what an institution is supposed to represent are two quite separate things; for the first is merely an empty shell, whilst the second is the reality. This is just one aspect of false perceptions of so-called public property. The nature of property can only be understood in its truest reality in a sociological context.

4 – True possession entails not merely legal ownership but control, but not necessarily absolute rights

The nature of possession entails not merely nominal or legal ownership but the right of control or use over what is owned. Nominal ownership without the right of control or use is meaningless. This is not to imply that the Absolute right of control or usage over property is an essential element of ownership, for in fact, the contrary is more usually the case. Absolute ownership is a modern concept, and it is now becoming increasingly clear that possession is and should be circumscribed by a variety of conditions. In the early days of the ancient Roman Republic, a father had the legal right in certain circumstances to destroy his wife or children. That is an example of absolute possession, and in our own time such a right would be repudiated as an outrageous barbarism. In contemporary Britain, however, a sole proprietor or a board of directors have the legal right to inflict millions of pounds of damage on their own property; and indeed, do this by demolishing factory roofs as a way of escaping the payment of rates on unprofitable enterprises. Much derelict property, in all parts of Britain, is made derelict by the conscious vandalism of proprietors, and as every builder knows, removing the roof of any structure, soon leads to its total decay. This, again, is an example of absolute possession, and again, is an action which should be made punishable by the criminal law, since the high and increasing cost of buildings puts them into the category of belonging to the capital wealth of our national assets - certainly transcending the rights of private property.

A man who in a tempter smashes up his own wrist watch or TV set, because they fail to work, does nobody any harm (except perhaps his personal reputation) since these things are of low value and easily replaceable; but a man who destroys a valuable painting or an irreplaceable antique bureau falls into another category *vis-à-vis* his relationship with property. If these things are his own, he has a legal right to do that, but since these things are unique and belong to the national (or maybe international) heritage, such actions should, again, be made criminally accountable. If, on the other hand, that same man tears out the windows of a listed building in a conservation area, replacing them with some hideous aluminium frames, he would indeed be liable to prosecution and a heavy fine and costs. As Walter Lippmann has maintained, "in the public philosophy an absolute right to property, or to anything else that effects other men, cannot be entertained.[33]... Absolute owners did damage to their neighbours and to their descendants; they ruined the fertility of the land, they exploited destructively the minerals under the surface, they burned and cut forests, they destroyed wild life, they polluted streams, they cornered supplies and formed monopolies, they held land and resources out of use, they exploited the feeble bargaining power of wage earners."[34]

---

[33] Walter Lippmann, *The Public Philosophy*, Hamish Hamilton, 1955, p. 106.

[34] Ibid., p. 109.

5 – Why property rights should be circumscribed

Whilst, therefore, the control and use of property is an essential part of ownership, the right to the use of property needs nonetheless to be circumscribed by the higher needs of the community in total as expressed through the general will. The needs of our highly technological interdependent society, increasingly emphasising the dependence of all upon all, is pointing to the amorality of the rugged laissez-faire individualism which first gave rise to the concept of Absolute ownership. The same principle also effects the relationship between masters and dependents or employers and employed, for as we shall later demonstrate, personal relationships have to be included within the principles of the sociological consideration of possession.

6 – The first function of property is to give emotional fulfilment

But the nature of property is not merely to be understood in terms of the relationship between owners and owned, but more significantly, in terms of its influence in facilitating smoother relationships in society and as a dynamic in assisting wealth creation. In other words, what should be the political purpose of property within the sociological context? What kind of property relations are necessary in ensuring that the individual and humankind are best fulfilled intellectually and emotionally? The answer to this question is more important and should be given a higher priority than the generalised abstract question usually posed by political thinkers: viz., What kind of property relations are necessary in best ensuring contentment and happiness? Such a question is merely nebulous. What is contentment? What is happiness? Contentment may mean - and is often made to mean - the death of the individual as an active participant in society - his consignment to a passive negative role in a community ruled over by the privileged few who enjoy all its fruits and pleasures. In such a society contentment means the spiritual surrender of the individual to the consolations of religion or to bread and circuses - a poor substitute for the relinquishment of natural rights and purposeful well-being. Whilst the question of contentment or happiness may be primary to the political thinking of arch-Conservatives and reactionaries (for its answer may be easily found in any anodyne available) the question of justice must remain primary to those in reforming politics, for only in such a line of enquiry can the eternal questions of truth be penetrated.

That is why the purpose of property in society should be to fulfil intellectually and emotionally the needs of the individual. What kind of society achieves this: a society where nominally the state owns everything; or a society where the bulk of property belongs to a restricted class of plutocrats? The answer is neither, and in fact there would be little to choose between the two. What society is more affluent: the society where the means of production and distribution is owned and managed by the state; or the society where the great conglomerates own and manage everything? Again, there is little to choose between the two, for whilst in the first we may see a gradual improvement in material standards from a very low starting base, in the latter we may see a gradual decline from a previously higher level.

7 – And to extend the personality and human potential

The purpose of property must therefore be to extend the personality of the individual as an aid to his self-development as well as that of society in its totality. Again, this returns us to Hegel, and we may repeat his contention that "the rationale of property is to be found not in the satisfaction of needs, but in the supersession of the pure subjectivity of personality. In his property a person exists for the first time as reason." What therefore are the necessary conditions for best ensuring that property achieves this purpose in society? They may be listed as under:-
1. That all property is as equally distributed throughout the community as is desirable in ensuring a democratic and classless society;
2. That property ownership be extended to as large a proportion of the population as is practicable;
3. That the state and local authorities be divested of as much property and direct executive authority as is possible; and,
4. That anti-monopoly policies in all sectors of business and public employment be effectively enforced.

8 – How to achieve this politically

How is the above to be achieved as it would affect the individual citizen? The following eight factors would need to be considered in some detail with regard to extending the individual's status of possession:-

1. Property as home-ownership
2. Property as the means of production
3. Non-owning employees, public sector and other
4. Communal or public property
5. Collective property, being that of independent associations
6. Rentier property, being unearned income
7. Inherited property and the question of taxation
8. Domination as possession.

Whilst pursuing the single principle of maximising the individual's status of possession, the following discussion, covering as it will a wide variety of factors in the life of the individual, will of necessity cover a broad canvas.

CHAPTER 11
Home-Ownership: Real and Illusory

"No one can doubt that the convention for the distinction of property, and for the stability of possession, is of all circumstances the most necessary to the establishment of human society."

David Hume, *Treatise of Human Nature.* Bk. III., Pt. II, para 2.

1 – Home-Ownership: Real and Illusory

Home-ownership is amongst the most important forms of private property, and to most includes the greatest material possession. The principle of home-ownership implies that not only is it desirable that there should be freedom from the obligation of paying rent to a private landlord, together with all the hidden threats that this entails; or the landlordism of the state, but that property prices should ideally be within the reach of the majority.

This means that mortgage agreements should be held within a low rate of interest so that full possession is facilitated within a reasonable period of time. Hundred per cent mortgages at high rates of interest for properties offered for sale at exorbitant prices, as we are now seeing in contemporary Britain, degrade mortgagees almost to the status of tenants of building societies, since it has become evident that their chances of achieving full ownership is highly questionable.

The full possession of a dwelling, and this should mean freehold rights, achieves the following:-

1. That the owner is free of those restrictions normally laid down by a landlord or local authority;

2. That the owner is thereby invested with a greater responsibility for the appearance and upkeep of the property;

3. That he (or she) is prepared to invest a greater proportion of his capital and time in maintaining the property;

4. That the property remains within the free market sector, so more easily facilitating exchange and the re-location of the owner;

5. That full possession confers on the owner the financial security of being a property owner including collateral for business or other requirements; and,

6.   That the dwelling may be passed on as inherited property in maintaining both the development and stability of family life as it passes from one generation to another.

Clearly, ownership in the above sense contributes to developing the mental and emotional potential of the individual in relation to his preserving, improving and even extending that property in his possession.. In contemporary Britain, the difference between council or rented property as compared with privately owned property, may be clearly distinguished by a cursory visual inspection: for whilst the first is often dirty and in disrepair and badly vandalised; the latter is cleaner, in better condition, with evidence of the different properties having received individual care. These facts, and they are irrefutable, should not be interpreted as a slur on the general character of council tenants - which they often wrongly are by the more affluent classes - but rather as the enlightening effects on character of those fortunate enough to be endowed with property.

2 – Need for intervention in maintaining home-ownership

The achievement of a universal private property owning society, however, cannot simply be attained through the laissez-faire of the free market.   On the contrary, extensive intervention would be necessary in creating such a society. This is because, as experience has demonstrated, the actions of the free market have led to an increasingly monopolistic society - in the private domestic sector no less than in the world of business. Monopoly in the house owning sector has taken the form of a rise in house prices above which the ordinary citizen can reasonably afford, or above which the free market could bear in tolerating the existence of a domestic property owning society. Borrowing for mortgage purposes has now exceeded six times average annual earnings – and this usually means the earnings of two persons and *not* one. The consequences of this tendency are leading to huge loans at extortionate interest rates whereby the reality is that property is falling increasingly into the ownership of the great building societies or financial institutions.

3 – Dispossession through usury

The late Tory government boasted that there were more home-owners in its day that at any time previously. It may also be noted that Britain at the present time has one of the highest home-ownership societies in Europe. Currently, some 70% of our people are nominally home-owners, although, of all ironies, this is exceeded by the ex-Communist state of Bulgaria with 80% of their population being home-owners. In Germany, on the contrary, only 38% of the population are home-owners. With regard to home-ownership in Britain, however, the greater reality is that a huge debtor class is being created by sure but subtle means; and the real beneficiaries of this insidious process are not the "pretend" home-owners but a small elite of well-to-do investors and the financial class who are serving their needs.

The building societies are currently adopting an entirely irresponsible policy with regard to lending *vis-à-vis* the ability to make repayments, although in fairness, it has to be said that the societies are not directly responsible for the inflation in property values, and it is inflation which places them in a different situation. If they embarked on a prudent lending policy, they would probably have to turn down some 80% of applicants. The building societies are therefore caught between two stools with regard to borrowers and investors. The truth behind the sticky situation of borrowers only slowly began to dawn on their consciousness as the recession bit deeper into the national economy, and the ordinary citizen found he had a decreasing proportion of funds for expenditure on food, essential utilities and other outgoings. This is already reflected by the fact that at the present time 10% of all homeless families are only homeless because of their eviction by the building societies to whom they were unable to keep up mortgage payments. In 1979 an average of 2,000 families were evicted annually by building societies. By 1987 this figure had risen to an annual average of 21,000, and in 2007 it was 31,000. The creation of what is alleged to be home-ownership under these circumstances, therefore, amounts to nothing less than a cruel swindle inflicted on the majority by the usurious activities of our existing financial system.

4 – The inflation-makers hurt both the economy and home-owners

What intervention is needed in achieving a real home-ownership society? Firstly, effective legislation must be introduced to discourage the rentier activities of our financial institutions: i.e. to ensure that investments are transferred from the passive non-productive assets of property and land values into the productive assets of domestic manufacturing and the international trade in merchandise. The massive investments of our quick profit-making financial institutions over recent years in land and property are not simply inflationary but are actually dependent for their profits (as we all know) on a high annual inflation rate. This activity entailing greater money-creation is, of course, the very opposite of actual wealth creation, as I have elsewhere clearly demonstrated.[35] Although the purpose of the present government has been to keep down inflation, and in this it has been successful, this is not in the interests of our rentier financiers and speculators to whom inflation is an important tool for their profits.

5 – Property restrictions should be placed on aliens in accordance with international practice

Secondly, restrictions need to be placed on the rights of aliens to purchase property in the UK in the same way that restrictions are placed on British nationals abroad. Today, Britain is a relatively poor country amongst the industrially advanced nations of the world measured in terms of equal wealth distribution, and a great influx of wealthy foreigners, as we are now experiencing, not only leads to a greater rise in property prices but to a shortage of desirable properties on the market available at reasonable prices for our own people. House or flat sales to aliens, for residential purposes only, should only be made under licence to those issued with visas and permits for work, study or retirement purposes. As soon as their employment or study periods have expired, or death puts an end to retirement, then the property licences would be revoked, necessitating re-sale of the properties at the price originally purchased, plus the inclusion of any inflation factor. This would be to prevent the possibility of any alien gaining a profitable return through property speculation. A total ban

---

[35] See Parts II & III of *The People's Capitalism.*

should be placed on the right to aliens owning rural land, whilst a maximum 49% share ownership should be placed on aliens engaged in the management or proprietorship of industrial or commercial enterprises.   The above two conditions would already be in accordance with international practice. No Briton, for example, would be allowed to purchase a stretch of the Arabian desert, or Finnish farm land, or even 100% share ownership of a small shop in the Sultanate of Oman, and yet aliens of all nationalities are freely allowed to purchase land and property in this country - and in fact are encouraged to do so.

The need to restrict house and land sales, and the right to business ownership, to our own nationals is not an extraordinary requirement, since many countries throughout the world, both in Europe and overseas, put onerous conditions on aliens wishing to participate in the national wealth of what, after all, belongs to their own people. This is because the reverse of this situation would in some degree entail the emergence of a "colonialist" status. Britain can no longer afford to lower her neck for such a yoke.   The manifestations of globalisation (which are malign) offer no arguments to counter the above proposals.

The need for home-ownership is vital to the principle of promoting private property. Those who would allay the fears of those recognising the undermining of home-ownership may cite the fact that between 1961-1981 home-ownership increased by 37% in Scotland and 65% in the South West, but these figures are, in themselves, of little consequence.   Their true import can only be understood in relation to the figures behind the terms and conditions of purchase. There is no difficulty at all in signing one's life away to the devil-on-earth, i.e., the taker-of-all our material possessions, if one so chooses. In the same report[36] from which the above statistics are taken, it is also noted that between 1976-1981 the average price of homes newly-mortgaged to building societies rose by 90%, and by as much as 96% in the North West.   These figures are truly horrific when their meaning is correctly interpreted. That is why powerful legislation is needed to protect the home-owner.   Horace Cutler, who is well-qualified to judge on these matters, has argued that, "we are rapidly reaching polarisation between two forms of tenure: owner-occupation

---

[36] *Regional Trends* - 18, 1983 ed., published by HMSO & Open University Educational Enterprises Ltd.

and municipal tenancy. There will be nothing in between. This is terrible to contemplate. Not only is municipal housing much more costly than home-ownership, but in my belief it is less socially satisfying, badly organised and maintained, highly restricted and politically charged."[37]

---

[37] Horace Cutler, *The Cutler Files*, Weidenfeld & Nicolson, 1982, p. 13.

CHAPTER 12
Wider Ownership In The Business Sector

"Curbing the monopoly powers of producers is ... important. When a company does well it is important that it should have an incentive to expand output and employment, rather than to set a high price for its product and to share out the resulting monopoly revenue in dividends to its shareholders and in wages to its employees that are out of line with those needed to attract capital and labour to the enterprise."

J.F. Meade, "The Restoration of Full Employment" in *The Rebirth of Britain,* ed. Wayland Kennet, Weidenfeld & Nicolson, 1982, p. 180.

1 - Freedom of sole proprietorships and partnerships   2 - Limited liability and the separation of ownership from control   3 - The company is a legal entity responsible only to itself   4 - Unanswered questions of limited liability status   5 - Employees' grounds for claiming a partnership   6 - Indebtedness of the company to the state are grounds for intervention on behalf of employees.

1 – Freedom of sole proprietorships and partnerships

Means should be taken to broaden the reality of business ownership amongst all employees through a variety of measures. All parties committed to the success of the business sector would thereby benefit, since, as we have noted, possession engenders a certain pride in what is possessed - irrespective of its purpose - and so in this sphere would act in some part as a stimulus to responsibility and goodwill.

As business ownership is manifested in many forms, this is a huge topic, and therefore it may best be discussed by considering the varying business structures in turn and as to how they reflect different property relationships.

a) *Sole proprietorships*, comprising small businesses of all kinds, clearly entail full ownership, and such proprietors are naturally subjected to least restrictions on the control and use of their business possessions. The sector should be protected, encouraged and extended by wise legislation, not only on grounds of promoting the principle of private possession for the benefit of the individual in developing his potential, but in the cause of - what has been proven through comparisons between leading industrialised nations - to best promote business efficiency and greater wealth creation.

b) *Partnerships*, these usually being the business structures most commonly found amongst the service   professions of   the law, accountancy, medicine, architecture, etc. Partnerships are the second most free type of business as regards discretion for its use and management - although GPs might dispute this by arguing that their hands are tied in many directions, but this rather stems from their obligations to the NHS and we have discussed proposed changes to this institution in Chapter 10.

2 – Limited liability and the separation of ownership from control

c) *Limited companies*: here we have to distinguish between two sectors, employers and employed.   Employers, or shareholding directors, have overall control over limited companies and they *act* as owners, although there is a distinct difference between the property of a proprietorship and that of a limited liability enterprise. Ownership of the latter is restricted according to the percentage of share ownership. This means that the directors of a company are often merely part-owners, and particularly in larger concerns, without the rights of any kind of possession. In general, the larger the concern, the wider the divide between the ownership of director-managers and the ownership of a separate shareholding body playing no part in the business of day-to-day management. In the largest concerns, it is very often the case that there is a complete separation between ownership and management, and so the directors of such concerns have a status differing little from that of their employees, for they are themselves employees although nominally described as employers.

3 – The company is a legal entity responsible only to itself

The greatest significance of limited liability, however, is that it creates a body which legally is only responsible to itself. The shareholding director is only responsible up to the value of his specific shareholding. When the company is in trouble, irrespective of whether it is financial or criminal (for example, through polluting the environment or negligently supplying dangerous or obnoxious goods) it is not individuals who ultimately are called to account, but the company as a legal entity. The artificially created abstraction of the limited liability company, which is a corporate entity only responsible to itself, is a very recent invention of hardly more than 140 years, and it was called into being as a protective barrier against financial ruin by those who wished to limit the personal risk entailed in managing a business enterprise.

4 – Unanswered questions of limited liability status

The existence of limited liability, however, raises a number of questions of moral, legal and political significance on the status of property that have yet to be answered.[38] When the ownership of an enterprise passes to a shareholdership which is   separate   from management, and that management or the directors are divested of possession, the responsibility for running that enterprise is passed to the shareholders.   This is the theory.   However, in practice, the management of the enterprise remains exclusively in the hands of the directors, and only in extraordinary circumstances can or would a shareholders' meeting call for the removal of the directors.   Beyond that, shareholders are powerless beyond the withdrawal of their capital.   In   practice,   the   relationship   between   directors   and shareholders is one of mutual trust and non-interference from either side.

5 – Employees' grounds for claiming a partnership

Since the directors of such an enterprise are not owners, their relationship to the enterprise, in regard to the rights of possession, is legally no different from that of the lowest echelons in their employment. The directors may retain huge powers of discretion in the   management   of   the   enterprise   entrusted   to   them   by   the shareholders, but that cannot possibly be interpreted as holding the status of possession. Since we can trace an evolutionary development and change in the limited liability enterprise from its inception through the Companies Act in 1862, and since we now see a clear separation between ownership and management, the next logical step would be for employees, at all levels, to claim some right to a partnership in the management of the employing enterprise. Such an

---

[38] For a discussion of these questions, see especially the books of my late eminent friend, the industrialist, George Goyder MBE, who has studied these matters for almost forty years, commencing with his book, *The Future of Private Enterprise*, Blackwell, 1951, and culminating in, *The Just Enterprise*, André Deutsch, 1987.

approach would be made to the management, with whom all industrial relations are concerned, and in such circumstances, the management could not:-

1. Claim the prerogative of ownership and on those grounds veto such a proposal; or,

2. Could not claim that they shared a management role with a share-holding body whom they would first have to consult.

The only function and responsibility to the shareholders of the directors in such a situation would be to satisfy themselves that the granting of such a partnership in the management of the enterprise would lead to greater efficiency. It would then only remain for the directors to satisfy the shareholders that the final scheme to be drafted was desirable and beneficial to all parties concerned. All this could be achieved without the intervention of any external authority.

6 – Indebtedness of the company to the state are grounds for intervention on behalf of employees

This would be the first step towards the employees' owning the enterprise from which they derived their livelihood. The second step would entail the intervention of a *deus ex machina*. State intervention in the conduct of the private and public sectors is already widespread on many fronts: not merely through taxation, Factory and Employment acts, but through training schemes and the offering of loans, grants and subsidies as aids to both regenerating communities and promoting international trade. The heavy investment of the state through the resources of the taxpayer in commercial enterprises both large and small is sufficient justification to force through measures for facilitating employee part-ownership. This is because the enterprise has already compromised its credibility for independent survival, both financially and morally, through its indebtedness to the state. It is morally bound to sometime return that which has been given and gratefully received - indeed, very often, that which has been begged from the state. Furthermore, it has to be noted that through limited liability an entity has been created that is not merely separate from but greater than that of any of its constituent parts. Whilst the directors cannot veto intervention on the grounds of ownership, workers cannot be prevented from claiming rights from an external authority since they cannot claim it from directors who no longer have it to give.

If part-ownership of the worker in the employing enterprise through a variety of alternative investment schemes would encourage greater commitment and diligence, in addition to the satisfaction of actual possession, then such a course should be pursued by the state in conjunction with the parties concerned. With the achievement of shared partnership through co-determinational industrial democracy and employee investment, workers would be granted the maximum possible ownership in real terms of their employing enterprises.

CHAPTER 13
The Problems of Rural Land Ownership

"It is ... obvious that men organised in small units will take better care of *their* bit of land or other natural resources than anonymous companies or megalomaniacal governments which pretend to themselves that the whole universe is their legitimate quarry."

E.F. Schumacher, *Small Is Beautiful*, Blond & Briggs, 1973, p. 32.

1 – The need for efficiency and Britain's success

T he use of rural land in regard to the question of maximising the existence of the private ownership of business property, or facilitating that as large a proportion of our people are enabled to come into the ownership of business property as is practicable, needs separate consideration. This is because a host of separate questions are raised that do not apply to other forms of property.

It is essential that agriculture should be pursued as efficiently as possible in producing produce that best serves the needs of the community.   Britain has perhaps the most efficient agricultural industry in Europe, if not throughout the world - although one would hardly think so in view of the widespread bankruptcy of farm holdings at the present time of writing.[39]   Britain, that several decades ago was dependent for her survival on massive imports of foodstuffs, is now not also self-sufficient but producing considerable surpluses. This, indeed, is praiseworthy progress! All this has been made possible by the fact that Britain has the largest farms in Europe, even though they may be minuscule by comparison with the great grain producing properties in the mid-Western States of America.

When the Briton looks to Continental Europe, he eyes the agricultural industries of the EU with cold disdain. Not only are they supported by huge government subsidies (but so too is British

---

[39] September 2007.

farming) but the majority of farm-holdings appear to be tiny uneconomic acreages in the ownership of "peasants." If most agricultural land (but not the number of farms) seem in Britain to be in the ownership of "gentlemen" farmers, those on the Continent seem to be in the ownership of the "backward part of humanity!"

2 – Why land ownership is more equally distributed in Europe

How have these contrasts come about, and what do they signify? Throughout Continental Europe and in Scandinavia, land is still owned by the ordinary people. There is relatively an equal distribution in the actual ownership of land, and monopoly ownership is rare. There are many reasons for this pattern of ownership: various legal systems effecting inheritance; special legislation following the many revolutions of the 19th century; and different forms of taxation according to land usage. British history, on the other hand, has followed a different course from that of the Continent. From the time of the Reformation, and particularly during the Industrial Revolution, and in Scotland, during the Highland Clearances, there has been an active process of dispossession, much of it pursued by the most ruthless means. In addition to that, English "gentlemen," or at least their eldest sons have "thanked God" for the English law of primogeniture. In the words of a distinguished French observer of the English scene, "the obvious tendency of British legislation and jurisprudence was to maintain in tact great landed estates."[40]

3 – British land ownership patterns no need for complacency amongst arch-conservatives

All these factors must be a great consolation to arch-Conservatives, and particularly to financiers and their vested interests. Here we have a situation where the grossest injustice has been allowed to flourish - the dispossession of great numbers of people from their inherited landholdings - in conjunction with agricultural progress emanating from a free market environment including speculation often entailing a high rise in land values. This would seem to justify laissez-faire as the path to realism and progress in the world of farming. This, however, would be a simplistic view of the true

---

[40] Elie Halévy, *England In 1815*, E. Benn, 1949, p. 205.

situation when the best future of land use is anticipated according to modern trends of thinking. Mere super-efficiency in land use through the specialised cultivation of high cash crops is not an end in itself since it does not necessarily reflect the best long-term economic needs of a community. This is because agricultural industry operates under conditions which are very different from that of urban industry.

4 – Agriculture dependent on intervention for market stability

Whilst urban industry, or manufacturing, flourished under conditions of competition and is able (or should be able) to adapt at short notice according to changing needs; agriculture, on the contrary, is always dependent on co-operation or intervention on a huge scale to ensure an approximate standardisation of prices for specific produce. This is dictated by the total impracticality of the modern farmer pricing his produce according to individual whim in competition with a thousand other similar producers of like merchandise. He cannot, like the manufacturer, adopt a strategy of under-cutting, for the latter is only faced by a limited number of competitors for his unique products. This in turn gives rise to the need for a macro-economic agricultural policy, either imposed or evolved through a nation's tradition. The agricultural pattern of a nation takes on a permanence of a kind not to be found in the realm of manufacturing. Not only is agriculture inevitably worked in an intensely conservative environment, entailing concentrated and repetitive labour offering restricted scope for change or expansion, but all these factors, together with the vast expanse of a nation's rural acreage, make change a slow and difficult process.

Nevertheless, there do occur occasions in a nation's history when change is made inevitable or desirable due to extraordinary circumstances. Over-production of a crop, or crops, due to the increasing specialisation of the agricultural sector, can produce economic repercussions that are far more serious in their long-term consequences than over-production in manufacturing which is anyway normally countered by the speedy response of the market to the laws of supply and demand and competition. It is then that prices slump and the agricultural industry finds itself at odds with conflicting economic interests. Today, for example, the agriculture of the American mid-West is in the midst of a major crisis due to the over-production of grain. This is causing considerable hardship to great numbers of farmers who are now being pressed by creditors for payment. Already a similar crisis has hit the farming community here. Government policies towards agriculture, therefore, are - and should be - very different from those towards manufacturing.

5 – The plateau for efficiency in farm sizes

Today there are many factors calling for radical changes in agricultural policy. These may conveniently be brought under five headings. Firstly, the recent research of Prof. Britton and Dr. Hill at Wye College, London, has pointed to the fact that there is a "plateau of efficiency" in farm sizes of between 100 - 300 acres.[41] This is definitive evidence pointing to the need for family sized farming units, and in the cause of helping to minimise the costs of produce, it is not only beneficial that such farm-holdings should be managed and worked by the family unit, but also, owned by them.[42] Daniel Green, a distinguished authority on the agricultural industry, and himself a farmer, has written passionately on the virtues of farm ownership, maintaining that, "farming represents, in a tangible form, both domination and survival. It also satisfies, and perhaps even created, his acquisitive instincts. A sense of territoriality is common to most animals. Landowning is a particularly definite way of establishing and protecting territory. No other form of property, not even house ownership, comes so close to satisfying the instinct, ineradicable in animals, to establish and guard territory."[43]

The same author has also maintained that "the British farming class is certainly the smallest and is probably the weakest of any in the world."[44] Therefore, the energetic pursuit of government policies aimed at breaking up the great landed estates and dispossessing the nobility and the millionaire *nouveau riche* classes, would not only

---

[41] See, the *Northfield Report*, Cmnd. 7599, HMSO, 1979, p. 36, for further elaboration of this.

42 In regard to desirable farm sizes, it is interesting to note that on the election as Tribune of Tiberius Gracchus in 133 BC, he announced his intention of proposing to the tribal Assembly that no citizen should be allowed more than 333 acres of farmland, or 667 acres if he had two sons.

[43] Daniel Green, *The Politics of Food*, Gordon Cremonese, 1975, p. 10.

[44] Ibid., p. 29.

strengthen the interests of an extended farming class, so helping to correct the contemporary imbalance between the rural and urban communities, but would assist in raising a higher proportion of taxable income from the land.   This in turn would help enrich rural areas through the provision of more and better services, particularly public transport and essential utilities.

6 – Scandal of land monopoly

To suggest that government should use its powers to *dispossess* may sound a shocking proposal of revolutionary dimensions. Our entire constitutional development over the past four hundred years has entailed the total rejection of such thinking.   Kings have been overthrown for just such measures.   Taxation alone has become the accepted mode for lowering the Too-high, but as we demonstrate in Chapter 16 of this book, taxation as a means for creating a more equitable society, too often fails when it is most needed to be effective.   The pattern of land ownership in Britain, however, reflects the presence of economic and social evils which have become impervious to change.   If the scale of land monopoly was known, there would be an outcry from all sectors of our population, but as a director of the reputable Hudson Institute has remarked, "it is not surprising, given the awesome political and economic power that goes with land ownership, that the details of its distribution are shrouded in secrecy. ... land, like knowledge, is only powerful while it is shrouded in mystery and esoteric privilege."[45]

The compilation of a new Domesday book is now nine hundred years overdue, but the idea of a serious land survey, including a table of land ownership, has always be vigorously resisted by the vested interest groups of the nobility, such as the Country Landowners' Association.   Fred Harrison, who has made a scholarly study of the land ownership problem, has contended that, "the paucity of information on land is a scandal, for it entails a serious limitation on the economic system to operate at an optimum of efficiency."[46]   Even the government officials who compiled the *Northfield Report* bemoaned that, "throughout our work we were hampered by the lack

---

[45]   James Bellini, *Rule Britannia*, Jonathan Cape, 1981, p. 114.

[46]   Fred Harrison, *The Power In The Land*, Shepheard-Walwyn, 1983, p. 34.

of detailed information on many of the topics we studied. It is disturbing that so little is known about the pattern of acquisition, ownership and occupancy of agricultural land and that governments should have to take decisions, which may have far-reaching effects on agricultural structure, on the basis of incomplete or non-existent data."[47]   The much-needed recommendations of the Northfield Committee that a full system of land registration be established as a final goal and that agricultural departments should be forced to take action to fill gaps in public knowledge, were conveniently ditched by the Tory administration after the election in 1979.

Only in Scotland, in recent times, has a land survey been carried out. That was in the late 1970s. The results were startling. It was revealed that 12 million out of 19 million of Scotland's acres were owned by a small group of landlords with estates above 1,000 acres, and that the top 10 landowners held more than 1,500,000 acres between them.[48] It is no wonder that after such findings, that no such survey would be carried out in England and Wales. We do know, however, that at the turn of the century there were 500,000 farm holdings throughout Britain, and that now there are well below half that figure. If a more historical view is taken, it will be found that there has been a gradual diminution of private land ownership since the early middle ages. In the words of the historian, L.F. Salzman, "medieval society was built upon the basis of land. ... a landless man was, at the time of the Norman Conquest, and for some centuries afterwards, a strange being, rarely to be found except in a few of the bigger towns."[49] By the 16th century land-ownership had declined to 50% of the population, and a hundred years later to 10%. What occurred at the end of the 18th and throughout the 19th centuries is too well known to be mentioned. This is a tendency which must be reversed.

---

[47] *Northfield Report*, op. cit., p. 109.

[48] See, John McEwan's, *Who Owns Scotland*, Edinburgh University Publications Board, Edinburgh, 1977.

[49] L.F. Salzman, *English Life In The Middle Ages*, OUP, 1920, p. 36.

7 – Ecological threat of large-scale farming

The second factor calling for a radical change in agricultural policy, stems from the need to preserve the long-term economic value of the soil. This is probably the most powerful argument of all for the privatisation of land ownership and management. At present, large scale farming methods entailing the rape and poisoning of the soil and water supplies in many areas, is a reflection of short-term expediency necessitating the sacrifice of long-term needs. Quick profits are pursued without any thought for the fate of future generations. Large scale farming comprising the management of thousands of acres with a minimal labour force but the use of sophisticated capital intensive machinery, is only practicable through advanced specialisation. Not only is the long-term value of the soil and water-bed ruined by synthetic fertilisers, but fields are enlarged to American-sized wheat growing acreages; hedgerows and trees are destroyed; and finally, the top-soil is simply removed through excessive exposure to the elements.

The author of this book, who has had occasion to drive regularly through the agricultural heartland of East Anglia, has witnessed areas that have been so denuded, that the roadside is often covered with a sandy layer of soil on every occasion the wind blows - a sandy layer that is deposited by a dust cloud over the open countryside, reminiscent, even, of the sandstorms of the Arabian desert. Such scenes should dissipate any remaining complacency that the dust-bowl phenomenon of the Western grainlands of America may not sometime also be visited on our own country.

The division of farmland into smaller more manageable economic units, in conjunction with the re-introduction of mixed farming methods, so as to replenish the soil through natural methods, and the rotation of crops, would put an end to the ecological threat now facing rural Britain. As Daniel Green has so powerfully argued, "it is impossible to deny that there are advantages that arise when a man farms land that he owns. He will farm for his heirs and for posterity as much as for himself and, will, as a consequence, be more concerned to maintain the fertility and productivity of the land than he would otherwise have been. Long-term improvements will be undertaken, the soil will not be abused for the sake of immediate profits, and profits themselves will be re-invested."[50]

---

[50] Daniel Green, op. cit., pp. 154-155.

8 – Organic farming needs smaller more labour intensive acreages

Thirdly, increasing health consciousness amongst our people, and greater knowledge of the causes of cancer and other diseases and ailments brought on by the dangers of synthetically grown and treated foods, has increased the demand for organically grown produce of all kinds. Recent research has demonstrated that increasing numbers of people are prepared to pay a premium for what are now categorised as health foods[51] but may later become the staple diet of the majority, as legislation is extended to promote the health of the public and subsequent generations. As organic farming is more labour intensive than current large scale automated methods, there is again an argument calling for smaller farming units to fulfil present and future needs. Rensis Likert has argued that, "if land is scarce and labour plentiful, agricultural methods can be changed to allow for that new balance. ... Methods of organic farming make fewer demands on fuel and fertiliser, but more demands on labour."[52]

9 – Need to conserve balanced rural communities

Fourthly, there is a strong movement amongst conservationists, ecologists, and ramblers concerned with the aesthetic appearance of the countryside to preserve trees, hedgerows and smaller farming units for a wide variety of reasons. It is urged by these varied bodies that the countryside is held in trust by the owners of land as a part of the heritage belonging to us all, and furthermore, that city and town dwellers have an entitlement to enjoy the refreshing air and aesthetic beauty of our countryside, and to the use of footpaths and bridleways. However pleasant the environment of our great industrial cities, and however varied their leisure facilities, there is nothing which can recompense the right to the enjoyment of the open countryside and the sense of space and freedom it gives to the average citizen.

---

[51] A report published in May 1986 showed that a large proportion of our population were already prepared to pay as much as 35% more for health produced foods.

[52] Rensis Likert, *The Human Organisation: Its Management & Value*, McGraw Hill, NY, p. 104.

But the countryside, in the mind of the city dweller, does not only consist of open rural areas, but also of villages inhabited by rural communities with their own distinctive ways of life, and it is these communities with their slow idyllic style of existence, so spiritually uplifting to the tension-fraught urban dweller, that are now being destroyed by the great institutional and private landowners who are both transforming and raping the countryside of its goodness. Ruthless financial interests are not merely inflating land values so that rural dwellers are mercilessly dispossessed, but the values of village properties are being so raised that they are out of the reach of locals, who are displaced by Yuppies with their second home "holiday cottages." Hence ancient villages take on an artificial museum-like reality, with a horrid Butlin camp-like ambience during the weekends; whilst for the rest of the week they are reduced to morgues. This, again, creates an imbalance in rural areas. If the countryside is to be restored to its natural balance, then this can only be achieved through ensuring the *personalisation* of farmsteads within family-sized economic units.

10 – All land should be put to a good economic use

Fifthly, it may be that too much land is given over to agricultural use or that much land is uneconomic for agricultural purposes. For whatever purpose land usage is put it is essential that the interests of economic utility, or productivity, are considered. Vast areas of our countryside, particularly in Scotland and Wales, are nothing more than a wilderness of denuded mountains or heathland given over to no economic purpose other than the sportsman's gun. It is in the public interest, in the cause of national wealth creation, that land should be put to a more natural use. It is a depressing sight to travel through the Highlands and Islands of Scotland and to witness the innumerable abandoned crofters' cottages, standing in ruin, their windows empty gaping holes, their roofs caved in. This desolation and empty countryside has resulted from the forced evictions of the Highland Clearances. Today, a huge proportion of rural Scotland is divided between a dozen or so multi-millionaire landlords, who have turned the territory into an open playground for the international jet-setting super-rich, who for an ample fee may enjoy the delights of the rod and gun. This, indeed, is easy money for the great landowners of the North - freed from the toils of cultivating the soil and harvesting and marketing its produce - freed from the cares of breeding and selling livestock for food and alternative industrial purposes. This is land which is put to an unnatural use.

11 – Benefit of afforestation policies

In view of the huge quantities of timber which Britain is forced to import from Canada and Scandinavia, and in view of the massive unemployment in the middle belt region of Scotland, great economic benefit would be gained by dividing the land into smaller ownership units primarily for mixed afforestation purposes. In this way, not only would Scottish land be returned to the descendants of those from whom it was unjustifiably confiscated, but unemployment would be reduced; the principle of *personalised* property be realised in practice; and most significantly, the economic value of the land immensely enhanced, not only through the domestic availability of pulp and newsprint, but of an assortment of soft and hard timber, for supplying our factories for the production of a multitude of wares.

In some countries, e.g. Sweden and Finland as well as here in Britain - forestry land has come under the ownership of the state, so serving as a useful source for government income. But it is our argument, in the name of economic freedom and in maximising the existence of personal possession, that the state should be divested of property in all practicable circumstances.

A final note on landownership must be made: if the personalisation of property is to be equitably maintained, then this is only likely to be possible if land is held under freehold licence for its productive and taxable use.

CHAPTER 14
Public Servants As The Non-Possessing Class

"There is no intrinsic reason why the social services should be provided by the state in an advanced economy. Housing, health, education and security can all be supplied by the private sector making use of building societies or of insurance policies."

David Galloway, *The Public Prodigals*, Temple Smith, 1976, p. 47.

1 - Defining the pure public service sector   2 - Abuses arising from the privatisation of tax collection or the armed services, etc. 3 - Power acquisitiveness of public servants   4 - Business sector acquisitiveness more laudable as it contributes towards national wealth creation

1 – Defining the pure public service sector

Those employed in the true public sector, i.e. in local and central government offices to organise the collection of taxes, and carry out inspection services, etc., cannot in the public interest, be made the owners or part-owners of their employing concerns, since they are in the truest sense servants of the community or state. Such a sector, as we would have it, it should be remembered, would in terms of personnel be far smaller than that existing today, bearing in mind that insurance, employment, social welfare, health, refuse collection, etc., would all be contracted out to private franchises of the state, circumscribed only by an overall *dirigiste* authority.

The remaining true public sector, or pure civil servants, would consist of those alone who were necessarily free from working in a competitive environment - other than exposure to the natural competition of individuals competing amongst themselves for promotion. They would be concerned with the administration of the state, executing the instructions of the legislature, carrying out inspection duties, and attending to the policing and defence of the realm. The judiciary and military, separate as they are and should be from the civil authorities, would similarly be servants of the community, free from the pressures of competition in the execution of their duties. It would be intolerable, for example, if policemen or judges were paid according to the number of convictions obtained. Such officers should therefore be obliged to work for and within the objective criteria of the state.

2 – Abuses arising from the privatisation of tax collection or the armed services, etc.

Government officials, law officers, the judiciary and the military are amongst the only exceptions of those in the community who should *not* own or part-own their employing concerns.   It is, nevertheless, hypothetically conceivable that certain of the above sectors could be managed on a free enterprise basis, in the same way as health, pensions or insurance (as is advocated in this book) but it would be wholly contrary to the public interest. Tax collection, as in ancient Rome, could be sold out to private contractors, but such tax collectors (as every reader of the Bible knows) - they were referred to as "publicans,"would be held in low esteem by society and hated by the majority. The army too could be financed through pursuing a policy of active imperialism entailing the collection of tribute. Such a policy, again, as in ancient Rome, would ensure that our generals were the richest and most powerful men in society, but again this would lead to an unhealthy rivalry and the ever-present danger of civil discord - not to mention a situation of constant war abroad. Therefore, it is impracticable to manage a society totally without a public sector.

3 – Power acquisitiveness of public servants

Nonetheless, it has to be noted that in all societies, public servants, the military and judiciary, because of the nature of their power, are classes in society instinctively regarding themselves as special in the community, and consequently, engage in a constant but silent struggle to expand that power and their spheres of authority. In Britain, this does not so much apply to the military, which for several centuries has been kept well beneath the thumb of the civil authorities, but our bureaucrats - certainly from amongst the Administrative class - undoubtedly see themselves as rulers rather than servants as they are properly supposed to be.[53] The upper echelons of all these classes, in addition to churchmen (whose status we have not yet discussed) have an unhealthy and clandestine yearning for political power for its own sake, that places them in a category quite separate from the rest of the

---

[53] See Chapter 24 sub-sections 12 & 13 where this topic is touched upon again, especially with regard to *pure political power* as differentiated from that of extraneous vested interests interfering with the political process.

population. The only other constituent of society to be excluded from the above generalisation are our elected representatives, but as their striving for power is explicit rather than covert, and as their power is anyway dependent on the popular will, they are to that extent a lesser menace in undermining our freedom.

Meanwhile, the lower echelons of all these classes, the soldiery no less than clerical class bureaucrats, because they are accustomed life-long to "following orders" and the formulae of rigid procedures, become dependent; losing that natural flexibility to exert individual initiative in pursuing personal interests. Consequently, they commonly fall into a habit of mind of resorting to government legislation in solving every human problem. Hence a society with too large a public sector loses the characteristics of a democracy as it is increasingly bureaucratised.

4 – Business sector acquisitiveness more laudable as it contributes towards national wealth creation

Business people, professionals, and those in trade, although motivated by a healthy ambition to succeed in their own spheres of employment, and to gain financial riches - a healthy and desirable instinct - are in usual circumstances, entirely free of the ambition to dominate and manipulate their fellow beings for the achievement of general principles, or to cry for legislation in solving their every difficulty. For all these reasons, if a nation is to remain free and not lose its hard won rights to encroaching restrictive legislation, it is important: firstly, that the public sector should be reduced in size as far as is practicable; and secondly, that the numbers employed in the sector should be minimised.

Although the acquisitiveness for power of civil servants may be used constructively in the public interest, the consequent expansion of the public organisation to which it too often leads, is at the same time an ever-present and overwhelming evil in society in terms of its cost to the taxpayer. The acquisitiveness for wealth of the business person, however, even when there is no altruism in the motive, is invariably in the public interest (except when rentier activities are allowed to predominate) since it entails employment expansion, the earning of foreign currency, and the creation and fulfilment of buying power.

CHAPTER 15

Communal, Collective and Rentier Property

"For the sake of the public, all public organisations should be looked at from the point of view of commercial viability."

Horace Cutler, *The Cutler Files*, Weidenfeld & Nicolson, 1982, p. 99.

1 - Nature of Communal property   2 - It must be justified by what is both democratic and ideal   3 - Collective property   4 - The need to monitor the wealth of independent associations   5 - Rentier property

1 – Nature of Communal property

This leads us to consider the several aspects of communal or public property. This usually comprises means of communication as roads, railways, telecommunications and postal services; street furniture and monuments; schools and other educational institutions; town halls and government buildings; recreational facilities: parks, sports centres, gardens, libraries, art galleries, museums and zoos. Communal property comprises services and facilities that either cannot or do not easily lend themselves to self-support through the free enterprise economy; or the erection and maintenance of monuments and assets of value to our heritage.

As we have argued, those things which can be put under private control and management whilst remaining under an ultimate *dirigiste* authority, should be so transferred, but there will always remain a limit to pursuing such a policy. The privatisation of our great museums and galleries, and even public libraries, is a theoretical possibility. A nominal minimal charge might be levied on visitors and borrowers, and the extended benefits could be longer opening hours until late in the evening; an extended programme of lectures and educational projects; and enlarged reading and study rooms for students.

2 – It must be justified by what is both democratic and ideal

The criterion justifying the existence of public property is its use and enjoyment by the majority. Clearly no discrimination of use should be exerted against specific sectors of the population on grounds of class or unwarranted privilege. Those facilities that in fact only lend themselves to the enjoyment of the very rich, are clearly undemocratic activities, and therefore do not lend themselves to use as public property. Public property is for universal use or enjoyment. It might be remembered, for example, that the common people of pre-Revolutionary France were generously allowed the privilege of wandering around the gardens of Versailles - although this is not to suggest that we in Britain should open up the smaller gardens of Buckingham Palace for the same purpose. However, the huge acreages of British heathland that are reserved for grouse shooting and hunting larger game is undoubtedly lent to an undemocratic use and would not be justified as public property if that was the case. In fact, of course, such pastimes are only pursued on the private lands of our great aristocrats and the wealthy *nouveau riche*.

By the same token, all public property of a recreational kind should be of an edifying nature. This means that the pressures of "populism" or "vulgarity" should be eschewed in the cause of higher standards and good taste. Only by holding up to example what pertains to the ideal (and so remains separate from association with specific groups) in line with the achievement of a classless society can public property be justified. What pertains in the competitive free enterprise private sector, in this matter, is of course, another question. Hence the purpose justifying the existence of public property in all its aspects, is that it should coincide with the higher objective needs of the community, so transcending the sectional or subjective interests of specific groups.

3 – Collective property

Collective property belonging to independent associations, entails property held in trust for political, religious, cultural and recreational clubs and organisations, i.e. bodies established for a non-commercial and usually non-profitable purpose. It is understood, of course, that such associations remain dis-established, since they are in essence associations of free groups of individuals independent of the state. It is therefore implied that the Church of England should be dis-established and made accountable to the state as any other free association. No department of the state should exist if it cannot claim an objective relationship with all those persons belonging to that state. This is because such a department would act as both an instrument of favour for and discrimination against special sectors of the population in that state. Furthermore, no independent association should be allowed the ownership of substantial property not put to the immediate use of the purposes of that association. This is because such property would be divested from the sum total of private wealth that rightfully belongs to the community - i.e. is divested from the national wealth creating sector.

4 – The need to monitor the wealth of independent associations

On these grounds, therefore, the Church of England should be dis-established, and its lands and property confiscated by the state for sale into private ownership. Responsibility for the good maintenance of church buildings of historical or architectural value would then be taken over by the state, but not on the grounds of satisfying the religious scruples of a minority, but on the higher grounds of preserving the national heritage for our people in total - for Jew, Catholic and Congregationalist alike. With regard to paying the salaries of our religious leaders this, as in other European countries, would be attended to by a church tax, out of which any citizen might be free to contract on grounds of agnosticism or atheism. The total revenue from this tax would be proportionately divided amongst the churches and sects, so that Hindu priests and Moslem mullahs would be paid salaries through the auspices of the state on the same grounds as the Anglican or Presbyterian clergy.

Such associations as sporting clubs that virtually take on a commercial role would be obliged to take on a limited liability status and be managed as taxable business concerns.

5 – Rentier property

The next category of property to come under our scrutiny is *rentier* property. The core of our philosophy is that the good of productive capitalism should be set against the bane of rentier capitalism, but it would be a gross over-simplification to argue that we were opposed to all rentier activities under all circumstances. As with the principle pursued throughout this book, it is argued that rentier activity and rentier property should be so democratised as to be actually in the possession of the majority.

Rentier property, as a significant economic factor in society, falls into two categories: firstly, the ownership of stocks and shares and their financial benefits; and secondly, rents from land and property. Employee share ownership and bank funding of industry, as we advocate it, would democratise - or reflect the democratisation of the capitalisation of industry. With regard to rented property, it has consistently been argued that the users of property should also be the possessors of it. There are exceptions to this, e.g. consideration should be given to the heavy demand for furnished lettings, particularly with regard to students and young single people who have been obliged to leave home for taking up employment away from the parental hearth. The demand for rented accommodation would for the most part be satisfied by repealing the Rent Acts, so allowing protection to house owners to rent out furnished rooms; and tenants for their part would be afforded the protection of an adjustable statutory ceiling on rents. The feeble minded and senile, in other words those incapable of managing the ownership of residential property, are other categories needing the protective umbrella of rented accommodation, where they may be kept under the benevolent surveillance of kindly landlords and landladies.

The ills of rentier capitalism with regard to the question of property, only arises in a society when a significant sector of the pre-retired population, as in Britain, is allowed to become more dependent on its unearned income than on payment for labour. In such a society, a creeping malaise infects the majority. In a sound society, free from the undercurrent of seething resentment, work alone must be the justification for the ownership of property and the enjoyment of the good things of life, although, as we shall see in the following chapter, it is necessary that what has been accumulated by hard labour in one generation, should be passed on through inheritance to the next.

CHAPTER 16
Inherited Property and Taxation

"A good shepherd should shear his flock, not skin it!"
(Boni pastoris est tondere pecus non deglubere!)

Tiberius Caesar.

1 – Perceived as illicit property

T he final category of property to be considered is inherited property. It is a popular notion of our time, particularly amongst the left and the "socially aware," that all inherited property is somehow illicit - an undeserved windfall for the fortunate.

Inherited property is often perceived as sapping the initiative of those related to the well-to-do, of those who prefer to loll out their days in easy repose in great expectations for an inevitable gift of large proportions. It is also perceived as a major bar to the achievement of a more egalitarian society, and in Britain, in the last century, ruthless measures were taken by many administrations to tax inherited property. A prominent civil servant, who has studied this phenomenon, has gone so far as to claim that, "in the matter of estate duty, ... the ancient Romans, with all their cruelty, were more humane than we are."[54]

2 – A poor measure for achieving egalitarianism

If death duties had really contributed towards the creation of a more egalitarian or democratic society, there might then have been an argument for justifying the measures that past administrations have taken. But that has not been the case. The poor and the middling majority have been stripped of their possessions to enrich the

---
[54] James Coffield, *A Popular History of Taxation*, Longmans, 1970, p. 49.

exchequer. Widows of the conscientious and diligent have been driven from their homes, whilst their hard-pressed children have been left a pittance. The wealthy, however, have been relatively untouched by these laws of dispossession, since through the skills of their accountants and the transfer of assets to different and special kinds of accounts, including businesses and even the creation of new charities (closed to all comers except to the family Trust), or the acquisition of a few invaluable works of art with which to fulfil all the obligations of the state, they have successfully evaded the work of the great leveller.

3 – Comparisons of personal wealth

This is easily illustrated by a few statistical comparisons. In 1911, for example, the wealthiest 10% of the population owned 92% of total personal wealth. Fifty years later (i.e. in 1960) and in spite of immense social changes in the intervening period, the wealthiest 10% still owned as much as 83% of all personal wealth - an insignificant drop in percentage terms. The following are some more detailed percentage comparisons of total wealth ownership in Britain:-

Top 5% of population		Bottom 90% of population
1911-13	87%	8%
1936-38	79%	12%
1960	75%	17%

In 1960 the top 1% still owned as much as 42% of total personal wealth. Thus although the bottom 90% of the population may have doubled their total wealth within a 50-year period, the top 5% still succeeded in holding onto three quarters of the total personal wealth of the country. The following table showing more recent figures is of even greater interest:-

Income group	£ bn.	%	£ bn.	%	£ bn.	%
1972		1976		Increase		
Top 1%	51.9	28.11	70.00	24.29	18.1	17.5
" 5%	99.5	53.90	132.90	46.11	33.4	32.2
" 10%	124.2	64.28	172.90	59.99	48.7	47.0
" 20%	152.1	82.39	219.60	76.20	67.5	65.2
Bottom 80%	32.5	17.61	68.60	23.80	36.1	34.8
Total personal						
wealth:-	184.6		288.20		103.6	

Therefore, although the proportion of the population owning the top 20% of all personal wealth declined by 6% between 1972 and 1976, that top 20% nonetheless enjoyed a percentage increase in its wealth that was double the percentage gained by the bottom 80% of the population during the same period.[55] All this demonstrates that death duties have not only had a negligible influence in democratising the circulation of wealth, but even less influence in diminishing the huge assets of the most wealthy. The function of death duties as a social leveller should therefore be seriously brought into question.

4 – Need for safeguarding inheritance

But before this matter is considered, a more urgent question demands discussion. Is the inheritance of property in any case contrary to the best interests of a free Social Capitalist and democratic society? To affirm that it is contrary to the interests of society would be a nonsense. All assets, improvements and the inventions of previous generations are inherited property. If society and individuals are to set long-term targets in best developing the land for agricultural and forestry purposes, or in building sound industries for the future, then the assets of inheritance must be protected from the rapacity of the state. Land and industries cannot be best developed for their long-term use by the efforts of a single generation. In times of rapid change, as we now see, this principle is of even greater significance. When people and businesses are faced by the crisis of change, they tend instinctively, out of fear, to conserve old ways and methods, arguing that "that will suit them" until their days' end. They tend not to think beyond their own time, since the effects of the capital transfer tax will anyway transform the pattern of ownership and control.

5 – Assists long-term productivity

If, on the contrary, inherited assets were protected, then there would develop a closer co-operation between the generations, and the

---

[55] The gross inequality of personal wealth in contemporary Britain has been well documented by Prof. J.F. Meade in his book, *Efficiency, Equality & The Ownership of Property* (published in 1964); also by J. Revells in his book, *Changes In The Social Distribution of Property In Britain In The 20th Century* (published in 1965), and most recently by A.N. Atkinson & A.J. Harrison in their book, *Distribution of Personal Wealth In Britain* (Cambridge UP, 1978).

father or grandfather would extend the horizon of their ambition, in working for that which could not be realised in their own lifetime. The short-sighted policies of British industries, the "make-do" attitudes, and the fatalistic or suicidal complacency towards the need for long-term investment in modernising plant, is in great measure due to our iniquitous taxation laws in dispossessing on their demise the diligent and ingenious. Friedman has aptly remarked that "without the maintenance of inherited capital the gains made by one generation would be dissipated by the next,"[56] but the reverse is equally true, i.e. without the maintenance of inherited capital the current productive generation dissipate their gains in dispossessing their heirs - not out of spite to their heirs but out of spite to the state, the effective inheritor.

6 – Alternative means of taxation should be used for achieving a more egalitarian society

Inheritance not only facilitates a healthier attitude towards the pursuit of long-term ends, but is also a great stabiliser in the community, in contributing towards a smoother continuity between one generation and the next. These may be startling ideas, and on their first impact, unpopular. They conflict with the entire thinking of the political establishment as to how we should most effectively achieve a more economically egalitarian society. It is the present author's opinion that other measures should be taken towards achieving economic egalitarianism, but not primarily through an inheritance tax - especially as it is anyway ineffective in achieving this.

Why should we only dispossess the super-rich on the point of death? Such patience implies that all the interim abuses, direct and indirect of superfluous wealth bearing down on the under-privileged should be tolerated without complaint. In creating a more just, equitable and stable society, it would be a better policy to initiate taxation policies that bore down on the undeserving rather than on the afflicted. The only rational criterion for such a distinction between the afflicted and undeserving could be made through taxing more lightly those who are gained in productive pursuits and interests (i.e. through labour and the direct investment by such earners in the long-term

---

[56] Milton & Rose Friedman, *Free To Choose*, Harcourt Brace Javanovich, NY, 1980, p. 21.

productive projects in which they are employed); and taxing more heavily those who are gained in rentier activities (i.e. the wealthy non-workers who earn their livelihood through general equity investments, often from a non-productive source).

7 – Examples of this

In such a society, the small landowner would be given an advantageous preference for the afforestation of agricultural acreages and heathland with a mix of soft and hard woods; whilst the small manufacturer may be debt financed for the purchase of machinery, providing only that he could give sound satisfaction for pursuing a viable business. Such policies would be in line with our belief in the need for productive capitalism and the need for the abolition of rentier capitalism. If it is thought that measures designed to bear down on the still-living over-rich are too reminiscent of Old Socialism, it might be useful to bear in mind that that great founding father of the largest democracy, Benjamin Franklin, went so far as to argue that no one had a right to his "superfluous" property, and that the public might dispose of it as it chose, "whenever the welfare of the Public shall demand such dispossession."[57]

8 – Taxation as the destroyer of initiative

Taxation policies should always be designed with the thought in mind that taxation is a destroyer of initiative, and that it is our intention to build a Social Wealth creating society dependent on work and the ingenuity of initiative. In the words of a distinguished journalist, "all taxation carried beyond a certain point must diminish the will, by effort and ingenuity to earn more. ... Slowly we have grown to accept the view that none of our money is our own, that the state owns all of it and is graciously pleased to allow us to spend an ever-smaller part of it. We are grateful for tax reliefs as though they were a present instead of a diminution in the amount confiscated."[58] In citing again the motto of an earlier chapter, the author of a recent

---

[57] Quoted in Dr. Leonard Peikhoff's, *The Ominous Parallels*, Mentor Books, 1982, p. 115.

[58] Paul Johnson, *The Recovery of Freedom*, Basil Blackwell, Oxford, 1980, p. 133.

history of taxation has written that, "the fiscal policies adopted this century have led to the destruction of private property on a large scale, to a strengthening of the executive powers of government and to the enthronement of big business."[59] This is a shocking indictment, not merely of trends counteracting the attainment of a more democratic society, but of trends counteracting a more productive society.

9 – How we compare unfavourably with Continental Europe

Lastly, with regard to tangible property, it needs to be pointed out that in the heavy burden of our death duties, we are quite out of line with our toughest industrial competitors in the EU. The following figures are of interest and are given without comment: viz., the effects of capital transfer tax, as in May 1977, in the case of a son aged 30 without children inheriting an estate with the following valuations:-[60]

	Value	*Value*
To pay -	£300,000	£500,000
United Kingdom	£144,750	£264,750
France	£ 54,599	£ 94,599
Denmark	£ 53,022	£ 93,022
Netherlands	£ 46,636	£ 80,636
Eire	£ 45,000	£137,500
Belgium	£ 39,106	£ 73,106
Italy	£ 34,723	£ 81,134
West Germany	£ 30,591	£ 52,591
Luxembourg	£ 23,975	£ 39,975

Although it is not being suggested that there should be a total abolition of death duties, it is argued that they should be so minimised as to be neither a lingering worry to either benefactors or recipients of inherited property.

10 – Inheritance of titles cannot be justified

Before leaving the topic of inheritance behind us there are two categories of intangible property that must be touched upon: viz. The

---

[59] James Coffield, op. cit., p. 252.

[60] Taken from Paul Johnson, op. cit.

inheritance of titles and honours; and the inheritance of political privilege, howsoever passed over from one family member to another.

There can be no rational justification in any democratic society for the inheritance of titles or honours of any kind, for it is the outcome of just such inheritance that is most responsible for the occurrence of anti-democratic tendencies in all their forms. It is therefore argued that the College of Arms and our hereditary aristocracy should be dis-established, and that measures should be taken (wherever they are thought necessary) for hindering the use of such titles or honours as sources of privilege or financial gain, and which titles or honours would then in any case be regarded as spurious. All Established titles and honours would therefore be life-created and based on merit, and the aristocracy comprising the membership of the House of Lords, or surrounding the Court, would solely consist of life peers and their spouses; their children having no more right to the use of any title more grandiose than plain "Mr," "Mrs," "Miss," or "Ms."

11 – Special place of the monarchy

The sole exception to banning such inheritance of titles or honours would be reserved for the monarch and her immediate family, but the children of those Princes and Princesses not destined for the throne would revert to the status of ordinary citizens. The entire institution of the monarchy would therefore be re-established on a sounder basis within the context of a contemporary democratic community. All the ugly and anachronistic aspects on the periphery of the present monarchical system - with their privileges, graft and injustice - would be shed forever, as the core of the monarchical system was re-integrated into the purpose of the wider community with its democratic beliefs in a freely competitive, Social Capitalistic, and egalitarian society. The monarchy would therefore become a "Nationalised" institution; as relevant, up-to-date and purposeful, as any other department of the state. These ideas for the establishment of such a Constitutional monarchy may sound startling in the Britain of the 21st century, but they would scarcely have raised an eyebrow in the Continental Europe of 150 years ago. Although monarchy *per se* can have little place within a radical doctrine, in a society where the overwhelming majority are still enraptured by its mystique (especially ordinary working people), Socialist movements as well as administrators must be prepared to circumscribe its limits with sensitivity until such time as empowered to authorise its demise through the popular will.

As the figurehead of the monarch, as currently accepted in law and custom, symbolises a universalising in terms of time and space in all things British; and as the ownership of all land - all houses, gardens, trees, rocks and even blades of grass on British soil, are in an abstract sense, the property of the monarch, there is no reason as to why the monarch or her reigning heirs should be granted any title to the ownership or use of private property. The private property of the monarch should therefore be divested of all that has been acquired or inherited, and divided and sold off to the public, and there is every reason to anticipate that the respect and popularity of the monarchy would increase in proportion to its divestment of material goods. The Japanese monarchy, for example, flourishes under just such conditions of modesty in terms of material possessions. The British monarch, of course, would retain the right to the use and residence of existing palaces, but the ownership of these palaces would be held in trust by the state.

In a modern democratic state there can be no rational argument whatsoever to justify a monarch's right to private property of any kind other than chattels or immediate personal effects. A monarch in a modern industrialised society can only take on value and purpose through fulfilling a spiritual function, and the extension of that function as it is exerted through the wider population, can only take on greater meaning as the poorest and most vulnerable members of our society may identify with that function. Hence the impediment of material possessions must in no way be allowed to intercept those feelings of affection or sympathy that the majority might feel for the first mortal in the land. This would entail the up-dating and democratisation of the monarchy under the most realistic conditions, and concurrently, it would help to establish and stabilise the monarchy on the soundest basis for the medium term future within the framework of a Social Capitalist society.

12 – Steps to prevent the inheritance of political privilege

This naturally leads us into the question of the inheritance of political privilege, for this factor is almost as real in contemporary Britain in blocking the development of a truly democratic society, as it has been over the past four hundred years. This is not to infer that the same handful of dynasties rule in Britain today as dominated political life in the days of Pitt, but that an unacceptably high proportion of our leaders across the political spectrum belong to a narrow elite with blood-related connections. This is unquestionably an unhealthy aspect of our political life, for the real power base of the nation is incestuously restricted to a chosen minority, and this minority must take on the characteristics of an oligarchy, even though it may resist that tendency and comprise of different groups in conflict.

Even the Labour party is corrupted by the nepotism of interconnected families, which not only facilitates the nomination and election of the mediocre, but more significantly, is responsible for a conservatism of ideas and the prevention of that imagination needed in creating a more progressive and intellectually alive movement. In a true democracy, political power should be as evenly distributed throughout the community as is practicable, and it is now clear that such an ideal requirement cannot be realised without appropriate legislation.

Of all occupations, the holding of political office cannot be claimed as a right; and of all abilities, the political ability of the individual can never be claimed as indispensable. There are few other occupations of which this may be said with such certainty. In their different ways, and according to their genius, the poet, the doctor, the business person and the teacher, can claim a certain right to their vocations through inclination and merit alone that none would wish to deny them. The politician, on the other hand, in the democratic community, can never claim this. He holds office solely on the sufferance of a majority vote cast through a secret ballot, and that office is only held for a limited period, subject to re-election at regular intervals. Although all should have the right to engage in political activity - and in a sense, even, have an obligation to do so - I believe it essential in safeguarding and furthering the cause of democracy, that legislation should be passed for preventing the election to central or local government the siblings, or parents or children, or first cousins of those already in office. In the case of two or more such blood relatives putting up for election on one occasion, and all winning office, then the legal condition should be imposed, that all such elections be judged invalid. In the case of a single relative winning, whilst others lose, then the former might take up office, but his other blood relations would subsequently be barred from standing for office, until the first had subsequently been defeated, resigned, or died.

Such proposed laws should not be seen as onerous on the ambitious or vociferous, since political activity - and even a political career - should always be regarded as peripheral to other and primary occupations. Certain it is that the intangible possession of political office, however Byzantine and obscure the course by which it is obtained, has become in Britain a significant factor of socially unfair and undesirable privilege.

The above proposals therefore indicate the need for urgent measures to ensure that a far greater proportion of our people are brought into the arena of active political life. If it is necessary that candidates should be paid by the state to stand for office, then this would be a worthwhile investment in breaking the stranglehold of inherited privilege, as well as in strengthening the force of *real* democratic power.

CHAPTER 17
Domination as Possession

"Domination in the most general sense is one of the most important elements of social action. Of course, not every form of social action reveals a structure of dominancy. But in most of the varieties of social action domination plays a considerable role, even where it is not obvious at first sight. ... Without exception every sphere of social action is profoundly influenced by structures of dominancy."

Max Weber, *Economy & Society*, Bedminster Press, NY, 1968, p. 941.

1 - Striving for possession motivated by pleasure   2 - Love, platonic and sexual, masks a lust for possession   3 - Even compassion conceals the enjoyment of power   4 - Perceived love and "mutual possession" is an illusion   5 - Identity of thinking is also an illusion   6 - Love is only realised through perceiving the good or the ideal   7 - When lovers fall out then reality shows through   8 - Function of humour, and realism of the Old Testament prophets   9 - But illusion is after all necessary for a tolerable existence   10 - Authority in society is dependent on projecting the ideal   11 - Direct personal power less dangerous than the abstract power of religious or political authority   12 - How the political problem of domination as possession can be resolved in society   13 - Conclusions

1 – Striving for possession motivated by pleasure

Having considered the different kinds of property as it is generally understood, we have now come full circle in our consideration of the origin and nature of property as a sociological reality. We now return to the consciousness of possession as the primeval force of life - to the basic instinct of possession as the condition for existence.

The striving for possession is motivated solely by the instinct of physical pleasure, acting often through illusion. It is a purely subjective activity - not necessarily of benefit to the seeker enjoying its pleasure. This applies to the striving for possession in its every aspect. For example, there exists a species of insects, the male of which is torn apart and consumed during the act of copulation. This, however, is no deterrent to the male in his striving to possess a mate. The human species differs little from these insects in the relationships which develop between the sexes. The same force is at work. The Freudian theory that the sexual instinct remains the life-long motivation for all our actions, is still sufficient to explain the striving for possession and the origin of property relationships in society. This theory stands even as amended by his followers and opponents up until the present day.

2 – Love, platonic and sexual, masks a lust for possession

Love in all its forms, physical or religious; Platonic or aesthetic, remains a purely subjective experience, and is therefore reliant on a magnificent illusion. Whilst it lasts, it is nothing more than the perpetuation of a beautiful dream experience. In reality its definition is finally reduced to a bodily chemical reaction, masking a lust for the power of possession. The courtesan and the saintly hermit stand on a similar footing in this one respect. Both strive for possession: the courtesan or the roué for a body to satisfy a natural or sometimes an unnatural instinct; the saint for supreme bliss in heaven that comes from God's recognition of a virtuous life on earth. The one may appear to have less altruism that the other, but ultimately, both are intent on satisfying their self-esteem and self-esteem is a kind of selfishness. Both are intent on seeking pleasure in its intensest form - albeit pleasures of a very different kind. The saintly priest will passionately argue that his rewards - although delayed for the present - are infinitely more satisfying than the pleasures of the flesh.[61]

Moreover, his earthly existence will meanwhile be made pleasurable by what he imagines is a greater peace of mind; the recognition of his inestimable goodness as perceived in the public eye; the satisfaction of ingratiating and fulfilling the wishes of the supreme being; and most significantly, the sense of power that must come from the confidence and knowledge of advancing supposedly the highest form of authority known to humankind. The possession of virtue through service to God - or rather, of greater sociological reality, the illusion of this possession - is no less an object of possession as a pleasurable stimulus, than say the warm rays of the sun were to Diogenes, or the enjoyment of a chocolate, a cigarette, a vision of scenic beauty or the pleasurable emotion evoked by a poem, play, novel, or even, the grandeur of a religious service. The obsession with sin and the need to trample it down, is a vital prerequisite in the struggle for virtue, and so this too - the consciousness of the struggle between good and evil - is a contributory factor towards the

---

[61] This theme has perhaps been most graphically explored by Anatole France in his great historico-philosophic novel, *Thaïs*, contrasting the ideals of dying paganism with those of nascent Christianity, and set in Alexandria at the start of the Christian era; and at a later date made into a great opera of the same name by Jules Massenet.

attainment of supreme bliss. In these comparisons we are not concerned with value judgements, for that is a matter for ethics which does not for the moment concern us, but only with certain sociological factors giving rise to human motivation.

3 – Even compassion conceals the enjoyment of power

Love, then, in all its aspects is the exertion of power, and compassion - that feeling of gentle consideration for the fragility in an adored or pitied object - is in reality powerlust in its primeval or earliest form.[62] Compassion can only be experienced through the consciousness of superiority over a pitied object. It is a subtle mechanism indicating an opportunity for the power of possession through arousing a sense of indebtedness in a fragile object. There are few things creating a tighter bond in human relationships, either individually or socially between different sectors of humanity, than that which exists between creditor and debtor. On the psychological level, the existence of social conditions where compassion can best flourish, reflects the dependence of the weak, and hence a situation is created of possession without freedom. That is, the one condition for those in receipt of compassion, is that they should remain in bondage to their disability. As soon as they rise above this, or their condition is transformed, they are no longer the object of benevolent consideration or the kindness of compassion. They are humiliated by the fact that their disability is the reason for the sympathy they arouse, and consequently, they find their humanity is circumscribed by this fact. It is for this reason that a patronising attitude is always resented as both distasteful and invasive.

---

[62] It has to be noted here that this definition of love as domination does not define the experience in its ideal or more desirable condition, but only as it is most commonly found in society. Social Capitalism, as I noted in Chapter 6 of *The People's Capitalism*, is not primarily concerned with transforming human nature, but rather with taking humankind at its worst and forming institutions which will constrain individuals and groups from oppressing or harming others in the community. If such institutions, over a period of time, succeed in transforming human nature, then that is an extra bonus, but otherwise men and women should be encouraged to develop their own forms of freedom. That, then, is our reason for emphasising the role of domination in the sphere of love. As for love in its ideal or more desirable manifestations, readers are urged to consult Erich Fromm's outstanding studies of this topic, especially, *Man For Himself*, Routledge & Kegan Paul, 1949. In this context, Fromm has achieved a perfect synthesis between the demands and truths of religion and those of psychology. This is a truly remarkable achievement.

In the most personal relationships between men and women, compassion is the psychological mechanism - the great trap - revealed as a gentle consideration for an adored object that cleverly conceals a huge powerlust for possession. Compassion is as an intrinsic a part of religiously inspired or Platonic love, as the sexual love between man and woman or the sexual love between those of the same sex. The powerlust of compassion is to be found in its underlying greed for the possession of the desired object. This greed is made evident through the eventual discovery of the undeserving nature of the adored object, i.e. its unobtainability to the lover due to his or her "unworthiness." It is then that the realisation occurs that more has been "taken on" than was bargained for; that the showering of such affection was excessive and absurd; that the feelings of the giver are not reciprocated; and that after all, an attempt has been made to capture something which was unobtainable and beyond deserving. Feelings giving rise to such affection in such a situation are a reflection of human greed in its most humiliating form.

4 – Perceived love and "mutual possession" is an illusion

The illusion of love as dominating possession is easily demonstrated in the realm of everyday life. Lovers - and husbands and wives whilst they maintain an equilibrium in their relationships - are proud to maintain that they "possess" one another. This possession is not merely physical, but mental, intellectual and spiritual, whereby all is shared, as they are supposedly tuned into the world on a single wavelength. The reality is different. The very concept is a contradiction in terms. No objects, in any sense, can possess each other, except for chemical substances which transform each other through sacrificing their existence in the process. Human beings cannot achieve this miraculous transformation, since they are separate, bodily and spiritually, as indeed are all forms of animal life.

5 – Identity of thinking is also an illusion

Nevertheless, the trick of love - the illusory chemical reaction - creates a feeling of identity on everything which seems of importance, but it remains merely a *feeling*, and may be as ephemeral as passing smoke. When lovers view a full moon; wax lyrical over a painting; are brought together by the emotions of a great drama; share the same political ideals; or feel a total identity as they take bread and wine at the altar rail, their thoughts and thought processes are no more identical than the cloud patterns in the sky from one hour to the next. The separateness of their individuality is an assurance that they cannot think alike. Those external things that seem to create a feeling of identity act merely as a medium through which sexual instincts are sublimated. Every aesthetic, religious, or emotive intellectual experience, sets off a chemical reaction which is *physical* in its effect, even though it may appear as spiritual or coldly abstract. Naturally, individuals may be categorised into groups as to what may attract their interest, and naturally crowds may be subjected to the common stimuli of an orator (this being communication in its crudest form) but this is very different from suggesting that common external stimuli give rise to identical thoughts in any two chosen individuals. All art and every aesthetic experience is both a stimulus and a decorative clothing for expressing, or sublimating, or concealing the sexual instinct.

6 – Love is only realised through perceiving the good or the ideal

In the sphere of consciousness, love is the realisation of the Good or the Ideal, and that which does not meet up with these qualities cannot be the object of love. But, again, the perception of what is good or ideal is purely subjective. A man may fall in love with a murderess and a whore, providing she has sufficient physical attraction, and he will perceive redeeming virtues through all her faults. It is the excitation inspired by the idea of the good or the ideal - and it is a sexually motivated instinct - which gives rise to the existence of love, and it is in this sense that Platonic and physical love are manifested as identical qualities.

The idea of goodness is in itself uplifting and inspiring. It gives rise to the desire for emulation which is a form of possession, and so when love is reciprocated, there is a desire for mutual possession. The contradictory essence of love is at the same time to possess and to be possessed, and such a relationship is inevitably fraught with latent conflict. It is only the idea of the good or the ideal as suffused through the adored object, that makes it possible for such a relationship to be tolerable, but the good or the ideal as held in the eye of the beholder is merely an anodyne in place of reality - a mere illusion.

7 – When lovers fall out then reality shows through

It is only when lovers, and husbands and wives, and friends fall out, that illusions evaporate to reveal the hard reality underpinning all human relationships. It is then that the scales drop from the eyes of the adorers and the adored. When that occurs one realisation only is brought to the consciousness of both: both have after all, all along, been dominated or taken advantage of by the other. Such mutual recriminations were never heard during the heady days of love and friendship, for each was prepared to sink his and her identity in the common melting pot of shared possession in the individuality of the other. During the blissful harmony of illusory love and friendship, neither felt that the one was dominating the other, but then suddenly, all appears in a very different light.

The one realises that at no time did she really share in the intellectual or aesthetic interests of the other, and neither did they share even in common feelings; whilst the other is disillusioned by the revelation of some apparent stupidity in the adored one. Both feel empty, disillusioned and embarrassed, and both feel duped and hurt. The blind irrational prejudice of love has alone been responsible for this confusion. What was once a pleasure now becomes a burdensome obligation, and the warm spontaneity of "mutual" feeling is replaced by hypocrisy and the calculating coolness of deceit. The simplicity of natural feelings and the trust in instinct is gone forever, as it gives way to the complexity of guile as a necessary mode in pleasing the other, and formal gestures are increasingly relied upon in maintaining tolerable relationships.

As an eminent American thinker has observed, "the emotion of love, in spite of the romantics, is not self-sustaining; it endures only when the lovers love many things together, and not merely each other."[63] Moralists and psychologists have argued that genuine sexual love is based on equality and freedom; and psycho-analysts who have given deeper study to all aspects of the question, have demonstrated that where equality and freedom have not prevailed in such relationships, then they have existed under the striving of sado-masochism, and the latter technically defines dominancy in human relationships. Our argument is that this ideal of equality and freedom in the closest of human relationships is unfortunately the rarest

---

[63] Walter Lippmann, *A Preface To Morals*, op. cit., pp. 308-309.

occurrence, and that inevitably, and beyond the possibility of conscious effort, degrees of sado-masochism (usually unbeknown to the subjects themselves) occur sometimes in most human relationships. Hence domination is the mark of all relationships and domination is possession.

8 – Function of humour and realism of the Old Testament prophets

In view of this, a sense of humour becomes increasingly important as each see more and greater faults in the other, and humour is when the absurdity of illusion is shown up in its true light, and every occurrence of humour is a momentary breakthrough of reality. But by the same token humour makes tolerable a remaining veil of illusion in concealing the abrasiveness of reality. If humanity was entirely illusion-free, and all were fully conscious of their faults and those of others, we would live in a world of mutual contempt and recrimination, for no one could then tolerate the faults of his neighbour - let alone his nearest and dearest. The hard realism of the *Old Testament* prophets in their consciousness of the unworthiness of humankind and their obsession with sin, was in no small part assisted by the sourness of their humourless disposition. They indeed saw humanity as it really was - in all its naked ugliness. In this sense the *Old Testament* prophets had a profound psychological insight into the true nature of humanity, but it is a vision that the ordinary man or woman in contemporary society would find very difficult to live with on a day-to-day basis. Today humankind is instead forced to view the world through the humanising lense of illusory optimism. In the contemporary world, few can tolerate for very long the constant battering of those who would endlessly remind them of their sins, omissions and transgressions. After a while those so bombarded become merely listless. The *Old Testament* prophets loved and worshipped God as the Yahveh of the ancient Jewish tribes - there is no doubt of that - but their love for humankind is open to question. They revelled too much in the "wrath" of God for that.

9 – But illusion is after all necessary for a tolerable existence

The ultimate truth, of course, is that a certain degree of illusion is a vital prerequisite as a binding element in all human relationships.

Linked to the need for illusion in smoothing the path for social relationships, is also the need for etiquette or manners, for ensuring that all human contact and communication of whatever kind may be made pleasant, agreeable, or at least tolerable in those situations in which dominancy is enforced. But in any case there are no social situations in which the inescapable reality of possession as domination can be simply dispensed with. In this context it is important to note, that in our contemporary society, this aspect of possession is as much under attack, or is as misunderstood,   as are all other forms of possession.

For example, the increasing public awareness of the need for claiming personal rights in regard to human relationships, and the emphasis on seeking self-fulfilment out of context with obligations, has in no small part been responsible for the breakdown of family life and widespread divorce on a greater scale than ever before. This has only occurred because rights in themselves are meaningless, and of no value, unless they are also linked into obligations within the design for a broader understanding of the purpose of society and the functions of its constituent parts. It is this design that is missing in so many industrialised societies today, which results in many feeling that they are oppressed by the domination of unjustifiable possession. Hence they have lost their freedom. But this topic is something that goes beyond the present enquiry.

10 – Authority in society is dependent on projecting the ideal

That which pertains between the closest relationships of two individuals - between man and woman - pertains between the individual and society at large. The individual in society is merely extending his most private *persona* to a different level of existence, and whilst he might take on a guise very different from that of his other "self," he nonetheless remains in every detail that same self. All religious and political creeds, law, administration and the world of work, are only maintained through the domination of authority, and ultimately that authority is represented by categories of individuals. Authority may be exerted through many styles, but ultimately, all authority in the open society can only be maintained through the voluntary or willing assent of those who are bound by it. But again, willing assent is only possible through upholding the idea of the good or the ideal. Every manifestation of authority must be supported by some utility justifying its purpose.

To ensure that every manifestation of authority passes through every sector of society smoothly, evenly and totally, it is necessary that those responsible for its legislation and execution are held in special repute. They represent the apex of society - its purpose - the goodness it strives to achieve. Therefore they are marked out as the representatives of high political and religious ideals, and those in the lower echelons of society with special functions for enforcing authority, are clothed in a special garb, like the priest or the policeman, or the high court judge. A uniform is a value symbol emphasising a specific function or ideal, and as such it de-personalises the wearer and transforms him into an abstraction or stereotyped representative of his real purpose. This, in itself, is the creation of power, for a uniform, whilst it helps conceal the personality helps also to transmit the awe of authority and the fear of the unknown.

11 – Direct personal power less dangerous than the abstract power of religious or political authority

The direct power of one individual over another in society - of the parent, the schoolmaster, the policeman - is innocuous, indeed necessary and beneficent, since it is simple and circumscribed by common sense, and when it is abused, it is recognised as such and is easily corrected. But the more abstract power of higher forms of authority, of political or religious leaders, call for greater circumspection, since its misuse may go unobserved and may be transferred to the whole of society. Historically, priestly power is the most absolute and has given rise to some of the greatest evils in society, but the advance of the secular world has diminished this power and brought about a more pragmatic and objectively moral aspect to the different churches and sects.[64] The evils of abstract forms of power derive entirely from their clandestine nature, i.e. through, a) The justification of authority which forbids query on grounds of utility (or social benefit), for, b) The pursuit of measures which may be of questionable value. This form of domination as possession - even if

---

[64] For an anthropological study of this topic, see especially the first two volumes of Sir James Frazer's, *The Golden Bough*, on priestly power and the origins of kingship.

only because of its scale - is therefore quite different from that of the parent or schoolmaster correcting the child, or the policeman apprehending the lawbreaker.

12 – How the political problem of domination as possession can be resolved in society

The political problems of domination as possession in society, as they effect relationships in the world of work, education, law and order, welfare, politics, etc., can only be successfully addressed through an intelligent consideration of the following factors:-

1. A sociological consideration must at all times be given to all human relationships, both individual and social. This is the first priority of all political activity if both justice and economic efficiency is to be its guiding purpose. This means that the prejudices of religion, and traditional ideals must, for the moment, be cast aside as humankind is considered from its most objective viewpoint.

2. Bearing in mind that all human relationships are dependent on domination as possession, and that this domination is only made possible through the fragile presence of illusion, power should be dissipated as far as is practicable through the creation of realistic democratic structures. In this way the principle of sharing is maximised. This implies that Illusion, although partially necessary and certainly ineradicable totally, is neither wholly baneful or wholly beneficent to society. Hence measures should be taken to undermine (but not destroy) its part in strengthening domination in society, and this can only be achieved through an active or living democracy. Democracy is thus in this respect a solvent on the bonds of society.

3. Measures should be taken by society to ensure that those deserving and competent to hold authority in their respective spheres are put in those positions. This means that both privilege and "populism" should be eschewed for good sense and the achievement of the ideal. Both practical and moral qualities should be looked for in those to be invested with authority.

4. Lastly, an ethical ideal must be projected so that all sectors of society may be unified by a common understanding and purpose. This is in recognition of the fact, that after all, humankind cannot exist without the need for love and ideals, and that society cannot progress smoothly or contentedly without the perpetuation of mollifying illusion. It then only becomes the responsibility of leaders to ensure

that those ideals are in harmony with the best long-term practical needs of the community.

13 - Conclusions

This section has been an essential contribution in completing this study on the politics of property. The nature of property and the conflicts to which it gives rise in society, cannot be properly understood without a consideration of the psychological nature of humanity. It is hoped that those who have carefully studied the arguments in these chapters, will now condemn as simplistic and undesirable, those perceptions which see as inevitable the need for a conflict between co-operation and competitiveness; sharing and profit; common ownership and private ownership; charity and acquisitiveness, etc., etc., since such concepts give rise to all manner of false hopes and ideals, political and other. The basic instincts of humanity are what they are, and remain impervious to change.

There are many who would - and have, enslaved the world in a vain attempt to change the nature of humanity. The problem of the politics of property is to recognise the unconstrainable energy and individualism of humanity, and irrepressible creativeness and striving for growth - the frightening but natural aggressiveness of both the individual and the group - and to design structures and confer property, so that humankind is neither mutually nor self-destructive. Only then can humanity achieve and maintain harmony and happiness.

The first prerequisite for a free society – indeed, the first prerequisite for developing the full potential of the individual, is the ownership and use of property in the many forms in which it is manifested. This is the basis for a fresh political outlook, with a greater promise for the future, but startling to those who have trodden the well-worn paths of the past. It is a new path, vital to the peace of the world if it is to flourish in prosperity for the future. In the words of Lord Acton, that most respected of men, "a people averse to the institutions of private property is without the first elements of freedom."[65]

**

---

[65] Lord Acton, *History of Freedom & Other Essays,* Macmillan, 1907, p. 297.

PART III
Democracy: Real and Illusory

"The politics of Britain have consistently deteriorated ... The old party structure, which for so long guaranteed the evolutionary character of our society, seems to me to have broken down. .. We are moving more and more in the direction of an elective dictatorship."

Lord Hailsham, *The Dilemma of Democracy*, Collins, 1978, pp. 20-21.

In Britain we have always been proud of our democratic history and traditions. They have been held up as an example to the world. They are instilled into us from early childhood, and we have been brought up to believe that it was Britain, by her example, that brought democracy and freedom to the rest of the globe.

But is that really a correct light in which to see our past? It is true that British constitutional history is taught and studied in schools and universities throughout a great part of the world; and it is true that in the previous century, we fought gloriously for the great world cause, but can we take such widespread credit for the creation of democratic ways of life in other societies, some similar to and some very far removed from our own cultural heritage?

And anyway, is our way of life all that democratic by comparison with other leading industrialised nations in the free West? If a snapshot comparison is made of the world, as it exists today, the answer must be a firm NO! British society by comparison with that to be found in Germany, the rest of northern Europe, Japan, etc., is very far from democratic on many counts. This factor may not yet be apparent to the majority of British people, but it is most certainly apparent to our European neighbours, and they are appalled by what they see.

What, then, has gone awry? Although we may be credited with the genius of having invented democratic structures for government in the early modern period, these have not proven conducive to the development of democratic societies. The thesis of these chapters is that whilst British institutions have acted as forces of conservatism in hindering social progress, other forms of government and other intellectual forces, in Europe and elsewhere, have through a circuitous process been directly responsible for the successful creation of societies more democratic than our own.

Our history must therefore be exposed to the hard criticism of a sociological or realistic viewpoint. The myths of our democratic heritage must be exploded, in the cause of revealing the inner truths which have made us what we are today. This may be a painful enquiry, but it is necessary for our own good. There is a general consensus amongst academics, that our present industrial decline and social malaise must be laid at the door of our past history. Even amongst our most cherished democratic institutions there may be found as much to be ashamed of as there is to be proud of. Therefore, our value judgements must be reformulated.

On turning to our neighbours with their very different historical heritage, and unravelling the causes for the success of their societies, we are confronted with implications of even greater interest. Questions of an uncomfortable nature rear their head - i.e. uncomfortable from the perspective of our own standpoint - and they demand an answer. They fly in the face of our own values, and demand that we review our own institutions and culture from a new and more constructive viewpoint.

This enquiry is an appeal to academics to re-write our history from an objective sociological perspective, so that the myths of the past may be discredited in pointing out the way towards a better future. Our anti-industrial ethos is only able to survive on the stagnant pool of our illusions from a dead but glorious past. These chapters are only a beginning, and can achieve little without the follow-up support of the world of learning and industry.

It has not been undertaken as an idle exercise in speculative thought. If the decline of British-based productivity is to be reversed, and if full employment policies are to be pursued through the regeneration of manufacturing industry and the dependent service sector, then not only is it necessary that we create a pro-industrial ethos, but a genuinely democratic society. The industrial society of the future will bear little resemblance to that of the past. The smoke-stack industries with their armies of proletarian operatives are gone forever.

The future is going to demand - demands now, that a far higher proportion of our population be educated to much higher levels of skill and technology than heretofore. This will transform the shape of our society. But the realisation of this is impossible without achieving the kind of fully democratic societies as now enjoyed by our toughest industrial competitors.

CHAPTER 18
The Erosion of Freedom

"Justice is the first virtue of social institutions, as truth is of systems of thought."

John Rawls, *A Theory of Justice*, OUP, 1972, p. 3.

1 - Trade gives rise to freedom   2 - Freedom is not an immutable national characteristic   3 - Our failing representative system   4 - Monopoly of the media   5 - Contrasted with Europe   6 - A fringe press is not sufficient evidence of a free press   7 - The secrecy of the state   8 - How it undermines democracy   9 - Elsewhere freedom of information is guaranteed   10 - Economic factors entail the greatest diminution of freedom   11 - Our erosion of freedom runs parallel with our industrial decline   12 - Dangers of institutionalised opinion forming and the Computercrat

1 – Trade gives rise to freedom

It has now become a common assumption that Britain enjoys less freedom than her advanced partners in the industrialised West. It is of significance that Britain's relative decline as a democracy by comparison with all the countries of northern Europe and Japan - several of which emerged from the status of totalitarian dictatorships - may be correlated with Britain's decline as an industrial power.

This is no coincidence. Freedom has always followed in the wake of commercial and industrial success, and not vice versa, although this is not to forget that capitalism too has given rise to its own social ills. But the activity of free enterprise, entailing the free exchange of goods and services, as it spreads throughout a community, giving character to a nation, is the very essence of democracy in its every manifestation. This is because the expansion of trade is dependent on universalising a system of law and contract, which in turn requires the breaking down of privilege and a broadening of equality of opportunity, and this gives rise to the granting of innumerable rights, and so eventually, to every aspect of speculative and intellectual freedom.

2 – Freedom is not an immutable national characteristic

It is absurd to cherish the idea that freedom belongs to a people as an immutable characteristic. But because we have a long tradition of free institutions, and because we are the home of the Mother of Parliaments, and because we developed these things whilst the rest of Europe lingered in a state of feudal bondage or revolutionary turmoil, and because we have a long tradition in song and prose flattering to our pride in freedom, it has, perhaps, become inevitable, that we should believe and trust that freedom, as an immutable characteristic, belongs to us selfishly and uniquely, as an island race that is somehow set apart from the rest of the world.

This, unfortunately, is an illusion from which we must be divested, if we are to face the reality of the future - that is, if we are to restore that real freedom we have lost. We cannot be excluded from that great wheel of history taking all peoples through good times and bad, through poverty and plenty, through tyranny and freedom. Nonetheless, we must strive towards a consciousness of our existing socio-economic status in the world, and that realised, we can then strive towards a better tomorrow.

3 – Our failing representative system

Britain's loss of freedom, both in relative and absolute terms, over the past fifty years, by comparison with our toughest industrial competitors, applies to almost every aspect in which freedom may be understood. The fact that Britain has contravened the European Convention on Human Rights on more occasions than any other of her EU partners, and has thereby been hauled before the Court in Strasbourg, is merely a superficial reflection of her failure to keep apace with those freedoms now taken for granted elsewhere. The frantic attempts of the previous Tory government to ban, censor and suppress information about Peter Wright's book, *The Spy-Catcher*, is but the tip of an iceberg in the huge on-going censorship by the authorities in covering up every malfeasance and aspect of administration. A political clampdown on such a scale - inconceivable in any other country in the industrialised West - makes the conditions for any true democracy impossible. Our dual party system of representative government is a travesty of democracy when compared with any other system in the free world, not only because the two great parties of the polarised extremes are less representative of the real interests of the community, but because the mechanics of the system fail to proportionally represent the declared interests of those electors who do cast a vote.

One of our most respected elder statesmen, after a life-time in law and Parliament, has sadly come to the conclusion that, "we are in fact governed by a bureaucracy of mandarins and their subordinates imposing on a people partisan policies devised by a government of amateurs who have achieved their position by a minority of votes under an unfair voting system, bringing to Parliament candidates selected by local caucuses of activists or outside bodies having little else to commend them but their party loyalties.[66] ... Our unwritten constitution is breaking down. This cannot be remedied by any *ad hoc* tinkering with this element rather than that.[67] ... My diagnosis is that the society we live in is in process of breaking down. This diagnosis does not differ profoundly from that of the extreme left, or the extreme right in politics."[68]

4 – Monopoly of the media

The media, i.e. the politically vocal press, including the weeklies, radio and TV, are not merely controlled by a tiny minority, but that minority so jealously exerts a closed-shop policy against outsiders, that the opportunity for the expression of new ideas or views on almost any topic becomes insuperable. The dissemination of information and ideas has therefore become the monopoly of a small professional elite of immense power, that has even gone so far as to implement its own regulations to prevent the free expression by a wider public through the media.[69] In addition to this, the editorial control of the entire national press, by a handful of men (and several women) is not merely undertaken for the pursuit of narrow financial vested interests, but is so cunningly conducted across what is allegedly supposed to be the entire political spectrum, that the public is virtually manipulated as to how it should think and act. A false consciousness is created, and great numbers of people are led to believe in those things that are directly contrary to their own best interests. This process, of course, is nothing less than the negation of freedom.

---

[66] Lord Hailsham, *The Dilemma of Democracy*, 1978, p. 160.

[67] Ibid., p. 203.

[68] Ibid., p. 217.

[69] See especially Nora Beloff's, *Freedom Under Foot*, Temple Smith, 1976, in which she demonstrates clearly how the unions are striving to impose their own censorship, as well as enforce a licence as to what may be written through the monopoly of their own control.

5 – Contrasted with Europe

How does our media compare with that of our great industrial competitors? Firstly, the dissemination of information and political views are expressed through regional and locally based newspapers, and those national dailies which do exist have a negligible profile by comparison with their British counterparts. This situation not only pertains in those countries with a comparable population to ours, as for example, Germany and France, but also in those countries with populations of only a few millions, as in Sweden and Finland, where even moderate-sized cities have their own politically vocal dailies. It is significant to note that some years ago in Germany, a huge protest campaign was mounted against the Springer Press, on the grounds that the press baron, Axel Springer, seemingly posed a threat to freedom through monopolising too great a proportion of political opinion-forming. This was democracy in action. But had a German populace mounted a similar protest against an infinitely more powerful press monopoly, as that existing in Britain today, if their indignation had been in proportion to the threat, they would have effected a revolution. In Britain, little has been said and less done to counteract the monopoly of the national press in its work in undermining the freedom of the British people. Might it not be suggested that we have become so drugged by the blandishments of the media as to no longer have the will to regain a consciousness for our own best interests?

A second factor that distinguishes the foreign press from our own is that their opinion-forming journalism is not the exclusive preserve of a professional elite. Apart from certain weeklies employing professional staffs covering specific areas of interest, the newspapers of Continental Europe have an open-door policy with regard to contributions from any source available. European editors have always thought that journalism - and certainly the opportunity for the free expression of ideas - should be more dependent on *La carrière ouverte aux talents*, than on the existence of salaried and permanent staffs. Continental editors have not entrusted their journalists with being the fountainhead of knowledge and wisdom on every conceivable topic to be covered in their papers and journals.

This leads to a third distinction between the Continental press and ours. The intensive professionalisation of British journalism and the entrenchment of this monopoly through trades union policies, have led to a situation whereby a great proportion of the trade, technical and professional press - especially those journals controlled by the several large groups - have been taken over by "pure" journalists and so dominated by them, that the true voice of the trades and professions so represented have been virtually muzzled.   In other words, professional journalists who are professional in nothing else, have hijacked the organs of many specialised occupations, and in the name of "streamlining" and "brightening up" the contents for greater readability, have in fact proliferated trivia to the sacrifice of serious content. Consequently, whilst a great part of the trade press has been reduced in quality, the relevant trades have lost their effective representation, and with it, their freedom as a collective body to best pursue their occupational interests.

6 – A fringe press is not sufficient evidence of a free press

It is said that there is a free press in Britain. There are open and free correspondence columns in all our papers, and plenty of criticism is vented. But the same held true for the papers of Soviet Russia, yet few would suggest that they were free. A protest correspondence column tucked away in our great national dailies is merely a harmless gesture - a valuable escape valve for expressing and sharing a natural feeling of dissatisfaction. Likewise, the protest columns of the Soviet press were as little feared by the Politburo secure within their palaces behind the Kremlin walls, as are our own press barons seated in their plush armchairs in the safety of their new Docklands location are afraid of criticism in their own papers.

It is also true that we have a huge fringe press, representing everything from the extreme Trotskyist left, and many variations thereof, to the lunacy of the fascist right. But the existence of these things is of little note to the cause of freedom. The lunatic fringe, of the right or the left, is about as innocuous as a fireside cat. This is because the lunacy of extremism flies in the face of the commonsense of the majority, and if it fails to arouse disgust, which it often does, it more often leaves an impression of cold indifference. To cite a wildly diverse protest press, advocating every eccentricity as evidence of a free press, is simply naive.

What Britain lacks is a critically objective press representing the radical left of centre: a press that strikes out at the vested interests of rentier capital; at the corruption of widespread graft and patronage; at the rottenness of our debased bureaucracy; and at the machinations of our powerful financial institutions which are directly responsible for undermining our economic welfare in exacerbating unemployment. Such authoritative, forthright journalism, sweeping away the myths and shibboleths of the tired old discredited parties would at once strike fear into the press barons of the now proverbial "Fleet street," and everywhere into the hearts of the establishment. Such a journalism, seeking after the objective truth, would be in the forefront of a free press. This is because freedom does not simply consist of the free expression of the untrammelled will, any more than the ravings of the insane can be said to be the voluntary expression of the free will. The free expression of the untrammelled will might pass for a vulgar definition of freedom, but it would certainly not pass the scrutiny of a philosophical or sociological approach to freedom.

True freedom is dependent on the reality that is revealed through a higher awareness of our true status in society; on the falling away of a false consciousness; and on the ability to identify the real barriers in our path to progress. The British people today are involuntarily in bondage to a media which has created a world of illusion and false values, and this especially applies to the sensuous embrace of the popular tabloids which intentionally set out to detract from the hard realities of ordinary existence. In the very attractions of the British press may be found its poison. The Continental press, by contrast, may be dull or even turgid; but it is factual, and it is relatively independent of powerful financial forces. The division of the press into many autonomous units on a regional and local basis, so that ownership is disseminated and competition ensured, inevitably contributes towards the cause of greater democracy. A centralised press, on the other hand, tied in with huge financial vested interests; close to the corridors of power of the bureaucracy and national government; extending its tentacles in gradually absorbing a diminishing independent local press in the provinces and metropolitan areas, cannot but be a bad omen for the future of democracy in this country. A former British premier in a careful consideration of the media as it relates to freedom, came to the following conclusion, that "the press is no longer the guardian of freedom in this country."[70]

---

[70] Edward Heath, House of Commons, 20th November 1985.

7 – The secrecy of the state

Turning from the limitations of our representative institutions to restrictions on the expression of freedom imposed through the monopoly of the media, attention may now be focussed on an even greater evil, viz., the suppression of free information by law and administrative edict.

The British bureaucracy, from the highest to the lowest level, and in every department and in all its manifestations, as it stretches out to effect the ordinary citizen in every aspect of his public, and what he (and she) might often consider, private life, operates on a level of secrecy not to be met with in any other country in the free world. Not only is the civil servant forbidden to discuss or reveal to other persons or authorities almost any kind of information regarding his own function or that of his department, but this in turn leads to the concealment of the way in which we are governed, and so to confusion and fear. This suppression of essential information in a country purportedly governed by the people, of course amounts to nothing less than the negation of democracy, since democracy by definition must be dependent on a full understanding of the way in which government works. If the existence of democracy was solely to be judged according to the operation of the electoral mechanism as it is set into motion from time to time,[71] then the East bloc countries could equally have contended that they were democratic, but of course such a criterion would be naive and absurd.

David Leigh, in a penetrating study of this topic, has maintained that, "the sum of secrecy in Britain is ... greater than that of its parts. Because we live in a society whose basic political culture has never been radically upended by revolution or war, these secretive components are heaped one on top of the other. ... Because of Britain's historical continuity, in which institutions are superimposed or grafted on to existing ones, and because of the habit of secrecy about their own powers and the limits within these institutions, the real mechanisms of government are hard to see.[72] ... Britain, nominally

---

[71] Rousseau argued more than two hundred years ago that democracy in Britain only burst into fruition during those brief periods when elections were held. His argument, unfortunately, holds equally true today.

[72] David Leight, *The Frontiers of Secrecy*, Function Books, 1980, p. 2.

a democracy, is in fact a complex oligarchy with a loose system of democratic supervision.[73]... It is very hard for a society to educate itself unless it can see what is happening to it. This is why the biggest secret of all is the precise extent of secrecy in government."[74]

The legal origins for the secrecy of the civil service stems from the Official Secrets Act hurriedly passed in its original form in 1911 following a spy scare. Since then the Act has been extended on a number of occasions to include an ever-widening contingency of eventualities covering the mundane functions of the bureaucrat, until today the manifestations of the Act when seen in its full implications have very little to do with its original purpose in safeguarding state security. The very name of the Act, when seen in the light of its real purpose, is little more than an example of *Newspeak*. It should be correctly re-named, the "Suppression of Information Act", for it entails nothing more nor less than that. On the prerogative of our civil servants in despotically pursuing their own functions, David Leigh has remarked that, "we apparently live in a country where unpopular and probably undesirable major policy changes can be proposed by 'neutral' officials who do not wish the public to know what they are recommending."[75]

On the state direction of the press through the D-Notice system and Section 2 of the Official Secrets Act, which is used to protect civil servants from every malfeasance for which they may be liable, he observed that, "despite lip service paid to the idea, genuine freedom of the press has never been seen in Britain as part of the constitution.[76]... Two fundamentally democratic ideas about information have never really been accepted in Britain even amongst many professional journalists - first, that liberty is indivisible, and crass, irresponsible or simply loathsome publications are inescapably part of it; and second, that knowledge about public affairs should be a right and not a privilege."[77]   Whenever the bureaucracy is cornered it "has two

---

[73] Ibid., p. 1.

[74] Ibid., p. 45.

[75] Ibid., p. 46.

[76] Ibid., p. 48.

[77] Ibid., p. 49. Regarding the first point, made by David Leigh, it may be apt to mention here that it has already been established that the Contempt law, used to prosecute

standard defence postures: the first is to assert metaphysical doctrines, such as 'ministerial responsibility' and defend them against all comers with a dogged scholasticism. The second is to bury reform in a procedural blancmange, whilst expressing loyal acceptance of whichever great alteration has been forced upon them."[78]

Another authority on the true nature of our administration, as well as having experienced life in the corridors of power, the MP, Brian Sedgemore, has aptly remarked that, "government in Britain today is so secretive that even the true nature of our Constitution is hidden not in the sense that it is unwritten but in the sense that those few people who are privy to the way in which, by whom, and in whose interests power is exercised are unwilling to tell what they know. In consequence half-truths, myths and outright lies abound.[79]... Top people do not trust each other. So they have developed a hierarchy of secrecy in government. Indeed our society can be likened to a pyramid in which the further away people are from the apex of the pyramid the less information they are allowed to have - officially.[80]... Secrecy is all pervading in our Constitution: it stretches into every nook and cranny in Whitehall and Westminster; it affects issues large and small; it shrouds policies of every kind; and it adversely affects the relationships between almost everybody, ministers, civil servants, members of Parliament and the public. ... Secrecy about how we are governed, how power is exercised in our society and the way in which institutions and individuals that buttress it operate can only lead to cynicism about the democratic process. It can only cast doubt ... on the validity and integrity of decisions on matters of policy which governments take. Secrecy may be a weapon that suits weak ministers and strong bureaucrats but it is of no advantage to ministers and public servants dedicated to a powerful, vigorous democracy."[81]

---

those who choose to "Publish and be damned," violates Article 10 of the European Convention on Human Rights. This was established by Judge M. Zekia in April 1978 during the *Sunday Times* case.

[78] Ibid., p. 13.

[79] Brian Sedgemore, *The Secret Constitution*, Hodder & Stoughton, 1980, pp. 11-12.

[80] Ibid., p. 13.

[81] Ibid., p. 24.

8 – How it undermines democracy

The anti-democratic nature of government secrecy is most evident in the fact that it raises a barrier of ignorance not merely between the public and the administration, but even between elected representatives and the administration, that effectively makes any intelligent appraisal, protest or participation by the ordinary citizen in the democratic process an impossibility. The ordinary citizen in Britain is not denied his democratic rights by any positive injunction, but by the subtle and equally effective means of the withholding of information. As the subjects for criticism are hidden from view, the ordinary citizen, in his frustration, is like a sparring partner in the dark. What is more common, however, is that the political life of the ordinary citizen - in so far as it can be said to exist - is lived out on a level of illusion, whereby all problems are only comprehended and responded to according to mythical and out-dated ideological thinking, that has scant regard for the world of contemporary reality. The explanation and slotting of all problems into the convenient rationale of the three great parties of the establishment, must be satisfying to power-wielding administrators, since it detracts all attention and blame from themselves, whilst concurrently seemingly to transfer all problems to the democratically elected representatives and so ultimately to the public themselves. In other words, the public are the makers of their own problems. Our entire democratic system is therefore, nothing more than a mirage, smoothing the way for an administrative dictatorship.

9 – Elsewhere freedom of information is guaranteed

How, then, does our public administration compare with that of the rest of the industrialised world? Firstly, there is nothing anywhere that quite compares with the Official Secrets Act. Secondly, there is an increasing awareness that all public administration inevitably entails an immense exertion of power effecting many aspects of life over the ordinary citizen. In response to this realisation, in safeguarding the rights of the citizen, many countries are introducing freedom of information acts to ensure more open government. In Denmark, for example, a number of laws were passed in the 1960s and 1970s enabling the public to have access to recent documents; whilst meanwhile, across the Atlantic, the USA originally passed its

Freedom of Information Act in 1966, and this was subsequently extended and made to have real teeth in 1974. Sweden passed her Freedom of the Press Act as long ago as 1766, and today in Sweden, a situation pertains whereby any journalist may simply phone a government department and ask for what in Britain would be categorised as classified information. No such realistic steps for increasing freedom of information are promised in Britain. In Britain, on the contrary, all the signs are indicating that we shall continue to regress in the opposite direction. In the words of David Leigh, "there is now a fairly general recognition among opinion-formers that Britain is out of step with many of the Western democracies."[82]

10 – Economic factors entails the greatest diminution of freedom

The greatest diminution of freedom of all, as if effects ordinary people, and undoubtedly that which hurts most, stems not from the limitations of our representative democracy, or the monopoly of the media, or even from the suppression of information as to how we are governed, but from the contraction of opportunity in the sphere of work and earning power. Unemployment and poverty is possibly the greatest loss of freedom that the ordinary citizen is anywhere liable to experience, short of being subjected to the tyrannical coercion of the state or being thrown into a detention centre as a political renegade. Nonetheless, in the free world, in terms of political reality, the loss of earning power is likely to remain the greatest loss of freedom to be experienced by the ordinary man or woman. Of course, if the other three freedoms were to be fully realised, then the possibility could exist for the collective democratic strength of the citizenry to restore that last and most important freedom of all - but that is another story. Clearly unemployment is the greatest loss of freedom, due to the absence of spending power, which is in no way offset by the compensation of the state.

---

[82] David Leigh, op. cit., p. 45.

Government policies for unemployment and Income Support and other benefits are designed to maintain the individual on nothing more than the barest essentials, including the payment of housing costs or the interest thereof - and possibly, even that benefit may be removed. The unemployed, therefore, find themselves restricted in every direction, since every useful activity entails expenditure and especially the seeking after new employment.   As almost any activity necessitates a cost, none more than the unemployed risk placing themselves in a debt situation, and they are frequently debts incurred in the very act of trying to extricate themselves from the status of unemployment. As the unemployed try to raise themselves from the mire, through self-help and greater effort, so they sink even deeper, only half-conscious of the fact that they are victims of economic forces infinitely greater than themselves, and at last they settle down into silent apathy in the discomfort of a new existence, a mere shadow of their former selves.   What could be a greater loss of freedom than that?

11 – Our erosion of freedom runs parallel with our industrial decline

This returns us to the argument at the start of this chapter: Britain's loss of relative freedom by comparison with our industrialised neighbours, has to be correlated with *our* industrial decline and *their* industrial success. At the end of the War, Britain was industrially in advance of all her EU partners.   Today, she is at the bottom of the league table - or very nearly so - in almost every economic rating touching on productivity and living standards.   The average Briton today earns less than the Mediterranean worker. Britain's decline is the most disgraceful example of economic self-defeat in modern history.   Here is not the place to analyse the reasons for that decline.   It is a topic which has been amply dealt with elsewhere.[83]

It need only be pointed out that as Japan and our European neighbours have reconstructed and materially improved their societies since the end of the Second World War, so too have they laid the foundations for sound democracies that have grown from strength to strength.   Several of these countries were transformed from the status

---

[83] See, *The People's Capitalism,* Parts II & III.

of dictatorships, but despite that handicap, they have developed democracies not merely in the mechanical sense of creating representative institutions, but in the more meaningful sense of creating democratic, open, and classless societies, seeking to maximise both liberty and equality of opportunity, whilst also ensuring the free dissemination of information.

Meanwhile, as Britain has sunk into a relative decline, so too has democracy here been on the retreat. As a phenomenon, this has not perhaps been markedly apparent during most of the last fifty-year period, since it has been masked by the greatest increase in living standards since the start of the industrial revolution. Nonetheless, a closer look at our society clearly reveals that democracy has been on the wane. If we take first our representative institutions, their character has changed dramatically for the worse over the past five decades. This is not simply reflected through the polarisation of British politics (both feigned and real), but through an internal breakdown of trust in the workability of the system. James Margach, after a life-time of reporting from Westminster, noted sadly towards the close of his career that, "there are today, and the 1980s will increasingly confirm this, deeper ideological differences between the two parties than ever existed in the thirties and with less tolerance and mutual respect. The more alike the identikits and profiles of the parties have become the more bitter and widely separated in political basics and humanities they have grown. ... The Parliament I leave at the end of the journey is much more inbred, introspective, impotent and self-centred than it was when I first appeared on the scene. ... Successive Parliaments and governments have displayed an obstinate resistance to modern change and reforms."[84] This is the classic description of a degenerate democracy immediately preceding its breakdown and transformation into some kind of oligarchical dictatorship.

If we take the politically vocal press, that is, the national dailies and the great weeklies, it is clearly evident that a great number of these papers have ceased publication over the past fifty years, never to appear again. This is a tragedy of incalculable proportions to the cause of freedom, for the thought-provoking depth of the written word can in no way be replaced by the ephemeral superficiality of the TV commentary, or by the plethora of local radio stations.

---

[84] James Margach, *The Anatomy of Power*, W.H. Allen, 1979, pp. 75-76.

As far as the loss of earning power is concerned, as it effects the diminution of freedom in contemporary Britain, nothing more need be said on this matter, since its implications are already so widely known.

12 – Dangers of institutionalised opinion forming and the Computercrat

There is another and last aspect of the diminution of freedom which must be touched upon, and that is the outcome of what I call institutionalised opinion forming. It is by no means unique to Britain but because of the exceptional power of vested interests in this country it is a problem which is made all the more acute here than elsewhere. Institutionalised opinion forming entails the cession of individual responsibility in the attempt to influence the public. Democracy is thereby sacrificed when representatives in political office are no longer cognisant of the ideas or pronouncements for which they are attributed. It occurs - and is increasingly occurring - in the following situations: when speeches are ghosted by specialised researchers; when books on policy or political matters are likewise produced; when correspondence is handled by third parties; when minor politicians remain totally unapproachable to answer or discuss questions put to them; when policy and power falls entirely into the hands of faceless committees so that party spokesmen become unwilling or incompetent to comment on controversial issues on which no formulated policy has been declared.

It is in these circumstances that statesmen, and even minor politicians, become nothing more than puppets on a string, and once they have surrendered their individuality, it is very often the case that they have already sold their souls or their integrity to powerful vested interests to whom they are indebted and to whom they are afraid to give offence. No institutionalised opinion former, or mouthpiece of some nameless and unknown authority, should be entrusted with democratic power. The telltale sign of a politician belonging to this category, is the man or woman who having delivered an apparently authoritative speech or statement on a specific issue, is then found to be entirely ignorant, and sometimes, even, uninterested in the topic on which he or she has spoken with such apparent insight. Institutionalised opinion forming reflects the de-humanisation of the political process. It occurs when the political representative is no longer prepared to express his own feelings or thoughts, for he has become instead a mere cypher or zombie of the political machine to whom all his loyalty is given.

Institutionalised opinion forming has arisen in response to the professionalisation of *political populism* or so-called spin-doctoring, i.e. scientific research by a political grouping as to how best it might win over or maintain the allegiance of the electorate irrespective of principles. The outcome of such research obliges leaders and activists of a political grouping, often against their own feelings and personal judgement, as to how they should act and present themselves and their policies, and hence they are sometimes reluctantly forced to follow a path which is contrary to their better inclinations. In this way, not only does deceit and self-deceit evolve through the needs of vote-catching, but at the same time, the integrity of the representative or democratic process is destroyed. If the needs of populism as dictated by a computerised system, grates against the instinct of those who have set the dreadful machine into motion for rehashing party policy to fit in with the needs of vested interests is allowed to predominate over personal inclinations, then democracy can no longer be said to function. Democracy is only workable when it is set within a framework of humanly workable proportions, i.e. when free from artificial barriers which prevent a spontaneous interaction between the real feelings and ideas of representatives and the people whom they address.

Those who advocate and initiate this de-humanised form of political power may be termed Computercrats. Their rationale for promoting this vacillating and faceless form of political power is that it eschews the dominance of the individual, so preventing the emergence of a charismatic-type appeal in the presentation of ideas or policy. This, of course, is in accord with the spirit of the age, when political character - in the East as well as in the West - is supposed to be held in subordination to a collectivist image of authority. The Computercrats, however, have carried this concept to its furthest logical conclusion, by attempting to create a system of power which draws its guidelines from opinion polls and focus groups, and the expediency of balancing and satisfying different vested interests, through which the political personality acts purely as a medium for their expression.

The Computercratic politician, therefore, still exerts enormous power, but it is through consciously abstaining from principle, conviction or vision, as he or she acts as a cypher in a computational capacity in transmitting a will which is non-individualistic - i.e. a will with which he or she does not personally identify. His relationship with the electorate therefore necessitates the projection of a false front - a false personality - a mere cardboard image, having no correlation with real ideas, convictions or policies. He is therefore perceived in the light of a TV personality - merely a pleasant visual effect, giving rise to pleasing associations of character. The amorality and essentially undemocratic nature of the Computercratic politician, as he thrives today, must surely be evident to us all. Everything about him is superficial, synthetic and evanescent.

There are many other freedoms which have been eroded over the past few decades which I have not attempted to touch upon in this brief introduction to the problem, but the above are possibly the most acute as they effect the majority.

So far, we have demonstrated historically that in the industrialised West in the post-War period, industrial success and improved material standards seem to have gone hand-in-hand with the advance of greater democracy; whilst on the contrary, relative industrial decline has been accompanied by the contraction of democratic standards. This has certainly been the case of Britain when compared with her comparable partners in the northern hemisphere. However, it would be the height of naivety to use this as a paradigm in citing democratic and non-democratic societies. Democracy is not - or should not be dependent on a nation reaching and maintaining a minimum standard of material existence. Democracy is primarily dependent on those factors cited at the start of this chapter, and although they are economic, necessitating a financial system for the free exchange and manufacture of consumables, they are factors which are qualitative rather than quantitative.

In any case, despite our relative decline as an industrial power, it has already been observed that living standards in Britain have vastly improved over the past fifty-year period. Therefore, the decline of British democracy cannot possibly be explained away in terms of declining material standards. It is very doubtful if a sudden increase in material welfare would do anything in promoting greater democracy apart from freeing those who are restrained from exerting their rightful spending power.

Hence we are obliged to look in another direction for the cause of Britain's loss of freedom. The cause, in fact, is far more deep-rooted than has already been suggested. The seed for Britain's self-destruction is concealed in the very heart of her representative institutions. Her wounds will be found to be self-inflicted. We must turn to another course of enquiry in diagnosing the real cause of the British disease. Comparisons will be made again with our industrialised partners in the northern hemisphere, but they will be comparisons from quite another perspective. The outcome may be shocking to the natural susceptibilities of our people. A malignant cancer will be diagnosed and surgery may be called for.

CHAPTER 19
When Old Prejudices Seem Vindicated

"In democracies, no man need feel ashamed of his calling, for all work is alike honourable - industry, trade, bodily labour; but, in England, the aristocracy as a body are neither engaged in trade, industry, nor bodily labour, and consequently ... society has agreed that persons following these pursuits are of an inferior caste."

J.B. Crozier, *Civilization & Progress*, Longmans, 1888, p. 297.

1 - Britain viewed from Europe   2 - Corrupt origins of the representative system   3 - Causes of our intellectual complacency   4 - Sound reasons for "disdaining" the foreigner   5 - But what lay under the democratic veneer?   6 - Why political reform failed to dissolve the class divide   7 - Our prejudices seemingly justified by 20th century events   8 - Contradictions of our divided society   9 - Social progress is not the outcome of political stability.

1 – Britain viewed from Europe

When our European or Atlantic neighbours view the political scene in Britain; when they see the polarisation of our party system; our industrial strife, and most of all, our appalling economic performance, they look at us in askance. How could we have got ourselves into such a mess?

Our complacency in view of these intractable problems is regarded as something bordering on dementia. Everywhere on the Continent, and elsewhere, the apparent extremism of our polarised politics with its dated ideological thinking, lately replaced by the anodyne forces of pragmatic non-principled spin-doctoring, is not merely regarded as delusive but with ridicule, if not disgust. Everything about the British political scene is considered as irrelevant to the needs of tomorrow, and those who view this country most kindly, look upon us with pity.

There is a huge irony in the fact that peoples from countries who laboured under totalitarian dictatorships just two generations ago, now boastfully proclaim the enjoyment of democratic rights denied to us in Britain, whilst feigning faint surprise at realising the various disabilities under which we linger. There is no hypocrisy in this. The younger generations of Germans and Japanese, born after the holocaust, to whom the past era is as distant as the Wars of the Roses, are genuinely democratic in feeling and intellect. They are as aghast at class privilege; political extremism; social conflict, and monopoly, in all their manifestations, as democrats anywhere, and yet here in Britain, they witness all these things, and much more, and in greater abundance than they ever knew it at home. If they are taught - or hear it taught - that Britain is the home of democracy and the Mother of Parliaments, they are mildly bemused, and begin to speculate on the values of most benefit to a community. Whatever their conclusions, they remain reassured in their belief that *their* societies come closer to representing, "justice as fairness" and that life may more easily be lived by the proposition that, "all social values - liberty and opportunity, income and wealth, and the bases of self-respect - are to be distributed equally unless an unequal distribution of any, or all, these values is to everyone's advantage."[85]

2 – Corrupt origins of the representative system

Britain perceives herself as the fountain-head of democracy and freedom in the modern world, and historically, in terms of our liberal representative institutions, this is true. It is true that after a series of bloody civil conflicts stretching across two hundred years, we did by the end of the 17th century, develop a mechanism whereby two conflicting vested interest groups could peacefully settle their differences. This was a huge advance in civilising political life, and of course, it conveniently coincided with the final demise of the feudal system. How much more civilised that groups of men should settle their differences by bribery and graft, lies and slander, than that they should resort to the sword or the block! At least civil bloodshed was averted. The vast majority of men and women may have been little affected by these changes, but that was of little consequence to the initiators of the new democracy.

But it should be noted that these conflicting groups or parties represented little more than the narrowest, most selfish and ruthless of vested interests, with the thinnest veneer or moral principle or concern for the best objective needs of the community. Each party had some small rightful justification for its existence, but in viewing the total claims of each in the context of their action, they were equally bad. Their overriding concern was power for the party against all other odds, and towards this end, they shifted their principles accordingly. These were to become the immutable characteristics unique to ourselves, and in different ways, they eventually were to poison every sector of society.

---

[85] John Rawls, *A Theory of Justice*, OUP, 1972, p. 62.

They were the basic ingredients of a sharply confrontational dual party system which has not changed a jot between 1679 (first emergence of the Whigs and Tories) and 1979 (election of the first Thatcher government) and that despite the many transformations of society during the intervening period. The very rottenness of this dual party system was perceived almost from the day of its inception. That great realist and most cynical of political philosophers, the first Marquis of Halifax - a man who drew his inspiration from the experience of life - judged all parties to be at best a kind of conspiracy against the rest of the nation, and party discipline to be incompatible with the freedom of private opinion. He maintained that a party had few if any principles, and that a loud profession of them was usually a pretence to cloak the pursuit of private or partisan advantage. A party was a "coarse thing," made up of expedients and compromises with hardly a proposition in it that was "not deceitful." Such, then, was the judgement of Halifax on the subjectivity of the government of the time, and this was already before the close of the 17th century. The situation has hardly altered, it might be added, between that time and the start of the 21st century.

3 – Causes of our intellectual complacency

Nonetheless, Britain had much to be proud of. Across the water, for well over a hundred years more, all the great powers of Europe were to be burdened down by such an oppressive feudalism, that any significant expansion of commerce, let alone of manufacturing (other than through mercantilist policies promoted by the state), was an impossibility. This gave Britain the greatest opportunity in her history, and she seized it by monopolising the trade of the world.

The greatest thinkers of the Continental enlightenment looked to Britain, with her freedom and prosperity, as the single country to be emulated for their own salvation. The great philosophers of France immersed themselves in all things and ideas English, before formulating their own distinctive theories for a changed world. Britain progressed unconsciously, oblivious to her expansion, and oblivious even to the very ideas which had given rise to her prosperity. She was too comfortable and too complacent to be bothered with theory. Action alone - not thought - had meaning; the practical affairs of business, invention and the improvement of processes were the things that mattered. She was too proud and self-satisfied to be concerned with speculative thought; and her attitude to philosophers was dismissive - as "not being of this world." These, too, were to become immutable characteristics of the British race, and it was to contain the seeds for our self-destruction. As long as expansion was to continue, and material standards maintained, all would go well in the world; but as soon as things went awry, then all would be lost.

Engrossed in our private and particular interests; obsessed with the pursuit of our narrow material aims, and confident in our superiority, we were not merely uninterested and dismissive of the world beyond our shores, but even of the condition and needs of other sectors in our own society. An unreflecting and unconscious attitude as to the direction of society and its purpose, from a surfeit of security, gave rise to the hidden growth of resentments and false values which would one day threaten to break out in the face of inevitable change. There was an unrippled calm over the flow of British domestic history, since the ingenious mechanism of our political institutions assured this, and because of this calm, there was nothing to stir the anxiety of a questioning mind, to stimulate the need for speculative thought. What sense - what need was there for philosophers?

It is significant that our greatest thinkers between the 17th and 19th centuries; both Hobbes and Lock, were motivated by great events from the past, to which they gave some rational explanation as an afterthought; the one by the Civil War, the other, by the Glorious Revolution; whilst the philosophers of 18th century France were all the precursors, and so in some part, the creators of their great event to come. As for our own Bentham, he lived in England in mean obscurity, contemptuously ignored, almost until the end, only receiving recognition and patronage in middle life in France and Russia.[86] David Hume, meanwhile, whilst he was lionised in the salons of Paris, saw his major work in this country received with a deadening silence. Such then has been the fate of the greatest thinkers in Britain!

---

[86] It would only be right in this context, however, to mention the esoteric influence of Bentham on public opinion with regard to legal reform during the first third of the 19th century. See particularly A.C. Dicey's first six lectures on the relation between, *Law & Public Opinion In England*, Macmillan, 1905.

4 – Sound reasons for "disdaining" the foreigner

When finally, the old regimes began to crack-up and collapse in Continental Europe, it was through the turmoil of revolution and twenty years of war. In Britain, shock waves of horror and disgust spread throughout society. How much better things had always been in England! Britain's most reflective statesman of the time, Edmund Burke, who had so recently stood by our rebellious cousins in the New World, was transformed into an arch-reactionary overnight, and damned the new French Republic and all it stood for. Conventional opinion on these events has hardly changed since the day that he wrote, and this philosopher of Conservatism, who was never a Tory, and this most English of Englishmen, who was never an Englishman, established forever that the continuity of tradition should be maintained forever, simply because tradition is its own justification as the best possible basis for existence.

> "Whilst he forewarns, denounces, launches forth,
> Against all systems built on abstract rights,
> Keen ridicule; the majesty proclaims
> Of Institutes and Laws, hallowed by time;
> Declares the vital power of social ties
> Endeared by custom; and with high disdain,
> Exploding upstart Theory, insists
> Upon the allegiance to which men are born."[87]

If any moral is to be drawn from the Napoleonic Wars with regard to the development of world history, it is simply this: there were two countries, and two countries only, that wholly and consistently, sought to crush the aspirations of democratic freedom, each advancing from the extremities of Europe: Tsarist Russia and Great Britain.[88] One of the greatest scientific and speculative thinkers of the 20th century has even gone so far as to forcefully declare that, "we were clearly wrong in our resistance to revolutionary France. If revolutionary France could have conquered the Continent and Great Britain, the world would now be happier, more civilised, and more free, as well as more peaceful. ... its early conquests were made in the

---

[87] William Wordsworth, *The Prelude*, Bk. VII.

[88] But even the Russian Tsar for a time toyed with the new freedom that was penetrating Europe. Witness the meeting of the three Emperors at Tilsit.

name of liberty, against tyrants, not against peoples; and everywhere the French armies were welcomed as liberators by all except rulers and bigots."[89]

The fact that the "balance of power" had to be maintained, or that Napoleon had a vain, mean and ruthless personality, are factors of little significance in the history of civilisation. The battles, victories and losses of Napoleon are merely of secondary importance. Of far greater significance is the *idea* which he represented. Everywhere he marched, he transplanted the seeds of freedom, and his every victory was secretly welcomed in the hearts of the European intelligentsia. The very greatness of Napoleon in history lies solely in the fact that he acted as a medium or an instrument for the development of the "World spirit," as one philosopher (whose very house was destroyed by the French bombardment) has expressed it. Britain and Russia alone were the arch-reactionary powers which sought to crush the aspirations of Europe, and they finally succeeded in restoring the Continent - albeit for a limited period - to a state of feudal bondage.

Having temporarily succeeded in destroying the political and social reforms of Europe, achieved during the previous twenty-year period - and this partly out of ulterior motives - Britain was able to further expand her overseas territory. Consequently, she became even mightier than and even more remote from the changing world beyond her shores. The new century with its new nationalisms, and turmoil and more revolutions, seemed to separate Britain even more distantly from any sympathy for the political or intellectual life of the Continent, as she settled down quietly to a century of almost uninterrupted peace.

5 – But what lay under the democratic veneer?

Still, she viewed herself as the most democratic of nations - but was she really? Undoubtedly she was admired for the success of her representative institutions - for their stability - their fine mechanism, and in successfully warding off civil outbreaks such as had occurred across the water. But already, by the first third of the century, her major cities and towns were blighted by more widespread poverty, by hunger, by foul housing and by appalling social conditions than were

---

[89] Bertrand Russell, *Principles of Social Reconstruction*, Allen & Unwin, 1916, pp. 99-100.

found anywhere else in Europe. Following the repeal in 1813 of the Elizabethan statute giving magistrates the power to fix wages,[90] the green light was given to injustice of a kind which was by now rare on the Continent, such as the abuse of women and children in our mines and factories; brutal workhouses, and murderous lodging places going under the name of "Schools." In addition to that, after the repeal of the following year of those articles regulating apprenticeship,[91] laissez-faire gave a licence to anyone to do almost anything under the cover of almost any trade or profession, so giving rise to innumerable abuses - many of which are known to us through the vivid pages of Dickens. Was this democracy? Was this justice? Foreign visitors to Britain - natives not from democracies but from constitutional or reactionary monarchies - were appalled by what they saw, recording for posterity their shocked impressions. These were sensitive men - men of humanity, and in their indignation, they all pointed the accusing finger of hypocrisy.

Meanwhile, at this time, the greatest intellect in Europe, a philosopher who was to inspire all the nations of Europe towards the goal of social and industrial progress, writing in his study in Berlin, on the great Reform Bill towards the close of his life, actually went so far as to argue, "that England is really the most backward country in Europe, because true freedom ... is sacrificed by the English system of representative institutions to *private and particular interests.*"[92] Had this "mere foreigner" actually laid his finger on the Achilles heel of British democracy? This servant of the Prussian state was damning in his indictment of class privilege, explaining that, "the reason why England is so remarkably behind other civilised states of Europe in institutions derived from true rights is simply that there the governing power lies in the hands of those possessed of so many privileges which contradict a rational constitutional law and true legislation."[93]

Here is food for thought: a professor, a national of an autocratic monarchy, by implication adversely comparing the outrageous

---

[90] 53, George III, Cap. 40.

[91] 54, George III, Cap. 96.

[92] Quoted from Sir Ernest Barker's, *Political Thought In England 1848-1914*, OUP, 1915, p. 21.

[93] Hegel's *Political Writings*, trans. By T.M. Knox, OUP, 1964, p. 300.

privilege of financial power in a democracy with the absence of that in a still almost feudal monarchy. The political criticism is aimed at the absence of "rational constitutional law and true legislation." Powerful vested interests were the bar to that. The social criticism is specifically aimed at a ruthless *nouveau riche* not bound by any social ties of loyalty, support, custom or tradition to any other part of the community. In which of these two societies was justice as fairness best to be found? In which of these societies was democracy as a social ideal best to be realised? Who was in reality the less oppressed: the proletarian factory operative in the smoke-filled slums of Manchester or the peasant labourer of Brandenburg?

6 – Why political reform failed to dissolve the class divide

A contemporary academic has remarked that this essay on the Reform Bill is, "one of the most scathing indictments of English social conditions to come from a Continental writer." He continues by aptly remarking that the "critique is aimed not only at existing conditions in early industrial Britain, but also at the liberal attempts to overcome them through a purely electoral reform of parliament. Behind those attempts (he) sees the self-interest of the new middle class which identifies reform with its own coming into power. (He) believes that English conditions could not be changed unless Britain underwent a social, as well as political transformation."[94] This acute analysis reflects a recurring response of our political institutions to social problems which have not changed to this day. It is a response of half-measures and botched compromises that leaves class divisions just as they were before.

The Englishman of greatest note during the first half of the 19th century who seems to have suspected the limitations of the Reform Bill in achieving significant social change, was the great philosophical jurist, John Austin.[95] In the words of J.S. Mill, he, "thought that there was more practical good government and (which is true enough) infinitely more care for the education and mental improvement of all

---

[94] Shlomo Avineri, *Hegel's Theory of The Modern State*, Cambridge UP, 1972, pp. 208-209.

[95] Husband of Sarah Austin, translator of several of the works of the great historian, Leopold von Ranke.

ranks of the people, under Prussian monarchy, than under the English representative government. ... Though he approved of the Reform Bill, he predicted, what in fact occurred, that it would not produce the great   immediate   improvements in government, which many expected from it."[96] Similarly, in 1838 Richard Cobden derided the "great juggle of the *English Constitution* - a thing of monopolies, and church-craft, and sinecures, armorial hocus-pocus, primogeniture, and pageantry," suggesting that for the majority of people Prussia offered "the best government in Europe."[97]

As Graham Wallas has observed, "Liberal administration, when the first energy of the reform struggle of 1832 was spent, showed a curious combination of national complacency and national inefficiency; we declared everyday that 'the schoolmaster was abroad,' and our educational arrangements remained the laughing-stock of the world; we idealised the British workman's home, and watched new slums growing under our eyes."[98] Political reforms have come off the statute book like leaves off an Autumn tree, but social reforms have been aborted monstrosities, only concerned with the immediate alleviation of material wants. They have achieved little towards creating a less divided society. The reforms of the great Liberal administration of 1906 and the Labour administration of 1945, for all their far-reaching benefits, did little to diminish class entrenchment or conflict.   The confrontational nature of our representative institutions saw to that. The rich today remain as sturdy and powerful as before, and the poor remain little less resentful and helpless than they ever were. There is no One Nation here! The incisive political analysis on the Reform Bill of the great German thinker, was never brought to the attention of British scholars and opinion formers until many decades later. Still there was time for complacency!

7 – Our prejudices seemingly justified by 20th century events

Time progressed, and by the middle of the 20th century, Britain had even more justification for reinforcing all her old prejudices.

---

[96] John Stuart Mill, *Autobiography.*

[97] See John Morley's *Life of Cobden*, Vol. I, pp. 130-131.

[98] Graham Wallas, *Our Social Heritage*, Allen & Unwin, 1921 ed., p. 170.

Continental Europe really did have nothing to offer! What lay in the wake of two world wars? Unprecedented destruction, totalitarian dictatorships of the worst possible kind, vile political creeds, oppression, and savage genocide on a scale never witnessed since the oriental monarchies of Biblical times. And how had this come about? Through obsession with abstract theories and speculative thought - or so it was sometimes said. How much better was a nation that stood by the empiricism of tradition! And yet, by the closing decades of the 20th century, all was not right with Britain. Even worse, we slowly awoke to the fact that our problems were far more serious and intractable than we had earlier imagined. Our economic decline was more than merely apparent, it was catastrophic. Festering resentments and social conflict was more real and acute than that to be found anywhere amongst our industrialised partners. Huge efforts at improvement - or so we thought we had achieved - were futile. Nothing stemmed our downward path.

8 – Contradictions of our divided society

There were strange contradictions in our society. We had what seemed the most polarised politics in Europe and yet nothing was achieved in bridging the class divide. Despite huge improvements in material well-being, there was no meeting of minds between the conflicting groups dividing the spoils of the realm. But stranger still, after many years of Labour rule - after administrations far to the left of those of our Continental neighbours (or so we were led to believe) the rich were still as rich as they had ever been; the majority only had fractionally more of the percentage of total personal wealth than their forebears at the start of the century; and privilege, titles and power were as widespread as in the feudal era. It was a topsy-turvy world - laughable to the foreign visitor - who saw archaic militant cloth-cap proletarianism alongside the mumbo-jumbo of anachronistic ermine-clad tradition. Those who were far to the left were no less ultra-conservative in their Marxist held beliefs, than were the ultra-Conservatives of the High church Tory right.

Behind the scenes, the reality of politics remained as corrupt and obscene as ever. As proletarian trades unionists doffed the coronet and a piece of spotted white fur, grateful for their recognition at last by a cruel society, in other quarters, huge pay-offs were made for this or that vested interest group. It was here that the contradictions of the class war were finally played out. But still the leftward march continued: the building of the great bureaucracies for the Welfare state, and the nationalisation of our largest industries. But there was no place in these Socialist bureaucracies for the participation of the workers themselves. It was to be strictly jobs for the boys, i.e. the middle class academically trained left wing intelligentsia. This was in alignment with the thinking of those greatest class conscious snobs of the far left, viz., Lord and Lady Passfield, otherwise known as Sidney and Beatrice Webb. No wonder the workers in our public utilities became the most dissatisfied and intransigent of all!

Worst of all was the corruption of patronage, which destroyed any pretence of moral principle behind the workings of our constitutional system. A prominent parliamentary journalist remarking on this has said it is, "the biggest and most dangerous growth industry in politics in my time. It is now on a scale which makes the abuses of patronage by earlier regimes, from Walpole onward, seem small-time by comparison. ... At the last count 7 cabinet ministers have between them the patronage, or gift of 4,233 jobs at their disposal, worth £4,200,000 in perquisites. There are between 6,000 and 7,000 nominated posts paid at rates of between £500   and £50,000 plus with further perks thrown in."[99] In this respect, things really have changed little since the reign of Charles II.

9 – Social progress is not the outcome of political stability

The foregoing historical sketch, critically reviewing the confrontational nature of our representative system *vis-à-vis* its stemming the growth of social justice or diminishing class conflict, only takes on a fuller meaning in the light of that comparison with the historically less visible, but more real, emergence of a greater social awareness and objectivity in Continental Europe.

There is no suggestion here that the British - or the English - people as individuals were, or are, intrinsically more obsessed with ruthlessly pursuing their vested interests, or grasping after material gain than their neighbours across the Channel or the North Sea. All the evidence points to the fact, and certainly it is reflected in the great fiction writers of the time, that the peoples of France, Germany, Switzerland, Russia and elsewhere, were no less mean, selfish and

---

[99] James Margach, op. cit., p. 85.

avaricious than their counterparts here. By the same token, the British had as much humanity, social conscience and genuine charity, as any people in Continental Europe. In fact, it would be easier to list the great reformers, and men and women of social conscience, active here in 19th century England than anywhere else in Europe.

Their names have spread throughout the world, and they are gloriously inscribed in our history. But conditions were different in Britain. These reformers did not arise to prominence because we were intrinsically more humane than other peoples, although that may naively be the commonly held belief; but because the crying shame of social conditions called them forth. If they had never been born, social conditions alone would have called others of equal merit into their place. The significant difference in the evolutionary development between the peoples of Britain and Continental Europe over the past three centuries, in producing the startling outcome we see today, stems not from the intrinsic characteristics of greater benevolence, charity, or a sharper social conscience, but purely from the framework of political institutions within which different societies were imprisoned.

These institutions have wrought their work in vastly different ways. Their value as a medium for social progress in the development of a nation, was and is to be judged ultimately not according to the ephemeral criteria of their appearance at any one point in time, but according to their eventual effect in transforming the nature of society. Therefore, by such criteria, stability is not necessarily in itself an indicator of good or bad times in the future history of a people. It may be argued that periods of instability in the development of a nation are essential for its social progress. But the British system of representative government has always been most admired for its imperturbable stability. The same criterion, I suspect, would never have been applied to praising the decaying Ottoman or Chinese Empires, howsoever admirable their stability. This is because it is common knowledge that the latter held back social progress in those empires, and if there was seemingly a modicum of contentment amongst the poor and oppressed of those societies, then this was accountable to a false consciousness; whilst in Britain it was always assumed (by ourselves at least) that progress was advancing in all directions.

The corrupt and bankrupt regime of pre-revolutionary France, superimposed as it was on a society with a high standard of civilisation, by its very badness offered an opportunity for a complete new start, entailing the greatest liberation for her people. Such discredited regimes across the face of Europe were to offer similar opportunities to a dozen oppressed peoples. By these criteria in tracing the social progress of peoples, we are therefore not concerned with drawing conclusions from a study of the bare dry-as-dust superficial facts of history, at particular points in time, for these are meaningless in themselves; and neither are we concerned with the conventional study of politics; but rather with the deeper undercurrent of sociological forces.

The moral of this exposition has been to show that stable institutions and regimes tend to generate complacent societies, apathetic to enquiry, and deaf to the expression of speculative thought (even when they are seated on a volcano); whilst political institutions given to turmoil are more productive of creative thought and inventive purpose. This has always been so, although it may only become evident in the more highly developed societies. It is because of this tendency that Jefferson once suggested that it would be a good thing for a nation to be up-ended by revolution every twenty years.

Slowly, then, the scales began to fall from our eyes, and the mists arose from Continental Europe. At first we could not accept or credit what we saw until it was forced upon us. Had the convoluted course of history really been so cruel - had it really reduced us to the status of a second or third rate power? Had our living standards and economic performance really sunk to such depths? Was our society really so less democratic than those of these foreigners? Was our representative democracy, after all, nothing more than a sham? To answer the last of these questions, we must now look into the meaning of democracy itself.

CHAPTER 20
Democracy: Reality and Myth

"However strong the case for democracy, it is not an ultimate or absolute
value and must be judged by what it will achieve."

F.A. Hayek, *The Constitution of Liberty*, Routledge & Kegan Paul,
1960, p. 106.

1 – Constitutional democracy defined

The definition of constitutional democracy is simple and unambiguous. It means government by the people, direct or representative. The reality of democracy is solely conditional on the mechanisms of power directed by the central and local authorities over the people within its territorial domain. Modern democracy is assumed to be dependent on universal adult suffrage of both men and women, irrespective of race, creed or colour, of all those holding nationality within the boundaries of the state.

Modern democracy is assumed to be only practicable through a representative system, i.e. through the existence of a number of parties, each representing a significant proportion of the population, and putting forward its own nominees for election. Representative institutions, however, need not necessarily be a condition of modern democracy. Small self-governing units, such as the Cantons of Switzerland, may operate direct systems of democracy, entailing governmental assemblies open to all citizens and referenda. In the future, computerised systems may facilitate direct forms of democracy for much larger states by plebiscite. New systems of direct democracy, if properly conducted, would certainly advance the cause of democracy by more closely fulfilling the will of the people, since the best forms of representation are necessarily limited by the very need for intermediaries who themselves have a separate identity, and are by no means merely simple delegates.

The limitations of representative democracy become most obvious when an alienation is felt by great numbers of people from any of the credible parties, or even, from the system itself.

Democracy is dependent on the free participation of the people, to express and propagate any aims and opinions, however foul, and to form groups for those purposes, short only of directly arousing sedition or harm to people or property. A democracy which prohibits an organisation openly intent on ensuring its own destruction even, is no longer a full democracy. A people, therefore, has every right to destroy its own democracy if that is its wish. In this may be seen the paradox of democracy: for whilst it may be perceived as the best or most just form of government, as an ideal, it can have no authority to prevent its own self-destruction. In practice, only the most advanced, highly educated, and civilised peoples are capable of maintaining democracies - although it would be bad manners to proclaim such a fact to the wider world.

A one-party state may still, in theory, be a democracy, but in maintaining that democracy, it would be obliged in practice to operate a sophisticated system of referenda whereby the people might regularly exert their direct authority in deciding on a wide range of popular and unpopular issues. Furthermore, such a one-party system would need to be so neutral in its image and purpose as to make an equally distributed appeal across the social spectrum. Such a democracy would most probably need to be a mix between a representative democracy and a direct democracy. Social Capitalist philosophy (as advanced in this book) might possibly form a creditable basis as a candidate for such a grouping in a democracy of a one-party state. The East bloc countries were not non-democratic on account of their one-party status, for that was a secondary matter, but on account of their suppression of free expression and organisation.

2 – Criteria as to the failure of our representative system

The degeneracy of British democracy is not primarily to be judged by the failures of the system *per se*. The mechanism of an unfair voting system, and the existence of parties which are unrepresentative of the *positive* will of the people, are secondary to other factors. It remains theoretically conceivable that the vast majority could be fervently divided into the parties of the right and left, and the system would still be passable, despite what would then remain as merely minor but tolerable faults in the system. If that was really the case then democracy might still flourish, albeit with a voting system which, in theory, was arguably fair. But that is not the situation.   The significant factor is that the vast majority of our population do not participate in the system with a *positive* purpose as consciously willing citizens of a democracy. This is demonstrated by the fact that over the past few decades the electorate has tended to cast its vote from a negative standpoint, i.e. to exclude from government the worst of several bad alternatives.

Election by protest votes, therefore, cannot possibly, by any definition, be said to be government by the people, since democracy is dependent on the exertion of a *positive* will. Government without the presence of this positive will can no longer be said to be democratic. Electoral procedures in themselves are not necessarily demonstrations of democratic activity. Our existing system of government is therefore in fact little more democratic than the electoral systems operated during the degenerate period of the Roman Republic or the early Empire, and all authorities are definitively agreed that such systems failed to   secure   the approximation of democracy and freedom which may have existed in an earlier period. Those who try to defend the present system can only do so by attempting to demonstrate that it does *still* represent the will of the people, but such arguments come up against the contrary facts presented by sociological research.

The prime reason why British government is no longer democratic, is that the two great parties of the left and right can no longer be said to represent the true interests of a significant proportion of the population. Time has left these parties behind, because the mental approach of their leaders in viewing our predicament and formulating policy, has been backward rather than forward looking. The parties, consisting as they do of narrow-minded caucuses, selfishly promoting their own financial vested interests (divided between big business, on the one hand, and supposedly, the dispossessed, in conjunction partly, with the trade unions) have through their excessive scramble for the spoils of the commonweal, lost contact with the real will of the people. If there is no disgust with contemporary politics amongst the silent majority of our population, there is certainly a deadening apathy. Consequently, because of this apathy, power slips into the hands of an ever-decreasing minority.

In addition to that, those remaining to promote the two-party system become less representative of the true will of the electorate on two counts: firstly, because they are there to pursue their own vested interests of big business or (as we find today) an undefined abstraction of the needs of the under-privileged; or secondly, because of a false consciousness whereby they wrongly believe their party is promoting their own interests or the good of the community. Whilst the first category may be covetous and deceitful, the second may be limited in their ability to distinguish illusion from reality. Meanwhile, both bring themselves and politics into disrepute with the wider public. Although the majority of our population may be lacking, in what may be termed "political literacy," that majority nonetheless possesses a natural intuitive sense which is sharp to distinguish between its real interests and false, dishonesty and truth. That majority, however inchoate its political will - and that will is ever latent - deserves a better deal or a better system, for exerting its own authority.

3 – Effective democracy dependent on majority participation

This is because democracy takes on increasing reality in proportion to that percentage of the electorate who are prepared to participate in its functioning. To ensure the workability of democracy, I believe it would be a good law (as exists in some parts of the world) which legally enforced a casting of the vote, even though a box on the voting slip would need to be made for recording an abstention. The concept of democracy is a call to all citizens - bar none - to participate in public life. The people of ancient Athens - the home of democracy - if they were to see our society as it existed today in Britain, would emphatically   conclude   that true democracy was non-existent amongst us, since by their standards, the public life of the majority in serving the community was lacking. The development of new techniques, however, may afford us in the near future opportunities for creating new and realistic structures for direct democracy on a scale not experienced since the days of Periclean Athens.

4 – Constitutional democracy is value free

This, then, is the definition of constitutional democracy and the conditions for its existence. As constitutional democracy can only properly be defined in terms of the mechanisms of political power, and is only concerned with the pure will of the people through the expression of majority *and* minority opinion, it has nothing to do with values or purposes in themselves. Democracy is not a value in itself. There is nothing moral in democracy *per se*. It is purely a medium for channelling ideas for action and implementing that chosen action itself.

There is no moral imperative to uphold the idea or practice of democracy, and vice versa, the defence of democracy, under any or all circumstances, is neither necessarily the reflection of a good or bad course of action. The execution of the righteous Socrates arose from his uncompromising criticism of democracy and his refusal to recant before the Athenian judges. Democracies can (and do) produce the worst of governments as well as the best of governments. A bad democracy can conceivably grant less freedom to a community than a good autocracy. Therefore, there are circumstances in which democracies can be socially oppressive whilst autocracies may be relatively free, although in both cases, such examples would tend to be exceptional rather than general.

5 – Democratic and autocratic oppression compared

The characteristics clearly distinguishing an oppressive democracy from an oppressive autocracy, is that whilst the first is de-personalised institutional oppression, the second is individualistic and prescriptive. The more covert oppression of democracy is felt through excessive taxation, bureaucratic restrictions limiting business enterprise, promoting unemployment, and the many social injustices arising from laissez-faire. In English history such arch-reactionaries can be identified, such as Sir Thomas More and Archbishop Laud, who fully recognised the problems of the new freedoms, and with sound justification, attacked those freedoms as oppressing the weak and the poor - although in the cause of having to give a more symmetrical pattern to our popular history, the latter has had to go down in posterity with a blackened reputation. Both, however, were beheaded. The overt oppression of autocracy is far more obvious, since through pyramidal forms of authority, it openly exerts a positive style of injunction that cannot be seen in any other light than the explicit restriction of freedom. Both forms of government oppression, as they hurt the individual or the group in society, may be as bad as the other, and so the one need not necessarily be any worse than the other.

The most curious paradox to be cited with regard to the benefits and dis-benefits of both democracy and autocracy, is perhaps the example of Napoleon's administration from the start of the 19th century. Whilst on the one hand the bureaucratic autocracy of Napoleon developed alongside the establishment of the first modern police state under the direction of Fouché, which incorporated an effective system of surveillance, was invasive, restrictive, and operated a strict system of press censorship (although in none of these activities approaching anything as oppressive as the 20th century dictatorships); on the other hand, the Napoleonic regime advanced forward in the vanguard of modernity, a just system of law, equality of opportunity, and the spirit of democracy. All this demonstrates the complexity of history and progress in illustrating the fact that freedom and democracy do not develop as unalloyed qualities within a specifically designed environment judged ideal for its growth.

6 – Democratic values defined

There is, therefore, something with a higher priority than democracy itself, if democracy is understood as constitutional government, and that is an appreciation of what are known as democratic values. For a proper understanding of the true needs of society, and in achieving greater reality, the two concepts must be distinguished apart. Although democratic values are the conscious creation of democracy, their existence is by no means its exclusive preserve. Nonetheless, the conscious creation of these values has inevitably and always focussed the attention of the world on all democracies as the natural home of freedom and justice. Democratic values were most succinctly summarised by the French revolutionaries with the cry of, *Liberty, Equality, Fraternity!* The first two of these are conflicting, and have given rise to opposing parties everywhere. The third entails the need for the successful interaction between all the economic sectors of society, or the emergence of what may be called a socially classless society. Democratic values entail, equality before the law; equality of opportunity; freedom of expression and organisation; freedom from censorship, interference or arrest by arbitrary authority; racial, religious and intellectual freedom, etc., and of most importance, the right to knowledge and the cultivation of an enquiring mind to which that belongs.

All these are democratic values, intrinsic to democracies but not exclusive to them. All those factors contributing to the freedom of conscience, expression and movement, considered as means rather than ends, are intrinsically democratic values, and no others can properly be said to fall into this category. The fact that democratic values are means to innumerable individual and collective ends in society, ensures that those values are in themselves dynamic and creative, and that is why democratic societies are so much more vigorous, heterogeneous and interesting than alternative types of society. However, it has to be noted that although democratic societies are found usually only in conjunction with democratic systems of government, this is by no means invariably the case. By the standards pertaining at the time, the urban societies of Imperial Germany and Austria-Hungary, as they existed at the start of the 20th century, were certainly democratic, although it would be questionable to argue that they existed within the framework of effective constitutional democracies.

7 – Limitations of Utilitarianism

The Utilitarian ideal of the greatest happiness of the greatest number, is not strictly a democratic value, since it is an end and not a means, the practicable achievement of which is left open to any interpretation. Besides this, the definition of the greatest happiness, despite the systematic analysis and conclusions of Bentham, is so much open to debate, that as yet, it has never been satisfactorily concluded - and in view of the most recent intellectual developments, it is now never likely to be concluded. It is no coincidence that a serious interest in Utilitarianism was first taken up by thinkers and rulers of despotic albeit enlightened Continental regimes.

Until very recent times, the Utilitarian emphasis on majority power as being of sole significance, has usually been accepted as a natural, inevitable and desirable reflection of democracy, but this concept is now increasingly coming under attack as the importance of the rights of minorities are recognised. It is no coincidence that Utilitarianism, conceived as the need to maximise the power of majorities, has always been most acceptable to those democracies operating a two-party system, for such democracies have tended to be dismissive of minority interests. The American philosopher, John Rawls, is the most prominent thinker of recent years to have pierced the armour of Utilitarianism in exposing its sham as a democratic value of consequence. Meanwhile, the eminent Israeli scholar, Prof.

Avineri, has interestingly observed that, "British Utilitarianism made the horrors of modern life into a new law of nature."[100]

8 – Why material values are a higher priority than democratic values

There is, however, something more important, even, than democratic values, and it entails those things adding to the quality of life coming under the heading of material benefits. Guaranteed intentions for the material well-being of the community, expressed in terms of housing, social security, reasonable pensions and good standards of education, etc., would be regarded today by the majority as a higher priority than the guarantee of those other civil rights listed above. However much we may view the situation today, the guarantee by the state of minimum material standards for the majority, belongs by no means to that category coming under the heading of democratic values.

Furthermore, in modern times, the initial introduction of material welfare as a concern of the state, has not been the product of any constitutional democracy but of an Imperial monarchy. Classical liberalism, which has always lain at the core of constitutional democracy as its inspiration, has until the present era used the democratic argument that when the function of the state extends to welfare, then the freedom and democratic rights of the citizen are eroded. Although in Europe today, such arguments may only be heard from those on the far right, American political sentiment remains overwhelmingly dominated by a bias which is critical of the welfare functions of the state, and this despite the fact that US welfare institutions are playing an increasing role in society. Nonetheless, the move to the right throughout Europe during the 1980s, tended to revive the older liberal calling for a limitation of state involvement in welfare on the grounds that this entailed a diminution of democratic values in society.

In contemporary Europe and Japan, however, the welfare institutions of society are not merely taken for granted, but are perceived, even - and rightly so, as essential to any democratic society, which, of course, is different from saying that they are essential to a constitutional democracy. To those few who might

---

[100] Shlomo Avineri, op. cit., p. 240.

argue that those civil rights should have a higher priority than the promise of material benefits, I would only point to those many hungry billions comprising the majority of our global population in the Third world, who would indignantly contend that our democratic values by comparison are the unnecessary luxury of a spoilt people with overfed stomachs living a cosseted existence. What right, they would cry, have you in the rich industrialised West, to pontificate on the virtues of the abstract rights of freedom of expression, whilst we are suffering and dying in a barren wilderness? We alone, they would contend, know the *real* priorities of life. It is only the rich and complacent who can demean the material values of existence by giving a higher priority to the secondary needs of free expression and organisation. The hungry must first be fed and clothed before the prophet can preach on the more eternal spiritual values of the democratic life. This, certainly, is the lesson of the Christian gospel – as also of the Islamic and Jewish faiths.

Therefore, we owe the introduction of the idea of minimum material standards as a "democratic right" in society, not to the reforms of a constitutional democracy but to the legislation of a militaristic state. Such a realisation may be a sobering thought, since we like to assume that all our values are owed solely to our constitutional democracy. But such an assumption is difficult to support, and our greatest philosophical historian of the 20th century has touched on this theme by arguing that the Prussian, "has managed to make his unpromising Kingdom 'the education of Europe' in certain matters which no good European can affect to despise. The Prussian has taught his neighbour ... how to raise a whole population to an unprecedented standard of social efficiency by a system of universal compulsory state education and to an unprecedented standard of social security by a similar system of health and unemployment insurance."[101] We are not concerned with the possible motives for such reforms, and it has to be reiterated - for we shall return to this in a different context a little later - that the granting of material benefits by the state does not strictly fall into the category of belonging to democratic values. Nevertheless, the undiminished values of material welfare were not to be implemented in Britain until almost a generation after the reforms of Bismarck, with the accession to power of the great Liberal administration of 1906-1911.

---

[101] Arnold Toynbee, *A Study of History*, OUP, 1951, Vol. II, p.58.

9 – Place of ethical values in society

Having in turn defined and evaluated, and noted the separate distinctions, of Constitutional Democracy; Democratic Values; Democratic Society and Material Welfare, there is one further factor, more important than all these, in ensuring the health of a community. It is a fact that is only indirectly of political interest, but it nonetheless, remains of overwhelming sociological significance. This concerns the moral condition and outlook of society in promoting the above four values, and in generally facilitating the smooth running, contentment and happiness of society. The ethical values of society and their spontaneous acceptance - even in an agnostic humanitarian society - ultimately find their origin in religious thought, as the imagination of society is stirred through the work of the churches, or as more often today, through the thought of non-organised religion. Although the moral condition of society may rise and fall, almost according to fashion, history has also shown that there is an underlying evolutionary moral development, through the gradual awakening of a greater consciousness and sensitivity.[102] These five values, therefore, comprise the essential criteria in judging the success of any modern industrialised community.

10 – Nature of political parties

Consideration must now be made of the real part that political parties play within their sociological context. Political groupings are only concerned with the achievement of specific aims through the exertion of power. Their reality only comes into being through those opposing forces giving rise to their existence, and hence their striving for power, ensures that their purpose is subjective and amoral. This applies, as we shall clearly demonstrate, to all parties on the left and the right of the political divide, and until now, to supposedly centrist parties also. The image of parties, however, as they are perceived by

---

[102] In this context see especially, W.E.H. Lecky's, *History of European Morals*, Longmans Green & Co.,, 1869; H.L. Mencken's, *Treatise on Right & Wrong*, Kegan Paul, Trench Trubner & Co., 1934; E. Westermark's, *The Origin & Development of The Moral Ideas*, Macmillan, 2nd ed., 2 Vols., 1912; and of course, Hegel's *Philosophy of History*, available in many editions.

the electorate or more often by their supporters, seldom matches with this reality. This is because every political grouping is protected by an attractive wrapping of self-righteous justification and a shiny veneer of moral platitudes.

Thus, for example, the wheeling and dealing of dishonest brokers, the ruthless greed of rentier capitalists[103]- activities undermining the objective economic interests of the community - may be justified under the falsified notions of liberty, free enterprise, democracy, &c. Likewise, the ballot-rigging of trades unions, the operation of Kangaroo courts, and violence and stone throwing by pickets and rioters, may be justified under the false front of equality, social justice, democracy, &c. There is no political action - even of the vilest sort - which is not undertaken without the justification or conviction of a good moral purpose.

The first evaluation of any political grouping, by an elector, should therefore be its dissection in separating the Myth from the Reality. This is not an easy task, since if properly undertaken, the sensitivity of intuition remains an insufficient guide. Considerable knowledge alone is necessary in reaching the maturity of balanced opinion. This is primarily why the objective appreciation of party politics makes for the most elusive of all studies in the realm of knowledge.

---

[103] For a comparison of Rentier as opposed to Productive capitalism, see, Part II of, *The People's Capitalism.*

CHAPTER 21
Unique Origins of The Social Divide

"There can be no more formidable symptom of our time, and none more menacing to popular government, than the growth of Irreconcilable bodies within the mass of the population."

Sir Henry Maine, *Popular Government*, John Murray, 5th ed., 1897, p. 25.

1 - Our toughest industrial competitors do not owe their democratic societies to Britain   2 - Our failure as a democracy is due to class entrenchment   3 - Class resentment traceable to psychological rather than material factors 4 - Unique origins of our class-based society 5 - How these cleavages were deepened at a later era   6 - Elsewhere the social organism was maintained through the old system   7 - Social effect of Britain's industrial revolution different from elsewhere

1 – Our toughest industrial competitors do not owe their democratic societies to Britain

Having dissected the various political elements natural to modern industrialised countries in the free world, we must again ask the question as to why Britain, by reputation the fountainhead of freedom and democracy, is today less free than her toughest industrial competitors.

How is it that countries with a recent past of totalitarian rule, which previous to that period, passed through short and feeble epochs of constitutional democracy (if they did at all) now thrive under more democratic societies and better constitutional democracies guaranteeing more extensive freedoms than ourselves? The explanation cannot simply be put down to the outcome of defeat in war, and the imposition by foreign powers of alternative modes of government, since the results are evidently more than merely the product of a superficial cause.

The democracies of these countries have not merely developed a character distinctive to their national personality, but reflect a diversity in many spheres of life; a depth of feeling, and a specific moral commitment (different from our own) that can only originate from the deeper undercurrent of their own tradition. The democratic susceptibilities of the German, for example, are often shocked by many things that he (or she) sees in Britain which whilst to him are counter-democratic are met by us with a nonchalant shrug of the shoulder. Such attitudes are hardly likely to have originated from the political re-educational efforts of a conqueror. Besides, it has to be noted that the character and forms of all democracies found in

Continental Europe, differ widely in most respects from our own. If it is imagined that we have anywhere in Europe influenced the shape or development of democratic institutions to any significant degree, then we are flattering our vanity. It is only overseas, throughout the Commonwealth, that Britain's influence as a democracy has achieved any real significance - and possibly, only then in Asia and the white Commonwealth.

2 – Our failure as a democracy is due to class entrenchment

The thesis being put forward in this chapter is this: the greater success of the European democracies - and we have particularly in mind the northern states - and the success of democratic Japan, is due primarily to factors stemming specifically from their own tradition. The failure of British democracy is due solely to self-destructive seeds implanted in her tradition in early times. The criterion for the success of European and Japanese democracy is to be judged according to their creation of relatively classless and democratic societies. The criterion for the failure of British democracy is to be judged according to the vicious entrenchment of class interests, operating within the framework of, what by the contemporary standards of the industrialised West, is an undemocratic society.

If Germany and Japan are isolated from the rest, and compared with Britain, we see something resembling the story of *The Ugly Duckling*. If the other European countries are taken, then they will be found to have had a democratic tradition as long, or longer even than our own, and no less glorious in their own right. The causes of this respective success and failure must now be unravelled in an attempt to find some lessons for our own future.

The British malaise is not something of recent date. It is not merely to be found in the distinctive circumstances of our early industrial development. Its origins are to be traced in the more distant periods of time. The tragedy of English history is that from an early period society has been riven by class barriers entailing a psychological divide far more deep-seated than anywhere else in Western Europe. The causes for this two-nation rift, clearly distinguishing our tradition from the rest of Europe, are clearly explained by unique historical conditions. The unbroken continuity of our history has done nothing to break down this psychological rift. The various turmoils of society, arising from economic changes or growth, instead of dissipating this rift, have channelled new interests into the old beds of national conflict.

The fact that that conflict gave rise to democratic forms at an early date is simply evidence that it was more than latent, so overflowing those bounds whereby it might otherwise have been contained within tolerable limits. The struggle for freedom, and the emergence of democratic institutions, arose solely through the sharp contradictions in our society. There is no more nonsensical illusion than the suggestion that freedom arises from the innate characteristics of a people. It does not come into existence as a substantive thing, but through causes that can only be explained in terms of sociological analysis. If there is any truth in Henry Ford's contention that "history is bunk," then it is to be found in the superficial interpretation of facts to fit in with the myths of the present or the recent past. A sociological approach in unravelling the events of our past has hardly yet been attempted, and must be left to a new breed of historians for the future. The early emergence of our democratic institutions is therefore accountable to psychological suffering and pressures in society which were greater than those to be found elsewhere, but those institutions, instead of resolving these pressures, merely channelled them so that vested interests might be maintained and pursued by separate and conflicting groups.

3 – Class resentment traceable to psychological rather than material factors

It is not suggested, it should be noted, that this suffering and these pressures in society may be measured according to acute material need. Material want in terms of famine, diet, warmth, clothing, housing, and the ravages of disease, were more extensive in much of Continental Europe, in earlier times, than here in Britain. The distinctive nature of the pressures we are now defining is predominantly psychological, to which economic causes nonetheless played a significant albeit secondary role. It is not suggested, either, that these psychological factors were exclusive to this country and absent elsewhere, but that in England, they coalesced to form a thread of tradition in such a way that differentiates our history from Continental Europe.

What exactly were and are these special psychological factors? They entail feelings of frustration, irritation, resentment and injustice, experienced in an acute form by significant sections of the community. The strength of such feelings cannot be only measured according to the rising and falling in the acuteness of material need; and neither can they be measured only according to the exertion of arbitrary or unjust authority; for other underlying factors, are clearly of greater significance. This, anyway, is the evidence of history. These are the factors which have marked our unique progress, giving rise to our national character. The only truly immutable characteristics of a people are their identity as members of a single human race, all made from one clay, shaped according to the exposure of psychological stimuli. There are no other truly immutable characteristics apart from our genetic make up. In this light can be understood the internal contradiction that the struggle and appreciation of freedom as a value is only experienced by those who *feel* they have it least. It was suffering alone which gave rise to the consciousness of the need for freedom. Might it not be suggested that the reason why the English and Jewish peoples have been long renowned for an all-pervading and irrepressible sense of humour stems from the fact that they of all peoples have been subjected to a greater sense of humiliation than most? If this is true, then humour is the most serious subject on earth.

George Orwell's contention that "Britain is the most class-ridden country under the sun,"[104] (and he was a man who had travelled the world) is as true today as it ever was. Those on the right - and on the left too - try to dispute this fact by arguing that material conditions have changed that situation, but as we have demonstrated, material conditions are not central to the issue. It is argued that all sections of society have undergone huge changes over the past sixty years. This is not disputed. It is silly to equate material progress when industrial unrest within the past two decades has been more intense than fifty years ago; when the most highly paid sectors of the proletarian workforce (e.g. the miners and printers) have expressed a greater and more violent anger and dissatisfaction with their status in life than the truly under-privileged and underpaid; and when there has been in the recent past a greater polarisation of opinion in our political life than at any time before. These are the things in our topsy-turvy world which cry out for an explanation.

---

[104] In George Orwell's, *The Lion & The Unicorn*, 1941.

There have been as many social changes in Britain over the past fifty years as elsewhere in the industrialised West, but they have been changes of the wrong sort - or at least deficient, judged in the light of a morally healthy society.   Whilst changes abroad have been accompanied by the growth of genuinely democratic attitudes for the creation of classless societies, in Britain those changes have been motivated by the protective interests of conflicting groups to reconstruct new class barriers in replacing old. As the shifting layers of society settle down after the irruptions of economic progress, new standards have to be found for distinguishing the "U" from the "Non-U," and all manner of subtle distinctions are re-created and enforced, in ensuring the existence of a community divided into its own tightly knit groups. Pretence and sham is raised to a pedestal whilst the real and essential is buried beneath the hypocrisy and empty conventions of society.

4 – Unique origins of our class-based society

The historical causes for these things must be briefly touched upon. They may be brought under three separate headings. The first, and possibly most significant of all, stems from the dreadful trauma of the Norman Conquest. Of all the cruel conquests which have afflicted Western Europe during the past millennia, the outcome of the Norman Conquest differed from that of the subjugation of any other people. Whilst all north south invasions in Continental Europe during the Dark and Middle ages led to the cultural assimilation of the conquerors, the invasion of the Gallicised Scandinavians led to the creation of a society which was to be cursed with a permanent social divide. This was already to become evident by the start of the 14th century, by which time the language of the two peoples had merged to form Middle English. But that language was in itself a lesson in the differentiation between two classes.   Whilst those words in the language referring to tools of trade, livestock, the simplest articles of furniture, agriculture, and indeed, productive labour of any kind, were Teutonic in origin, those words referring to luxury, opulence and good living, and even the names of animals when destined for the table, were exclusively of French derivation.

The etymological evidence of our language alone, therefore, demonstrates clearly the development of two quite separate mental processes and two contrasting perceptions of the world we live in.

Through the formation of language alone, class consciousness went to the depths of our national soul. Two societies had thus been created, each quite different from the other. Nowhere else in Western Europe can such a paradigm be found. In the words of a great 18th century pamphleteer, "conquest and tyranny transplanted themselves with William the Conqueror from Normandy to England, and the country is yet disfigured with the marks."[105] But this is not to imply, it should be noted, that tyranny was greater during this period and hereafter in England than elsewhere, for the outrages and cruelty of arbitrary authority was as hard - or worse - on the Continent than here. The underlying distinction, however, is that whilst injustice throughout the rest of Europe was perceived as individualistic and the work of hated bishops and princes; in England it was not simply perceived as the work of a conquering race, but eventually, of a privileged class, and it was this which stuck in the gullet of the English people - piercing the national consciousness to the depths of its soul. Every minor ordinance became not merely an irritation but a crying humiliation. Generations buried their resentment - only occasionally breaking out in sporadic revolt - until the emergence of new grounds for conflict centuries later, when new class structures arose, awakening the age-old consciousness of a class divide. In every local community, the poison of resentment penetrated to every sector of the community, even in an upward direction, so that even the conquering race was infected by its servile multitude, and rose up with mailed fist and battle axe against Kingly rule.

Due to such unique historical circumstances it was only natural that class differences should come to be seen as the most real factor dividing one man from another. Therefore, conscious efforts were made in all spheres of life to sharpen rather than lessen these differences, as a protective mechanism in defending what were perceived as the interests of those classes, for those interests were identified as the essence of class itself. So today the class divide is to be found in the world of work which is still differentiated into acceptable and unacceptable spheres of employment in a way which does not bear comparison with any other country in the industrialised West. The divide is even carried over into the world of learning, in science and technology, where a preference is given to *Pure* over *Applied* studies - again, concepts unique to Britain. Everywhere there

---

[105] Tom Paine, *The Rights of Man*, Pelican ed., p. 97.

is a snobbish preference for the theoretical and invisible over the practical and visible. In the world of business, financial services and banking are socially acceptable, whilst engineering or manufacturing is most definitely not. Is it any wonder that a country which places the productive industries on such a low level in the occupational hierarchy, should now find herself in severe economic straits?

5 – How these cleavages were deepened at a later era

The second cause for our divided society stems from the injustices and social turmoil arising from the early breakdown of the feudal system in English society, entailing the loss of those cohesive and protective social forces which united all sections of society through a set of mutual obligations engendering a better co-operative spirit. Those very freedoms won through the extended alienability of land wrought havoc in society, and their injustices obsessed the mind of such men as Sir Thomas More. Following the sack of the monasteries, Abbey lands were put onto the open market, and guild and chantry lands followed a decade later. This alienation of land, some of it bought at absurdly low prices by needy courtiers, led to a decade of mania land speculation, much of it acquired by middlemen, who bought up scattered parcels, held them for the rise and disposed of them piecemeal for a good offer. In the words of R.H. Tawney, "much of it passed to sharp businessmen who brought to bear on its management the methods learned in the financial school of the City."[106] Social injustice and suffering was the inevitable outcome as groups of London merchants formed syndicates to exploit the market, resulting "in rack-renting, evictions and the conversion of arable to pasture land, for surveyors wrote up values at each transfer, and unless the last purchaser squeezed his tenants, the transaction would not pay"[107]

The huge tensions and resentments so created in Tudor England - in reality amongst the most miserable, in reputation the most glorious era of our past - as a new and more vicious class structure took shape, kept the authorities on a constant alert to the threat of open rebellion. By the 17th century, at the time of the Civil War, a further step was

---

[106] R.H. Tawney, *Religion & The Rise of Capitalism*, Pelican books, p. 144.

[107] Ibid., p. 145.

taken in stamping out the cohesive force of the old order, with the abolition of feudal tenures when lordship was turned into *absolute* ownership. In the words of an industrial historian, here "was the decisive change in English history which made it different from that on the Continent. From it every other difference in English society stemmed."[108] The new landowners were ruthless men with no obligations, moral or otherwise, to the now vulnerable tenants whom they cruelly crushed. The new Parliamentary cause, raising the flag of freedom, was quickly exploited by the vested financial interests of the City. Those who had been falsely led to believe that here was a real opportunity for the liberation of the oppressed, the Levellers, Diggers and other groups, were soon brushed aside. As the Royalist cause was defeated, the last remnants of feudal law and tradition, protecting those at the base of the community, evaporated; and the religious hypocrisy (with its atrocious doctrine of predestination) of an arrogant middle class, was used to justify kicking the labourer and the poorer artisan. This may not be the common view held today of those looking back at the mid-17th century, but they were certainly the views of the men and women of the time. This is not to imply a bias for the lost cause, for both had their righteous justification whilst both were unjustified. The juggernaut of history crushed good and bad alike in weaving our nation's fate.

6 – Elsewhere the social organism was maintained through the old system

On the Continent, meanwhile, and for almost two centuries more, feudal values and institutions were to ensure a greater harmony in society, uniting lord and peasant towards the idea of a common purpose. Even though material standards were everywhere worse in Continental Europe - apart from in the Netherlands and in the great urban centres - a strong sense of communal unity was nonetheless retained. Amongst the sandy plains of the north east, if the peasants lived in grimy poverty, so too did the dominating nobility live a meagre existence, giving little cause for resentful envy. All the states of northern Europe were poor, small or provincial, and since the emergent wealthy commercial classes from the great Hansa and other cities, were confined as citizens to city states, they were denied the

---

[108] H.J. Perkin, *The Social Causes of The British Industrial Revolution*, 1968, p. 135.

opportunity for developing an entrepreneurial rentier capitalism, in the buying and selling of rural land, which still remained the domain of a feudal nobility. Consequently, Continental societies maintained a more unifying homogeneity in both urban and rural regions than here in Britain. Whilst the nobleman or ruler of the pocket principality maintained the willing subservience of its fawning populace; so the great oligarchical merchants and artisans in the more sophisticated towns, maintained the loyalties of their subjects and apprentices through the ideals and practices of the guilds. As yet, nothing seemed to threaten or undermine the stability of the centuries' old fabric of society. When the old order did begin to collapse, it was in the populous and centralised bureaucracy of a mighty monarchy that the shock waves of a revolution were first to reverberate.

But then the cohesive power of English feudalism may never at any time have exerted that unifying power and magic over all sections of the community that it had in Europe. Recent research has revealed that the feudal system had a weaker influence on society in times of peace than was earlier believed, for already by the 13th century much land was already alienated as witnessed by considerable population mobility. These recent revelations would fall in naturally with the argument that the Anglo-Saxon and Norman populations were never wholly integrated into the stability and domiciliary fixity of the feudal system. The discontented and oppressed are always on the move - or would be if they could be - for that is freedom in itself, and certainly the evidence of our medieval literature suggests a wayfaring life more colourful and vigorous than that in most of Europe.

In summary, the significance of Continental feudalism as a great cohesive force in counteracting the growth of those social factors giving rise to class divisions, cannot be under-estimated.   The remarkable cohesive power of contemporary Japanese society - so astonishing to the West - is the single most significant factor contributing to the industrial might of that country, and its origins are to be found solely in the complex feudalism of the old order. That order was still extant in the mid-Victorian era, and by the last quarter of the 20th century, the attitudes and structures entailing the loyalties and obligations of a medieval system were transposed almost in their entirety to the most modern industrialised society on earth. In Germany, also, the healthier remnants of feudalism existed until very recent times, certainly up until 1870 in the north east and possibly even up until 1945. Furthermore, it was that part of Germany responsible for national unity and embarking on a programme of heavy industrialisation which experienced the attitudes of feudalism until the most recent past. There is, therefore, a certain irony in the fact that in the most despised aspect of medievalism - as commonly conceived - may be found a clue to the dynamic for the modernisation of the world's two most successful industrial nations.

7 – Social effect of Britain's industrial revolution different from elsewhere

The third cause of Britain's socially divided society stems from the consequences of her situation as the early pioneer of the industrial revolution and the ambiguous attitude of the capitalist class towards industry *vis-à-vis* society. The industrial revolution was so sudden and ubiquitous, that within a period of a hundred years, the poorer landed classes were torn from their roots, dispossessed by circumstances beyond their control or understanding, and transplanted to murky cities often a great distance from their places of birth, where they soon sunk into a condition of unbelievable degradation. In the words, again, of R.H. Tawney, the "free play for the capitalist seemed to menace the independence of the small producer, who tilled the nation's fields and wove its cloth. The path down which the financier beguiles his victims may seem at first to be strewn with roses; but at the end of it lies - incredible nightmare - a regime of universal capitalism, in which the peasant and small master will have merged in a property-less proletariat."[109] The existence of that great benefit to freedom, laissez-faire, meant that the factories, mines and mills were managed with few considerations for the humanity of those they employed. Friedrich Engels' book, *The Condition of The Working Class In England* (published in Leipzig in 1845) is still the most vivid descriptive account of the proletariat of that time.

Meanwhile, the conflict of conscience and taste of the capitalist class towards the world of industry awoke a desire to escape from this sordid industrial environment as soon as it was profitable to do so. This was partly motivated by the snobbery of wishing to emulate the landed gentry, for the capitalist was haunted by the spectre of what he may falsely have perceived as his own "vulgarity" or "lack of breeding." Consequently, as a result of social striving towards "self-

---

[109] R.H. Tawney, op. cit., p. 168.

improvement," by the second or third generation, and partly with the help of that new institution, so useful to the *nouveau riche*, the Public School, these Bounderbys from Coketown emerged as smooth middle class gentlemen, whose education had taught them to despise and so to distance themselves from the manufacturing environment. In the words of an American academic, "as capitalists became landed gentlemen, Jps, and men of breeding, the radical ideal of active capital was submerged in the conservative ideal of passive property, and the urge to enterprise faded beneath the preference for stability."[110] From this may be traced the great social divide which was to occur between the different layers of management and the shopfloor - social divisions which remain as real today as at any time before. Because of this it became psychologically problematical for these great factory proprietors to offer a moral leadership over their employees, or to inspire in them a spirit of devotion, trust and loyalty. Meanwhile, the inevitable response of the resentful and rejected workers - rejected since they could never experience the appreciation of their purpose by the employer - was to organise into unions, inspired only by hatred of the exploiting class and bourgeois values, and determined to destroy the capitalist system. In the words of Anthony Sampson, "the earlier industrialisation of Britain left it with a more solid and self-conscious proletariat than on the Continent, as the core of a single working class party."[111]

The historical development of industry and capitalism on the Continent, Japan and elsewhere, followed an entirely different course. Firstly, the development occurred at a later date by which time the world had developed a sharper social conscience; and secondly, it occurred in the light of the English experience which had been a lesson to the world. Everywhere, class divisions were less differentiated, and almost invariably, governments were astute enough to ensure that the change from a rural to an industrial society would not entail such a traumatic upheaval as had occurred in Britain. Meanwhile, the capitalist classes themselves happily accepted the status in which their livelihoods were staked, and had no pretensions to the gentility or a leisured class, as in England. They remained

---

[110] Martin J. Wiener, *English Culture & The Decline of The Industrial Spirit*, Cambridge UP, 1980, p. 4.

[111] Anthony Sampson, *The New Anatomy of Britain*, Hodder & Stoughton, 1971, p. 234.

unabashed men of business, and consequently, could far more easily identify with the spirit of their employees, and vice versa, and so could offer genuine leadership. In addition they were assisted by a spirit of intensive nationalism, which at the same time seized every country on the Continent and elsewhere, but which at no time had need to inspire the peace time imagination of the British who succeeded in a commercial conquest of the world not through the spirit of nationalism but through an "absence of mind."

These, then, were the differing paths of social development from early times, in Britain and elsewhere, as they contributed towards the growth of democratic societies. As yet little has been said about the contrasting development of constitutional democracy, for this too, has evidently contributed to democratising society. It is to this topic that we must now turn.

CHAPTER 22
Revolutionary and Evolutionary Progress Compared

"Despite spectacular material improvements there persists in working-class communities a malaise, an anger, a bitterness."

Jeremy Seabrook, *What Went Wrong?*, Victor Gollancz, 1978, p. 13.

1 – Revolutionary change has a different effect on society compared with evolutionary change

It is well known that whilst the development of English democratic institutions and society has been a slow and evolutionary process, entailing an unbroken thread from Simon de Montfort in the 13th century onwards; the development of democracy elsewhere has proceeded over a much shorter period of time, and more significantly, has more often been a product of violent revolution.

The term revolution is here to be understood in its broadest sense, meaning the emergence of new regimes under changed social conditions. Germany is often cited as the country which has never experienced a successful revolution, on the grounds that her regimes have never been overthrown by spontaneous uprisings of her own people against constituted authority. The revolutions of Germany have usually been achieved through her conquest, although this is not to imply that it is usual to see defeat in war in the light of a revolution. A revolution not simply entails the emergence of a new regime or the change of authority to a new power, but more significantly, reflects a ferment of ideas on the nature of society and its government. Those events which took place in Germany in 1806, 1870, 1918 and 1945, certainly gave rise to factors that were nothing less than revolutions, since not only was German society up-ended, but in each case it was accompanied by a ferment of new ideas. 1848 has not been included in the above list, since the events of that year marked a failed revolution. Despite the apparently adamantine nature of German society in response to change, the greater truth is that Germany has experienced a ferment of intellectual ideas from 1789 until the present. Moreover, those ideas have achieved far more radical changes in the attitudes and nature of society, than have been achieved here in Britain through the gradualism of an evolutionary process.

It is nonsense to formulate a value judgement, in terms of a general principle, as to whether an Evolutionary or a Revolutionary process is preferable in achieving greater progress for society, since all societies are in a continual state of flux, experiencing good and bad periods in their history. There are also good revolutions and bad revolutions. Those great revolutions in 19th century Europe, however bloody, were undoubtedly beneficent in their long-term outcome, since they assisted towards the implementation of desirable reforms and democracy. Those revolutions in the 20th century, on the contrary, have tended to be tragic, since if they have not given rise to oppressive dictatorships and ossified societies, then they have often merely entailed replacing one military dictatorship with another, whilst bringing limited or even no benefits in their wake. Nevertheless, there is a difference between an Evolutionary and a Revolutionary process in advancing the ends of society, and it is not without significance that whilst the first conjures up an image of the dinosaur, the second evokes the hope for more real changes in the Here-and-Now rather than in the nebulous unknown future.

2 – How a dual party representative system exacerbates the class divide

But the contrast between the two processes entails far profounder differences than these. An examination must be made of the origin of the processes before an understanding can be grasped of the contrasting ways in which they influence the mental attitudes of a people and the direction of society. The evolutionary process of our British democracy is most distinguished by the fact that it has always entailed the selfish pursuit of vested interests by powerful economic sectors in the community. Since our institutions have always and only enabled the existence of a two-party system of representative government, this in turn has actively accentuated the divide which has existed in our society from an early period. And since that divide has always been of a dual nature, splitting society into two camps, which if not of equal size in terms of numbers have always been approximately equal in terms of power, this has traditionally tended to create a situation whereby almost every individual in the land feels that he naturally belongs to one camp or the other. This feeling of political-class identity has not necessarily gone hand in hand with party commitment, but has merely reflected a magnetic influence arising from a sense of inherited belonging to one party or the other. Resentments or discontents may be felt with a party, but as with family relationships, there is often an uncritical feeling of belonging - sometimes, even, a feeling of cold apathy, but the connection remains. These vague feelings and relationships of an electorate for its democratic institutions are typical of a two-party system steeped in generations of tradition where old political loyalties remain undisturbed.

3 – Its contempt for minority opinion and anti-intellectualism

Of more significance to our argument, however, is that all of this is reflected back to the parties themselves. Since there are only two parties assuming either the loyalty or enmity of an entire population; and since their confidence is strengthened by a long tradition; and since each possesses great influence by the fact of its size alone, there is an enormous concentration of power by each.

This power and sense of security gives rise to several characteristics: contempt for minority opinion either within or outside the group; an anti-intellectualism; an impervious resistance to new ideas; and the growth of oligarchic structures confining opinion-forming to an exclusive elite. In addition, since these parties form complementary parts in a dual system, facing opposition from one direction only, this exacerbates the antagonism of each, and as the grounds for conflict are heightened, this inevitably leads to the greater polarisation of the groups. If the grounds for conflict between the two parties appear to diminish, or in fact, actually do so, then artificial means for conflict have to be resorted to in stoking up the flames of controversy, so that, firstly, power may be maintained or won, or the cause justified; and secondly, so that the outcome of elections may be successful. For these purposes, each party has to attractively package its cause in a wrapping of myth.

4 – Its eventual breakdown in the perception of reality

The intensity of such a confrontational, i.e. two-sided conflict, cannot but lead eventually to a breakdown in the perception of reality, and that is what has occurred in Britain today when we view the parties of the two extremes. A gradual breakdown in the perception of reality means a decreasing involvement in the representation of those substantive issues needed to solve the greatest (usually economic) problems of the time. Therefore, such a breakdown can only be correlated with a breakdown in the effectiveness of our democratic institutions, for the mechanism of democracy is then reduced to a meaningless facade. This is the argument behind Lord Hailsham's contention, that we are in fact governed by what would be more correctly termed an elective dictatorship, and such a system and its unrepresentative nature, cannot be properly called a democracy.

5 – Subjective vested interests give rise to many ills

The greatest criticism of the two party system in Britain as a sociological phenomenon in its undermining the democratic nature of society, or in preventing the emergence of a democratic consciousness, or the need for a classless community, stems from the exaggerated concentration on the pursuit of subjective vested interests. These interests have always been economic, entailing the greedy pursuit of financial gain, and irrespective of whether they were parties of the left or right. If the struggle between the Whig and Tories in the 19th century is viewed from the perspective of our own time, it would be difficult to say which of those two was the less greedy or cruel to the downtrodden and oppressed. Perhaps the Tories might come off a little more lightly, since some of the greatest philanthropists were listed amongst their leaders, and the One-Nation call of Disraeli was marked by a genuine sincerity as a move towards unity. The Whigs of an earlier period, however, used the call for laissez-faire as an excuse for the most ruthless exploitation and for opposing the introduction of the Factory Acts. Of course, it would only be fair to add that the Liberals, at the end of the century, were a far cry from their Whig predecessors. In our own time we have lately experienced a Tory party in power which was only concerned with the pursuit of pure financial interests as against developing the long-term profitability of the productive sector; and until the very recent past, a Labour party which was only concerned with, or was in the pockets of, a powerful trades union movement only out for its own narrower gains as against any other interests.

As we have observed, all political parties are only concerned with the achievement of specific aims through the exertion of power, and they are basically subjective and amoral; but when the ruthless pursuit of vested interests is added to those other considerations of representation, then there are even fewer grounds for standing by moral principle. But in Britain, the vested interest character of our political parties has a more wide-ranging and adverse influence on society, than those of other parties elsewhere. Many organisations in the world of work and labour are drawn into the vortex of serving these vested interests: financial institutions, employers federations, trades unions, etc., and so in any attempt to judge the autonomy of parties, it is difficult to know as to whether it is the tail or the animal which wags the dog. This naturally gives rise to unlimited suspicion and mistrust, and especially in a country, such as ours, where the evils of patronage are conducted so brazenly and on a scale of such unprecedented proportions.

Furthermore, there is a cold cupidity and matter-of-fact practicality in the approach to our dual-party system from which all idealism and sense of higher purpose had been drained. Consequently, those of questionable character are drawn towards a political career. Principle is laughed at as illusion or hypocrisy; whilst expediency is lauded as a virtue. The truth is that no representative democracy can exist without principle, as principle is the sole guiding base for the loyalty of the elector. Without it, the shifting sands of change would deny the elector a firm hold of understanding through which he or she could effectively express his "Yea" or "Nay" via the democratic machine. This, then, is the character of our system through which all its weaknesses may be perceived.

6 – Different character of representative institutions abroad

The above, however, can only be seen in its true perspective if a comparison is made with those political parties abroad in their very different sociological setting. It is significant that Britain is the world home of representative government - its inventor - for representative government does - and can only mean the representation of vested interests. The criticism of our own institutions stems not from the representation of vested interests *per se*, but from an exaggerated emphasis on their pursuit against any consideration for the higher or more objective interests of the community. Although we may press our own credit for the invention of the representative party system, those systems which arose abroad were of a very different character, and indeed, arose through quite different circumstances.

As the major systems of representative government abroad arose through the turmoil of revolution, or through changes in society of revolutionary dimensions, and everywhere appeared as sudden creations to fulfil an immediate need, their sociological significance was uniquely different from here in Britain. Since they were the products of world-stirring events: of the collapse of the *ancien régime*; of struggles for national identity; of wars against a foreign oppressor, etc., and were thereby inspired by such general abstract ideals as liberty, equality, justice or nationhood, appealing to all classes in the community, they were less concerned with subjective vested interests. They were created far more as conscious entities for the pursuit of the common welfare, as opposed to the spontaneous groupings in England which arose through a sordid squabble for spoils, each naming the other "Thief" or "Outlaw" in different dialects of the Celtic tongue.

7 – English revolutions have been failed revolutions

Our so-called revolutions or allegedly "progressive civil wars" have ultimately all been failed revolutions. The 17th century philosopher, James Harrington, who was imprisoned for his views, already in his own time argued that the Great Rebellion had failed due to the failure to re-distribute land, since the large estate constituted an aristocratic society, on which it was impossible to construct a democratic state. Dicey, at a later date, pertinently remarked that, "Puritanism ... missed its mark. In no sphere is this more obviously true than in the sphere of legislation. Many Puritans perceived that the law needed reform, yet the Puritan revolution did little for the amendment of the law. ... The Puritan worship of the Common law barred the path which might lead to its amendment. Their rightful dread of arbitrary power blinded them to the necessity for the changes which were gradually and awkwardly introduced by the development of equity through the Court of Chancery."[112]

---

[112] A.V. Dicey, *Law & Public Opinion In England*, Macmillan, 1905, p. 169, note 2.

Burke in the 18th and Macaulay in the 19th century both clearly demonstrated that the Revolution of 1688 was not revolutionary but conservative, since in the words of the man now regarded as the greatest British historical scholar at the turn of the previous century, "it was little more than a rectification of recent error, and a return to ancient principles. ... The Revolution was mainly the work of Conservatives, that is, of churchmen who, where church interests were not threatened, strictly upheld authority, and reverted to their original doctrine when the crisis was over. No change took place in the governing class. The gentry who managed the affairs of the country managed the affairs of the country after 1688 as they had done before. There was no transfer of force from the aristocratic element of society to the democratic."[113] On the Whigs, the same author makes the pertinent observation that, "they became associated with great interests in English society, with trade, and banking, and the City, with elements that were progressive, and devoted to private, not national ends. ... They were a combination of men rather than a doctrine, and the idea of fidelity to comrades was often stronger among them than the idea of fidelity to truths."[114] The great French Revolution, on the contrary, not merely entailed the total transformation of society and property relationships, but was supported by all classes in France - even by the closest blood relations of the unfortunate king. In Britain, party politics began with the greedy pursuit of financial gain and has remained so ever since. On the Continent, Japan, and elsewhere, although vested interests naturally played a limited role, there remained a stronger underlying sense of the need for upholding national interests and promoting the material welfare of the community.

8 – Vested interest nature of British administration contrasted with more objective oriented European bureaucracies

There is also another reason why political parties on the Continent, and elsewhere, were less intensely influenced by private vested interests, and hence tended to be more nationally oriented, more objective and more adhering to principle than those parties

---

[113] Lord Acton, *Lectures On Modern History*, Macmillan, 1906, p. 231.

[114] Ibid, op. cit., p. 217.

operating in Britain. Whilst in Britain administration (as well as government) remained in the hands of an unpaid gentry and aristocratic class until the middle of the 19th century, the Continental countries had already long been governed by paid officials operating within bureaucratic systems. These bureaucratic systems, answerable to authoritarian monarchs or princelings , may have been oppressive or even arbitrary, but they did have the quality of having no other pretence than serving the cause of a single master or the state. The most notable systems were those developed in France and Prussia, each undergoing revolutionary reforms to meet the needs of a new epoch, viz., in France after 1789 and in Prussia, those of Baron vom Stein shortly after the start of the 19th century. In England, no such system arose until the formation of the Civil Service in 1855. Until then administration had been in the hands of dilettantes, without any formal qualifications whatsoever, and the entire system depended on the corruption of patronage, sinecures, and the satisfaction of the private interests of the leading families in the land. Hence, in contrast with Continental Europe, there developed no objective conception of the state or sense of national purpose to act as a focus for existing political parties.

Consequently, in England both the legislative *and* the executive spheres of government remained firmly under the control of private vested interest groups until a very late date. The Northcote-Trevelyan reforms of 1855-1870, far-reaching as they were, were not of sufficient impact to effect a transformation in thinking on the nature of political power and the requirements of democracy in serving the national will. Therefore the vested interest nature of our political parties continued unchanged as before. Furthermore, the British Civil Service, in contrast to those systems on the Continent, was not subject to statute regulating its constitution or organisation, and so this was another factor which prevented a natural integration (within a desirable democratic context) between the powers of the executive and the legislative. Naturally this helped to ensure that British political parties remained as subjective in pursuing their own selfish interests as they had ever been.

In general, parties elsewhere were more closely influenced in their thinking by the speculative writings of philosophers, economists and other pamphleteers. Consequently, more open-mindedness led to the development of less conservative parties (on the left as well as the right) and ultimately, to wiser and better government. A further factor contributing towards greater democratisation arose through the multiplicity of parties in many states, for this not only broadened the representation of interests, but countered the chances for the dictatorial domination of one or several parties over the rest. Each party was thereby not merely kept within manageable proportions, but if it was to exert any influence at all, it needed to maintain a realistic flexibility whilst also upholding its principles. History has demonstrated to date, beyond doubt, that of the two categories of representative government, that existing abroad has proven more realistic in better serving the true needs of the community.

9 – Confrontational and Participatory representative democracy compared

The main distinction between the two styles of representative government, is that whilst the British system is Confrontational, foreign systems tend to be Participatory, and that whilst the first encourages the entrenchment of interests, the second more easily facilitates change and social advancement towards modernisation and industrial efficiency. In contemporary Britain, therefore, the great social divide and class conflict is politically promoted most of all by our parliamentary dual-party system, and then by every group embracing the subjective vested interests of one side or the other. The rectangular form of our parliamentary chamber as contrasted with the circular forms of the parliamentary assemblies of the majority of peoples in the Western world, together with our first-past-the-post electoral system, inevitably perpetuates a confrontational as opposed to a participatory style of democracy. Confrontational democracy not only emphasises the prerogative of majorities in oppressing minorities, but also means that decisions are reached between two combatants of approximately equal size by a punch-up played according to the sporting principles of the Queensbury rules. Since all arguments pro and contra are the monopoly of two parties only, so narrowing the potential consideration of any issue by contrast to the broader discussion in a multi-party chamber, principle is more easily sacrificed to expediency.

As there is less diversity in the representation of opinion, and as there are fewer checks and balances of a multi-party presence, the ruling majority of the two party system, with less sense and less objectivity, can in the end impose what its own vested interests dictate. The brute power of personalities, and the absence of any necessity to compromise, generally ensures that real issues remain unresolved; whilst the very polarisation of opinion makes the badness of each tolerable to the other, since the political exploitation of the electorate in the short term, in terms of noise and clamour, is more desirable and realistic than the actual exertion of political power in the longer term.

All this vulgarises the political scene in conveying more an impression of play acting than the actualisation of practical business, as is most clearly illustrated during Commons' Question Time. And in fact, play acting it is, for the combatants, remain the same combatants, and are permanently at odds. There is no possibility of compromise, and because of the extent of the polarisation, there is no possibility of appealing to reason in creating a likeness of minds. Stupidity, intransigence and hatred is the trinity upholding the very system. The combat is interminable by the very nature of the Confrontational process, and it takes on a form of destructive proportions. Two stags have their antlers inextricably intertwined, and every movement of each is an act of struggle against the other, and both are doomed to destruction. None of this is mere theory. It is witnessed in the every day practicality of our contemporary institutions, A political party, for example, which continues to create hereditary peerages for its servants, or argues that work motivation for the majority can only be effected by wage restraint, whilst work motivation for the privileged can only be effected through substantial salary increases, cannot under any pretence contend that it is intent on creating a more democratic or fairer society. Likewise, a party in the hands of the great trades union barons is possibly sacrificing responsibility for the national welfare to the vanity of uncompromising proletarian power.

A participatory democratic style, as exists on the Continent, Scandinavia, Japan and elsewhere, is markedly different. A circular shaped parliamentary chamber, and proportional representation - now in some form almost universal in the non-Anglo-Saxon world - and a multi-party system, are all factors contributing towards a greater consensus in feeling and policy, not only amongst the elected but amongst the electors too. There is nothing in such a system dictating as of necessity, as with us in Britain, that a permanent class divide should run through society. And in fact we see in these countries, moderate, reasonable and mature parties, democratic in outlook, irrespective of the label under which they choose to pursue their aims. Therefore, whilst confrontational democracy is in essence divisive, participatory democracy is essentially unitary in spirit, purpose and outcome; and in that unitary spirit is implied a common concern for the welfare of nation and people. As William Rodgers has noted on those operating within the former, "politicians have failed largely because they have been prisoners - sometimes willing prisoners - of a political divide which is itself based on outworn social assumptions."[115] The confrontational method of settling disputes is even reflected in our judicial system: viz., the adversarial system of English law as contrasted with the more objective truth-seeking inquisitorial system in the Continental countries.

Whilst the outcome of confrontational democracy is more directed to settling merely the differences between conflicting groups; the outcome of participatory democracy is more directed to settling substantive issues as they actually exist in society and irrespective of their relationship to different social groups. In this is to be found the profoundest contrast between the two styles of constitutional democracy.

---

[115] William Rodgers, *The Politics of Change*, Secker & Warburg, 1982, p. 164.

CHAPTER 23
Democratic Society As a Realisation

"The extremes are opposed both to the mean and to each other, and the mean is opposed to the extremes."

Aristotle, *Nicomachean Ethics*, Welldon's trans., Macmillan, 1892, p. 53.

1 - Economic egalitarianism cannot be equated with social egalitarianism   2 - The class divide is widening   3 - As representative democracy has failed as an agency for social reform other roads to social freedom must be sought   4 - The value of objectivity in unifying society   5 - When representative government is used as an instrument for social oppression   6 - Continental thought giving rise to the idea of the classless society

1 – Economic egalitarianism cannot be equated with social egalitarianism

The prime motivation for undertaking this enquiry, is not simply because of the ineffectiveness and breakdown of our democratic system, howsoever acute that situation has become, but because of a ruinous social malaise destroying society itself. It is this question which is more urgent than the former. We see, today, not the diminution of class differences, but in certain situations, their accentuation.

This factor is masked by the existence of an economic egalitarianism, expressed not in terms of the distribution of total available wealth, but in terms of standards of living. In this sense, excluding those obviously deprived minorities, there is a greater equality in the distribution of essential material needs for a tolerably comfortable existence, than at any other time in world history. But as we have already noted, material egalitarianism is quite different from social egalitarianism. Although De Tocqueville's contention that "the desire for equality always becomes more insatiable in proportion as equality is more complete,"[116] is a controversial argument, it is nonetheless true that there are many precedents in history illustrating social conflicts which did not owe their origin to inequalities in material circumstances.

---

[116] Alexis De Tocqueville, *Democracy In America*, Vintage Books, NY, 1945 ed., Vol. II, p. 147.

2 – The class divide is widening

The recent research of leading sociologists, however, has definitively demonstrated that class barriers are widening rather than closing.[117] Goldthorpe has summarised his research by stating that, "the results of our enquiry lead clearly to the conclusion that ... no significant reduction in class inequalities has in fact been achieved. ... the only trends that may arguably be discerned are indeed ones that would point to a widening of differences in class chances." A former director of the Hudson Institute reaches similar conclusions in his researches, when he writes, "all the evidence points towards the return to a class-based lifestyle. ... Britain's class structure is held together by a thread of myth and magic that puts ritual before practical value and status before any ideal of social progress. The result is a country where sentiment rules and where two different realities exist side by side. On the one hand there is Britain as it appears to outsiders: a country in which the evidence of economic and social crisis is now overwhelming; on the other there is the dream world created by Britons for themselves."[118] In this kind of crisis, therefore, any justifiable means are warranted in solving these social questions.

3 – As representative democracy has failed as an agency for social reform other roads to social freedom must be sought

All these issues can be reduced down to the problem of freedom as justice in the community. In Britain, since the inception of democracy, the path to freedom has been institutionalised through representative government. Representative democracy means the pursuit of vested interests, and it has always been taken for granted that the pursuit of vested interests is a natural, desirable, healthy and essential element of constitutional democracy. But the pursuit of these interests in Britain, has become vicious, morbid and destructive to society itself. Therefore, in responding to this reality, we must look to an alternative course for expressing our freedom and resolving our socio-economic and political differences.

---

[117] As shown, for example, by John Goldthorpe and others in, *Social Mobility & Class Structure In Modern Britain*, and Halsey, Heath & Ridge in, *Origins & Destinations*, both published by the Clarendon Press, Oxford, in 1980.

[118] James Bellini, op. cit., pp. 163 & 166.

This may not be a simple task, since as a practical earth-bound people, there is a suspicion of speculative thought that may whisk us away from the immediate commitment to our material needs. Whatever may be the faults of representative government in regard to the pursuit of our vested interests, at least it has the tactile virtue of tangibility - of easy comprehensibility. The babe resents the snatching of the plaything from the security of its grasp! But freedom does not properly consist of the pursuit of vested interests - and has never done so. The creation of our institutions - our unique invention - was only intended as a medium for a higher purpose and never as an end in itself. If we have lost our way with regard to any ideal we may have cherished of freedom or democratic values, then surely it occurred through a confusions of those ideals, in grasping at an empty shell after the spirit had flown. These are the searching questions we must ask and answer. For this purpose, we must dive into the realm of speculative thought - a final sally into the recent past - in exploring those factors which contributed to Continental freedom. In what aspects does their freedom differ from our own? Irrespective of our findings, we shall not attempt to revive the truths of any metaphysics from the past, but merely display those findings in the light of a sociological understanding of the most basic needs of the British community today.

4 – The value of objectivity in unifying society

In this final excursion into the past, we might not do better than return to the Berlin study of that philosopher who had so remarkably criticised the English Reform Bill. There is some compunction in returning to this authority, since for some fifty years of the previous century, his name has not merely been under a cloud of misunderstanding and distortion, but of calculated misrepresentation and unjustified abuse, perpetrated even by some of the best minds of the age. Happily, however, this cloud is now passing by, to reveal bright rays of sunlight, as scholars worldwide, from Israel to Canada, are realising not only his invaluable contribution to the intellectual development of Europe, but qualities of historical learning and a penetrating grasp of society, which was never fully discerned before. Here, we are only concerned with his consideration of representative democracy and his concept of freedom. The most distinguished contemporary student of this philosopher in the English speaking world has remarked that, "Hegel's philosophy is an important step in the development of the modern notion of freedom."[119] Another distinguished commentator has suggested that with the emergence of Hegel, the world had not produced a more imaginative philosopher since Plato, and that he was "a profound social and political theorist and also a profound psychologist."[120]

The relevance of Hegel's thinking to our contemporary condition is, in the words of Charles Taylor, to be found in his "vision of a world reconciled to the spirit."[121] His entire system of idealistic philosophy - and he equates the Ideal and the Real as identical concepts - is directed towards an objective understanding of existence. This means identifying Reality, and defining the place of man, as a free being, within a society in which he felt a total identity of purpose. This is no simple achievement, and many volumes were filled in expounding a new logic and a new system that was free of contradiction. Hegel is attributed to have triggered off that line of thinking giving rise to Collectivism, but to associate Hegel with political Collectivism, in its various forms, as we know it today, would reflect a naivety in misunderstanding his true purpose. It would also entail a gross misrepresentation of his philosophy to take at face value those apparently transparent pronouncements on the issues of his time, since these are so often only comprehensible within the deeper context of his philosophy. The misrepresentation of his political philosophy, intentional or otherwise, has frequently originated from the naive seizure of isolated statements, that were then falsely interpreted as statements of general opinion. In this world nothing is simple, and a first perception of anything is seldom a reflection of its true reality. Hegel knew this, and consequently, much of what he wrote and said is conditioned by a variety of factors.

5 – When representative government is used as an instrument for oppression

His thoughts on representative government, however, have a crystal clarity, and present a striking relevance for our time. His

---

[119] Charles Taylor, *Hegel*, Cambridge UP, 1975, p. 570.

[120] John Plamenatz, *Man & Society*, Longmans, 1963, Vol. II, pp. 202 & 131.

[121] Charles Taylor, op. cit., p. 544.

underlying concern is with the problem of freedom and justice. He fully comprehended the divisive nature of our system, although he could hardly have anticipated the extent of its damage to society in our own time. In the words of a contemporary scholar, his paper on the Reform Bill is, "one of the most informed and radical critiques of English social conditions. Hegel is well aware of the immensity of England's social and economic problems and cognisant of the inadequacy of purely technical and political solutions. His essay reads like an agenda for social reform in England. ... (He) called for a restructuring and remodelling of an antiquated social system which used political power for social oppression."[122] That system has not yet been restructured or remodelled, and in terms of measuring the relative social advance of England and the Continent since that time, the gradualism of our evolutionary process has set us back even further.

An American historian has remarked that, "English parliamentarism appeared to (Hegel) to be merely a modified form of class-government by an aristocracy. ... A thoroughgoing dislike of government by an hereditary patrician oligarchy was one of Hegel's earliest political convictions. ...The representation of individuals upon an arbitrary territorial basis appeared to him to be almost meaningless. ... What needs to be represented ... is not the individual but the significant spheres (*Kreise*), or interests, or functional units, of civil society. ... In its larger social aspects the Hegelian theory applied to a situation in which the progress of industrialism and modernised government depended not on a policy of laissez-faire but upon strong political leadership."[123] If the advocacy for all these things had been made but yesterday, their originality would have appeared as new ideas for tomorrow.

6 – Continental thought gave rise to the idea of the classless society

But Hegel was himself but part of a larger Continental tradition, influenced as he was by the French Revolution and the European

---

[122]   Shlomo Avineri, op. cit., pp. 219 & 220.

[123]   George H. Sabine, *A History of Political Theory*, Harrup & Co., 1937, pp. 642, 643-644 & 645.

Enlightenment. The Continental philosophers had no concern with the squalid issue of the pursuit of subjective vested interests. In creating a new order, they were concerned with the humanity of man in ideal circumstances - his own best interests beyond the context of his existing situation. The old order was dead, or dying, or to be destroyed, and so the nonsense of superimposing mutilated reforms and compromises on a rotten substructure was not to be. Rousseau, in his wisdom, formulated the concept of the General Will, whereby all men in a free democracy were to be united by a single overriding purpose. There was no room here for class distinctions! In this there was unanimity amongst the great thinkers of the Continent. At a later era, Hegel was to formulate his own philosophy of humankind united in identity within the all-encompassing embrace of the benevolent state. The consciousness of true freedom was only to be experienced through the life of the state. Was this to be the origin - the sole pathway - to the achievement of the classless society? May be.

The four demands of the German philosophers of the Enlightenment: Unity, Freedom, Communion with Man, and Communion with Nature, entailed a universality for the humanity of man in political thinking never realised here in Britain. In Britain, such idealism went no further than the Lake poets. Its ethereal quality was laughable to those who had their vested interests to pursue. But thinkers such as Schiller and Novalis had a great message for humankind, and although their words were not transmitted into political action, their message sunk permanently into the consciousness of the intelligentsia, to be reformulated at a later era as a basis for genuinely democratic societies. Schiller gave deep thought to the sociological analysis of humankind in his search for discovering the true nature of individual freedom in society and in his attempt to trace the origins of class divisiveness. In the words of Charles Taylor, "Schiller in his 6th Letter on the *Aesthetic Education of Man* traces cleavages which man has suffered in the evolution from ancient Greek to modern society. Modern man has divided up the faculties which were united in men of classical times; and in doing so, men have become specialised, so that instead of expressing the whole, each is only a fragment (*Bruchstück*) of humanity. This specialisation, fruit of the dichotomies of the understanding, is in turn linked to the divisions in society between classes, which are each confined to a function. This division into classes transforms the living unity of society into a mechanical interdependence. Running the complex machine of modern society cannot be left to the spontaneous initiative of the members, but must follow bureaucratic formulae. Men are treated no longer as concrete beings but as mere intellectual constructs, and in return they can feel no identification with the state, which finally loses all authority and sinks to mere ruling power."[124]

If this penetrating analysis, packed with meaning, on so many aspects of the class divide, had been written but yesterday, it would have constituted an original text book guide to the problems of our own contemporary society. These were the thoughts, and these the men, who laid the foundations for true democracy as a way of life. It was this which gave Continental Europe her social advance.

This cursory sketch of those intellectual influences which so deeply affected European thought and attitudes on the unity of humankind, so implying the underlying need for the creation of a classless society, can only be comprehended in its correct perspective if a comparison is made with the intellectual poverty of 19th century England. All the great political intellectual movements of the 19th century of any note, arose on the Continent. This not merely applies to such peripheral movements, as Syndicalism and Anarchism, but to all the different categories of Socialism as cited by Karl Marx - Owenism being the sole exception. Of course we produced political thinkers, but they all lacked that intellectual will required for formulating a systematic ideology for action. If J.S. Mill is regarded as the greatest thinker of the period, his entire life was spent on shifting ground, and this greatest of Utilitarians ended life by virtually repudiating the precepts of this creed as formulated by his father and his father's friend, Jeremy Bentham. As for Carlyle, Ruskin, and others amongst their circle, despite the urgency and relevance of their message, they were merely listened to with bemused respect and then quietly forgotten. They passed on nothing to posterity in the realm of practical politics.

The intellectual influences which did finally percolate through to exert some direction on our political parties were passed through a strainer of so fine a mesh as to make a very weak brew. British party politics, from first to last, was to be dominated by the force of subjective vested interests, seemingly made respectable under the flag of empiricism. This not merely amounted to the rejection of

---

[124] Charles Taylor, op. cit., p. 28.

speculative thought, but inevitably outlawed the possibility of ever achieving radical social progress.

CHAPTER 24
Democracy For Tomorrow

"The House of Commons should have cross benches, as in the House of Lords, and the sooner the carpenters are brought in to bridge the actual physical divide in the chamber ... the sooner the chamber will lose its two-party adversarial rituals."

Dr. David Owen, *A Future That Will Work*, Penguin, 1984, p. 183.

1 – Britain cannot survive in a vacuum

The central argument of these chapters takes on its full significance only within the context of those needs to develop a free and democratic society in meeting the demands of a modern industrialised state.

If Britain existed in the world as an isolated or independent unit - in a kind of vacuum - it would be of merely secondary importance that she should change the nature of her institutions. But Britain, of all countries, is most certainly not an independent entity, however much she would like to be, and however much in a past lost age she may have had no need to care much about how the rest of the world progressed or regressed. Our present complacency stems not purely from the fact of our situation as an island race, but more significantly, because of an unconscious ingrained pride originating from an imperial past. Our dependence on foreign trade for our very existence has brought about a situation whereby a careless nonchalance on the extent of the great industrial competitors facing us today is nothing less than suicidal. Events must force us to ask ourselves as to the How and Why of our failure in the face of foreign success - of those who have overtaken us at breakneck speed.

2 – The challenge must be met

All our values must be brought into question in the cause of building a modernised society, not primarily for meeting what is so commonly referred to as the "needs of the 21st century," but more urgently, for meeting what already exists as intensive international competition.   In the past we have prided ourselves as a nation of amateurs and dilettantes, suspicious of professionalism with its intensity of purpose and the principles of rationalism which direct it. The value of efficiency in meeting the needs of competition now makes it imperative that we change our attitudes   on   work   and society in all its aspects.   A great French observer of the English scene, reflecting on the reasons for our having slipped behind as an industrial nation already before the end of the 19th century, has remarked on that power most noted for its efficiency in the modern era that, it was "the most 'progressive' state in the whole of Europe from whatever point of view it was regarded - scientific or military, industrial or social - (it) was the democratic absolutism of the Caesarion pattern ... based on the double foundation of a hereditary monarchy and a democratic parliament, and every other nation was attempting, more or less clumsily, to imitate in every sphere what he may call the Prussian model; and not only the Continental nations. ... In Germany, one great name dominated the entire history of this political and social development, the name of Hegel. ... If England was vaguely apprehensive that the success of the Prussian model might degrade her to the position of a second-rate power it was perhaps because she had not paid sufficient heed to Carlyle."[125]

3 – The democratisation of society is the road to its modernisation

The reasons for this advance can only be correctly understood in the light of the greater democratisation of society; of the breaking down of the values and psychological divisions of class, and a huge broadening of equality of opportunity. These things were not brought about by laissez-faire, or through the democratic struggle between conflicting vested interest groups, but by the imposition of state authority which took a protective caring role in developing the potential of its people.   In Germany, Japan, and indeed elsewhere in northern Europe, the state took on an almost parental attitude in ensuring the democratisation of society, and in response to this, the people were to experience the realisation of their freedom through a dynamic self-motivated co-operativeness in every sphere of life.   This

---

[125] Elie Halévy, *Imperialism & The Rise of Labour*, E.Benn, 1951, pp. 139-140.

becomes most starkly evident through work attitudes everywhere in northern Europe, Japan and elsewhere, and such attitudes are accountable not primarily to more democratic institutions in work and labour organisations - although they too are significant - but to a sense of belonging, security and human dignity actually instilled into the individual by a benevolent state.

This is why a greater commitment is felt and given by the Swede, Dutchman or German to the world of employment. There is a sense of confidence and natural pride that can only arise in an open society which has rejected utterly the older concept of class privilege with all its injustice. If the British worker feels resentful and intransigent, looking upon employment as having no more purpose than a necessary obligation to earn a living wage, it is not because he has been demoralised by political manipulators, but because he senses the injustice of a closed society, with its exclusive class-dominated elites, wielding supreme power through a soulless state with no personal feeling for his welfare. In these circumstances, the cynicism of the intelligent British worker is not merely natural but inevitable. The road to contentment or happiness is to be found elsewhere! The psychological status of the manager in regard to the world of work is no less regrettable than that of the manual worker. Although those employed in the higher levels of employment may reveal no open intransigence, there is nevertheless in Britain, an attitude that places work on a low rung in the scale of values. Status for its own sake is a priority over purpose, and work is seen more in the light of a means than an end.

4 – Bankruptcy of the confrontational party system

How can our elective dictatorship be brought to an end, and how can society be democratised? The first essential step is the reform of our institutions so that the powerful vested interest groups of our polarised society are dissipated. It is, as we have noted, the dual-party divide of our democratic system which has exacerbated the sharp divide of our country into two conflicting halves. Whatever the realities or myths behind the two great parties of the left and right, they are perceived by each other in the popular imagination as follows: by the committed as a conflict between good and evil, and by the uncommitted as a conflict between evil and evil. Because of this fixed duality and the entrenchment of class interests over a very long period in our history, the conflict is far sharper than that to be found in the countries of our toughest industrial competitors.

The conflict is perceived by the majority in the following light, and such perceptions, for all their falsity, are in a great degree encouraged by each of the two great camps: of the poor versus the rich; of the oppressed versus the free; movement versus stability; change versus conservatism; novelty versus tradition; rebellion versus authority; equality versus liberty; a planned society versus a competitive society; bureaucracy versus democracy; the new versus the old; permissiveness versus convention; fundamentalist beliefs versus catholic beliefs; agnosticism versus religiosity, and an anti-business ethos versus a pro-business ethos. Of the above 28 values, 3 of which represent social ills, viz., the poor, the oppressed and an anti-business ethos, none of the other 25 are absolutes, and all may have certain positive qualities in a defined context. Listed as they are as beliefs associated with the left or the right, they are nothing more than psychological states of mind. They are a nonsense as a basis for any rational divide in the sphere of politics, and only cast a veil of darkness and confusion in the attempt to elucidate any order of real substantive values. An electorate deserves something better than this.

5 – Imperative need for Social Capitalist centrism

How can this divide in society be ended and our institutions reformed? There is only one way: through the accession to power of radical centrism - not through the fudged thinking of Liberal Democrats, but through the ideals and policies of Social Capitalism. New and higher ideals must be appealed to in awakening the conscience of the British people to a better future, based on ideals of justice and freedom, both morally and emotionally, appealing to those on both sides of the traditional divide.

6 – Problems of centre parties

Several significant problems, however, may be brought about through the emergence of a Socialist inspired radical centrism, and here we may say something about centre parties in general. Firstly, they are liable to the accusation of being all things to all people since they set out to make an appeal across the entire political spectrum. An allegedly centrist party may attempt to evade this problem by declaring itself either left or right of centre, but of course if that is so in actuality, then that party is no longer truly centrist. Secondly, a centrist party intent on extending its appeal across the spectrum may, in certain circumstances, be suspected of undermining representative democracy itself, if, as in Britain, the prime or only purpose of such democracy is perceived as the need to exploit vested interests. This, possibly, is the main reason why the SDP and later the Liberal Democrats called upon themselves the virulent dislike of both the Tory and Labour parties, who would rather have entered into co-operative arrangements with each other - despite the polarisation of their views - in keeping out this new third grouping so threatening to the *status quo* of the old system. Thirdly, a centrist party which sets out to appeal to the goodwill and reason of men and women from all sectors of the community, in all areas, can only best succeed through a system of proportional representation, since it is to be anticipated that they should be more widely spread on a geographical basis than those owing allegiance to the older class-based parties, which tend more to find their support in concentrated pockets of population. Proportional representation therefore becomes an important issue for radical centrism, irrespective of whether the idea of supporting a third grouping is accepted or not. This is because the principle of PR is only concerned with fair play and not with balancing one power group against another, although that may inevitably become part of the process during the course of government.

7 – Failure of the SDP Liberal Alliance

With the formation of the SDP and the emergence of the Alliance, millions of well-intentioned people in Britain were offered the hope of a new vision in politics and the start of a great movement to reverse our industrial decline. This, at last, was to be the political grouping that was to eschew the vicious representation of vested class interests. The Roy Jenkins Dimbleby Memorial lecture, *Home Thoughts From Abroad*, given before an audience of millions on TV, was an indication of great things to come, and for some months following the Limehouse Declaration, a year later, everything seemed to bode well for the future of British politics. At the time, the author of this book, was falsely led to believe that the establishment of the SDP Liberal Alliance was possibly the most significant political event in British domestic politics in the four and a half decades of his life-time.

Since then, much has happened and after many vicissitudes, the emerging Liberal Democrats have proved an unrealistic alternative to the other parties.   Firstly, they have not begun to give serious consideration to our most urgent political issues.   Whilst acknowledging that the regeneration of British industry was at the "top of their agenda," they have added nothing to the debate on the restoration of this sector. Secondly, whilst spewing forth a vast plethora of policy papers (so putting the lie to the contention that they were a party "without policies") they have remained a party without vision.   They have never attempted to formulate a philosophy, and indeed, have been opposed to the very idea.[126] Consequently, all their policy papers have fallen still-born from the press, and have hardly been read by any except for the keener activists.

8 – The vice of political "professionalism"

What, then, went awry?   Almost from its inception the SDP fell into the trap of sharing the worst faults of both the major parties. Logically, the emergence of a centrist party should seem to imply the creation of an objective political movement, intent on the solution of *real* communal or national problems, transcending the narrow vested interests of specific groups - but then politics is seldom logical.   None of these hoped-for things occurred.   The opportunity of a life-time was thrown to the wind.   Instead, it was decided that the SDP should be run on "professional" lines, together with the aid of a computerised system.   The fact that subscribers during the first year never received their membership cards, due to the breakdown of that system, is of such minor significance that it need hardly be touched upon, but what is significant is that the party leadership set about the establishment of something that was to be nothing more than an electioneering machine.

---

[126] The sole exception being the brave attempts of Dr. Stephen Haseler, who put up for election for the Presidency of the party during the first year of its existence. This far-seeing scholar wanted to give the party intellectual depth on being appointed editor of the newly founded Open Forum series of pamphlets. Shortly after accepting for publication a contribution from the present author, the party decided to close down the project for "lack of funds," and Dr. Haseler hurriedly left for America to take up an academic post to the great loss of the SDP. In the light of his fresh approach to politics, he is perhaps the one person who might have established the party as a serious new force in British politics.

Firstly, this meant correctly reflecting the views of its membership. Since the overwhelming majority of its active membership comprised middle class public sector employees, and those from the service professions, this meant that industry and major economic questions were to have a low-interest profile. Secondly, to ensure the effectiveness of the electioneering machine, it was important that the party should be quick on its feet and flexible. Without this, expediency would not be possible. Therefore, the idea of developing a philosophy or ideology was to be ditched from the beginning. The trouble with a visionary approach to politics is that it points too strongly towards a specified direction, and is therefore liable to upset those whom one hopes to win over to the cause. Besides, it is also "unprofessional" if the intention is to maximise the ratio of vote-winning opportunities. Hence "principle" was to be thrown to the wind.

9 – How it became a vested interest party

What then was to be the outcome of this? Since the active membership included a large number of well-intentioned professional people from a wide variety of interesting backgrounds, the great assemblies of the Council for Social Democracy were guaranteed to produce intelligent, level-headed, and sometimes, lively debates. A wide variety of issues were to be brought before this august body of some 500 people, and the party was to be given the impression of being truly democratic. Besides questions of devolution, transport, CAP, Third World debt, etc., etc.,there were also to be debates on Gay Rights and Animal Liberation, as one speaker followed another in endless succession. On those few occasions when the economy or industry came up for discussion - questions of overriding importance to Britain's future - these occurred in circumstances with a very different aspect. As the hall emptied there would be a rush for the bar, but this did not mean that the debates were conducted for want of speakers. Clearly these rare occasions - scheduled for a minimum time slot - were invariably stage-managed.

A coterie of City financiers would be called to the rostrum, followed by an odd selection of handpicked speakers, such as clergymen and social workers, assured to know little about the topic (for this was the case) and so safely assumed not to raise controversial issues, or cutting points, into the discussion. The City financiers, directors of merchant banks and stockbrokers, would deliver emotional socially-aware speeches, projecting an acceptable left of centre bias. Clearly these were humane men, always given a loud applause as they left the rostrum, by those remaining in the hall.[127]

However, when they were afterwards approached to reveal their *real* views behind the empty rhetoric (as they were by the author of this book, in his capacity as an elected CSD representative) they were found to have no sympathy whatsoever for British manufacturing or the primary industries, and were invariably opposed to any suggestion that changes should be made to our financial institutions in encouraging greater productive and so job-creating investment. I often wondered why these urbane people condescended to present themselves at these SDP conferences. Only later did I become cognisant of the fact that of course it was necessary that the City should send in its denizens to wish the new party a "successful future." Friendly and intimate relations had to be cultivated with the SDP leadership. There had to be a rubbing of shoulders, an exchange of pleasantries, and some good-humoured banter, just to ensure that this "new political grouping" was not going to rock the boat or upset the *status quo* in the future, or come up with new ideas which might stir the anxiety of the City. Meanwhile, whenever the SDP leadership spoke on the economy, they always adopted a grave demeanour, and whilst pronouncing that the "regeneration of industry is the most urgent issue of our time," have admitted, "that the situation is so severe, that there's almost nothing to be done about it." The City financiers could not have agreed more! And that was the sum total of the SDP's efforts to reverse our industrial decline.

The following conclusions have to be drawn: as far as the economic policies of the SDP were concerned, the party fell entirely into the lap of the conservative City magnates; and the apathy of party activists towards questions of industry was such, that not a whimper of protest was heard against this tendency. It was just too unimportant to

---

[127]   The above paragraphs may seem to give an unfair picture of the percipience of the Council for Social Democracy. It is only fair to add that when this coterie of financiers, together with their hangers-on, introduced the Share Ownership debate at Torquay in 1985, the proposed plans were attacked by speaker after speaker as being little more than a sham. When the debate was finally wound-up by a man described by one of the Gang of Four as an eminent "grocer" (who has long since re-joined the Labour party), he beat a hasty but defensive retreat, by saying in effect, "don't take the proposals too seriously, they're only a draft anyway."

be bothered with! The SDP always boasted of being financed by its rank and file membership, as contrasted with the business financing of the Tories and the trades union financing of the Labour party. This presumption of membership-only financing, however, only tells one half of the story. The party was hard-pressed for finance and wanted to win over the great merchant bankers. Nothing was to be said or done by the party which was liable to upset the conservative views of the financial institutions. The SDP was successful in maintaining such a stance, and corresponding with this, was its failure to expose and discuss the real issues surrounding Britain's industrial decline, or to formulate positive policies for regeneration.

10 – Actions not words must be the criterion of a party

The SDP measured its value against the faults of the opposing parties. This was good electioneering politics in view of the fact, as remarked in an earlier chapter, that for the past few decades voters have tended to Vote-out a party rather than to Vote-in a party. But negative values are no values. No party can claim objective credence for its existence by arguing that it is the least of the pitiable alternatives on offer. Several leading manufacturers at the time (and this was twenty years ago) confided to me they were opting wisely to change their allegiance to the Labour party, since despite any perceived short-comings of the latter, the Labour party appreciated passionately the need for regenerating the UK-based productive sector. Ultimately, a party must be judged according to its real intentions or actions rather than according to its rhetoric.

There have been many changes within all the parties over the past fifteen years. We have expended considerable space on the history of the SDP. This has not been without purpose. The present Labour party is often compared with the old SDP. Does the SDP stand as a metaphor for New Labour? The answer has to be "Yes", for Blair's Labour government has repeated all the fallacies that its predecessor might have pursued had they succeeded in controlling the reins of power.

Where does this leave us, in view of all we have argued in these chapters? Parties which promote the vested interests of one sector of the community against another, as do the Tories or Old Labour, are clearly bad for the country. But the SDP Liberal Alliance/Liberal Democrats, were or are in this respect, hardly any better. The Liberal

Democrats may not represent the hard-pressed against the well-to-do, but what is little less reprehensible, they represent the public sector and service professions - not to mention covert support for the City institutions - against the wealth creating UK-based productive sector, which includes everyone from the factory operative to the entrepreneur.

11 – Hope for a merging or withering away of parties

The hope of centrist radicalism expressed through the emerging power of Social Capitalism may be seen as an attraction to those from all the old parliamentary groupings. This may have already been made evident by those MPs, and others, who have foresworn old allegiances in moving over to support the cause of other parties. This could conceivably result in the eventual merger of all parties, or contrariwise, the withering away of parties as new technologies facilitated the introduction of more direct forms of democracy. The long-term viability for a merging of the major political groupings towards a more objective goal, may be seen in the fact that there are certain major principles with which the parties are already in agreement. For example, there is unanimity amongst the parties, in theory at least, that British manufacturing must be regenerated if our economic decline is to be reversed. At present, the differences only occur as to how this is to be achieved, and if the thinking and policies of all parties on this issue is only leading to failure, then there is the opportunity for a third and more realistic force to enter with its own programme and ideology.

The eventual accession to power of a radical centrist majority, either through a merging of the existing parties or their withering away, would in the long term achieve changes of a truly revolutionary nature. It would be an essential prelude to creating new and more effective modes of democratic power for the New Millennium. The idea of class-based parties are already anachronistic and distasteful to the electorate and there is a need for more balanced forms of representation to take their place. Today, it is already obligatory on our members of Parliament that they list their directorships and other financial interests. This ruling (motivated by fears that are by no means exaggerated and by a recognition of all that has been said in these chapters on vested interests) has achieved little in real terms. Tomorrow, public opinion will possibly demand that all our elected representatives and public servants, both central and local, be forbidden directorships, the ownership of shares, or involvement in any other financial interests, on pain of criminal prosecution. This is because no democracy can be impartial, or hold to the promises of its representatives, unless it is free of the graft and corruption to which we have become accustomed.

12 – Representation through pure political power

If the power of electors is to be maximised through their representatives, then this can only be achieved through *pure political power*, for only this is truly democratic if an intermediary is to stand between the elector and legislated power. Pure political power is defined as that which is uninfluenced by extraneous vested interests separate from party principles as commonly understood. The principle of pure political power also requires that there should be a complete separation between the administrative power of civil servants and the financial power of the free market, other than those powers proposed for a reconstituted Department of Trade & Industry, elaborated in Chapter 21 sub-section 8 of, *The People's Capitalism.* There should be no mutual patronage between the world of government and the world of financial markets. Vested interests have always been poison to democracy whether we speak of democratic values, constitutional democracy or a democratic society. Elected representatives - even in fairness to themselves - if they are to maintain integrity to their own principles, must be free of extraneous influences, so that they are facilitated to fearlessly and uncompromisingly advocate those ideas and policies in which they believe in their innermost hearts. Only then can the electorate place trust in their integrity. Only then will they thereby come closer to taking on the role of delegates.

This immediately raises another question. Since Burke's famous address to the electors of Bristol it has been generally accepted in this country that a representative, once he has been elected as a member of Parliament, is no longer a delegate, for he then takes on an autonomous role. This is true, but it should not be used - as it has - as a cover for every nefarious change of principle and as a salve for the conscience of those who accept gratuities or directorships. Furthermore, if democracy is to become more real or direct, then this would be assisted by our representatives perceiving themselves more in the light of delegates.

13 – As a step towards the achievement of direct democracy

But the accession of representative democracy exerting *pure political power* should only be seen as a preliminary step towards forms of direct democracy in the more distant future. With the raising of educational standards to levels far higher than those now contemplated, and with the aid of new technologies and more decentralisation, it is to be hoped that government in the future will increasingly be directed by various systems of referenda.

It would then follow that political parties would fulfil a diminishing role in the community, as in their place would emerge, in the words of the philosopher, the representation of those innumerable "significant spheres, or interests, or functional units, of civil society." Although the state would remain forever as a fabric through which the community expressed its will, political parties might wither away when once they had fulfilled their appointed purpose as a stepping stone to better systems of direct democracy, or what is now commonly referred to as *people power.*

***

PART IV
The Road To Constructive Politics

"Our world will not get upon its feet again till it lets the truth come home to
it that its core is not to be found in active measures but in new ways of thinking."

Albert Schweizer, *Civilization & Ethics*, A. & C. Black, 1929 ed., p. 205.

The greatest hindrance to solving the major issues of our time
cannot simply be put down to the wrong-headedness of our
politicians and statesmen of any or all parliamentary factions.
The problem goes very much deeper than that.

There is little likelihood that any of our existing political parties,
Left, Right or Centrist, can begin of their own volition to formulate
long-term cures for Britain's ills - let alone reverse British industrial
decline. In a certain technical or practical sense (leaving doctrine or
values aside) no existing political party is at present any better or
worse than another. This is not simply because of their resort to short-
term expediency or vested interests, or because of the limited
understanding or misjudgement of our political leaders (as touched
upon in earlier chapters), but because the entire framework for our
political thinking entails a false intellectual perception of reality.

This means that the greatest mental efforts or the very best
intentions of our political leaders, working within the intellectual and
institutional structures of our time, are doomed to miserable failure.
The empirical demonstration in support of such a telling statement is
made evident through the past sixty years of our history, viz., our
relative decline as an industrial power by comparison with all other
advanced countries in the Western world. The purpose of the
following chapters is to identify those false intellectual perceptions of
reality and modes of thought, responsible for our regression, and then
to point the way out of our present impasse.

The thinking and actions of our contemporary political leaders,
together with the organisations supporting them, operate at the surface
level of forces tracing their origin to far greater depths of our cultural,
moral and intellectual consciousness. There are elements in those
forces - of distant origin - which no longer satisfy the demands upon
our mental resources in facing the challenging needs of the New
Millennium. We all know this, but hate to admit it because we feel

impotent in the face of impending decline. As a nation, are we doomed to relinquish our prestige to those who are better and more deserving than ourselves? There is no doubt that the said elements in those forces of ancient origin contain the seeds for cancerous growth, and now in the face of the vastly changed circumstances of the new world now coming into being, that that cancer will take hold of our people and civilisation with a destructive grasp.

Such cancers of the body politic, of course, are nothing new. They can be traced and analysed in civilisations and nations from time immemorial. All peoples, it seems, possess certain specific weaknesses in their collective make-up that only become apparent to themselves when it is too late, and the rot has already gone too far. But today we live in a world which is different from any other. Today we are blessed with a greater knowledge and a fuller consciousness for collective self-understanding than any previous era in history. Consequently, it is in our power, with the aid of good fortune, to take our fate into our own hands.

How is that to be achieved? It entails adopting a fresh intellectual world outlook - more inspired, purposeful and constructive - so that we are given the willpower and the strength to rationally resolve all those issues which threaten our well-being. It may be a consolation that nothing more than this is required in facing those endemic problems which have undermined our relative prosperity over the past five decades - but it is a truth that nothing more is needed. It is a fiction to apportion blame for our decline to the greater material resources of others. History has demonstrated that spiritual power always prevails over material forces. After all, our enemies at the end of the last War, arose from the ashes to defeat us in peace in the economic sphere, and they achieved this in the face of every disadvantage. We cannot now complain about their greater material power. We can only acknowledge their greater strength of spirit. And this spirit stemmed from an intellectual and moral perception of the world which is different from our own.

If we want to re-adjust matters we must begin by looking critically into our own intellectual, cultural and moral values, and identify where we have erred. We must ditch those values which have served us badly, and construct new foundations for our own renewal. Only then may we once again take our stand as equals amongst our partners in the industrialised world. The following chapters make a start towards such a new beginning.

CHAPTER 25
The Unseen Real Issues of Politics

"The wise man is informed in what is right. The inferior man is informed in what will pay."

Confucius, *Analects*, Jothill's trans., Yokohama, 1910, Vol. I, p. 237.

1 - Failure of modern politics to solve substantive issues   2 - Government policies fail to reflect underlying causes of ills   3 - Examples of superficial problems perceived as underlying ills   4 - Demonstration of the false perception of these issues   5 - Deceit behind such false perceptions   6 - Public acceptance and hardening of these false views   7 - This compounded by anxiety of self-justifying to others   8 - Consequently, the truth in political discussion and thought is poisoned   9 - Hence the intellectual paralysis of political life

1 – Failure of modern politics to solve substantive issues

It must be plain to anyone who has given any thought to the matter that contemporary British politics has failed to solve our most serious and endemic problems. Furthermore, in this respect, we see today the failure of all parliamentary groupings. If the contemporary situation is not an entirely new factor in our political life, it is a phenomenon which has become far more acute today as we witness Britain's relative decline as a modern industrial state by comparison with newer and even much smaller countries in the industrialised West.

If the fact of Britain's failure to solve her greatest problems is plain to all, the reasons for this failure remain hidden from the majority. The prime purpose of the following chapters is to analyse and expose the true nature of this failure, for it lies at the core of all our problems as a nation state. The second purpose is to point the way out of the dilemma facing us.

2 – Government policies fail to reflect underlying causes of ills

Britain's failure to cope with *real* or substantive problems, as for example with unemployment, with an appalling imbalance of payments, and with falling relative living standards and actual increasing poverty, is most clearly manifested through government policies and the manifestos of most political groupings which are concerned with issues failing to reflect the root causes of those problems. That is, the entire process of politics has come to concern itself with peripheral issues which although seemingly important in themselves, are in reality irrelevant or of negligible significance as starting points for examination or discussion. This has occurred through the adoption of illusive political ideals thrown up during the process of conflict between different vested interest groups.

The consequence of this is that conflicting political interest groups are more intent on the activity of opposition, and perceiving the world through the eyes of such conflict, than in comprehending the true nature of our substantive problems. It is ironic to reflect that the activity of political conflict has alone been responsible for bringing about this situation. This is further compounded by the fact, as Bertrand Russell has noted, that "politicians do not find any attractions in a view which does not lend itself to party declamation, and ordinary mortals prefer views which attribute misfortune to the machinations of their enemies."[128]

3 –Examples of superficial problems perceived as underlying ills

The following may be cited as some of the peripheral or surface issues with which recent governments have come to be obsessed, in the false conviction that such problems are substantive that in themselves are always of paramount importance:- most monetary and fiscal policies; call for a higher exchange rate for the pound sterling; the pressure for better wages and conditions; the poor performance of the stock market; the "over-heating" of the economy and the need to cut back consumer spending; and the fight against inflation. All these problems, although they may give headaches to many people in powerful positions, are only symptoms of other underlying ills to which modern governments have been partially if not totally blind. In treating surface issues in the belief that they are the causes of the underlying economic maladies is like applying unguents to syphilitic sores in the hope of reversing such a disease. In reality, of course, it does no such thing. Inevitably, therefore, the government approach to problems often tends to compound rather than resolve them.

4 – Demonstration of the false perception of these ills

It would be useful to look a little closer at these superficial problems, the solutions of which have come to be perceived as ends in

---

[128] Bertrand Russell, *Sceptical Essays*, Allen & Unwin, 1928, pp. 13-14.

themselves. In referring to the last example, viz., inflation, it has to be said that this is not at all times and under all circumstances an economic ill. There are periods when it is inevitable but by no means baneful, e.g., during times of accelerated resurgence of productivity. Japan experienced raging inflation during the 1970s, but this in no way damaged or threatened her economy. It was a natural if not a necessary process in the particular circumstances. During less hectic periods of industrial growth she has, of course, succeeded in wisely maintaining one of the lowest inflation rates amongst the world's leading economies. Hence inflation may be tolerated during periods of surging growth within a *profitably* productive economy.

The "Over-heating" of the economy may be cited as one of the most absurdly contradictory situations with which contemporary Britain has been faced. This should be apparent to any thoughtful person on the proverbial Clapham omnibus. If on one day we are told that Britain's problem is sluggish productivity and on the next we are told it is consumer spending, so implying that the "ill-gotten gains" of an improved productivity undermines the economy, there must be a reason to stop and question such an awkwardly paradoxical phenomenon. It is reminiscent, of course, of the even more paradoxical phenomenon of the Stop-Start policies of the Ted Heath government in the 1970s. Both are connected, reflecting Britain's greatest economic problem, viz., the lack of profitable productivity. This problem, however, is never even recognised by governments of any hue. It is far too embarrassing, and the reasons for this have been elaborated in detail in Parts II & III of, *The People's Capitalism.*

5 – Deceit behind such false perceptions

The term "Over-heating" of the economy has been evoked as a deceitful image to convey a false impression of our real situation. The first ill is not the over-heating of the *real* economy, i.e. of home-based productivity, but on the contrary, the demise of productivity. The second ill is not simply consumer spending but only spending on imported merchandise. The third and overwhelming ill - a factor rarely recognised by governments for fear of offending the Most High - is the actual over-heating of the rentier (or *phony*) economy, viz., all those inflationary activities entailing the making of money out of money. Consequently, British governments never even begin to solve the real difficulties behind the problem they euphemistically describe as the over-heating of the economy. In fairness they are unable to if restricted to their present remit of power, since it would necessitate their challenging the powerful rentiers of the financial establishment, and this they would hardly dare to do. No policies within the possible scope of any Chancellor of the Exchequer, or for that matter, within the ordinary powers of any other Lord of the Treasury, are likely to have any serious long-term effect in improving the *real* economy.

6 – Public acceptance and hardening of these false views

When these superficial and ephemeral problems are seized upon by the vested interests of the powers that be, and endowed with a reality they do not possess; and when these same powers choose to cast a blind eye on the underlying and substantive ills of the commonweal, then delusion replaces true sense and irrationality sound reason. In these conditions a finely woven complex of lies is needed to bolster the vested interests of pure rentier capitalism. Both pro and contra groups take their place in the political forum; both equally self-deluded; and in this sterile intellectual environment, White becomes black and Black becomes white. Worse still, both sides maintain an inner as well as an outer faith in bolstering their own self-delusions, and stubbornness gives the final stamp to this myopia and stupidity.

7 – This compounded by anxiety of self-justifying to others

Words, phrases and even concrete concepts, take on distinctive political colours, taking on the false appearance of reality in the mind's eye, so that in any discussion between a number of individuals, there is the tendency of each to ask him- or herself the question not "What is the right or wrong of this issue,?" but, "What is the underlying party political sympathy of the other in putting across a point of view, or what is his ulterior motive?" When that question has been answered, a supplementary self-question is put, "If indeed the other seems to share a sympathy with a political grouping with which I disagree, then should I not guard myself against agreeing with that line of thought (irrespective of its intrinsic rightness or wrongness) as otherwise I may be tarnished by a brush with a colouring not of my own choosing?"

It is a sorry situation when so many, when applying their minds to political questions, are more concerned (even if unconsciously) to justify their thinking in the light of a power group, or their peers, and to tread the line of conformity, rather than dare to think alone and independently in seeking out the truth. One of the tragedies of political life is that it is too often the silent or passive majority who remain the independent thinkers in society, whilst those who actually manage society, i.e. the political activists, the power wielders, the councillors, members of Parliament, administrative civil servants, and others, are the unimaginative conformists, timid traditionalists, and even bootlickers of different modes of established thought. Little hope, therefore can be expected from them in terms of new ideas or wise reform.

8 – Consequently, the truth in political discussion and thought is poisoned

In this way not only is all political discussion but even all political thought is poisoned, simply because so many are locked into the political prejudice of their chosen environment or vested interest. In this way the search for objective values is nipped in the bud, and the original or independent political thinker - the individual who wishes or dares to transcend the enslavement of narrow party prejudice - often treads warily, in constant fear of being tarnished with a brush of one colour or another, when really his only true and honest intention is to identify and promote the truth.

9 – Hence the intellectual paralysis of political life

Much has been written in previous chapters about the myths and illusions - the totem poles - of our contemporary political life, and how these have compounded the greatest problems confronting us. These false trails and ideals are no concern of the present chapters. We are now concerned with identifying the causes and nature of what has become the intellectual paralysis destroying the positive effectiveness of British political life - or at least, that effectiveness needed in promoting the best interests of the community.

Britain is now in a parlous political condition, and is seen to be so by informed people throughout the industrialised world. If the term, "Britain in decline," is now heard as one of the kinder epithets of foreign observers, amongst the unkinder or most common, are, "a people living in the dreamland of the past," "the problem nation of

Europe," "the degenerates of the West," or even, "the near bottom nation of the Western world." In Britain these terms are angrily repudiated, not because they may contain a grain of malice, but because they express a half-truth which cuts too near the bone.

CHAPTER 26
The Causes For Our Intellectual Disability

"The reaction of human thought in all things which makes us swing from extreme to extreme, satisfies in a manner one of our intellectual virtues, the love of justice, and seems to sweep mankind all with it, leaving him no time to reason."

C.F. Keary, *The Pursuit of Reason*, Cambridge UP, 1910, p. 83.

1 - Our problems may be blamed on an intellectual disability   2 - The poverty of new ideas   3 - Comparison with the political creativity of the 19th century   4 - The eight causes for our intellectual paralysis   5 - I: The polarisation of political life   6 - Group conflict buries truth   7 - Multi-party systems tend to alleviate conflict intensity   8 - SDP Liberal Alliance was unable to break the mould   9 - Britain's system different from other dual party systems

1 – Our problems may be blamed on an intellectual disability

The single consolation stemming from our parlous condition, or in confronting the above allegations, may be that all our problems stem primarily from a total intellectual inability to analyse and solve those problems, and that inability is caused by nothing less than an extraordinary intellectual paralysis.

In a world where we not only possess greater knowledge than ever before - and knowledge which is readily available to the power wielders in the community - but a greater ability for scientific, social and economic research - and research which is in fact in constant progress - it may seem extraordinary to the ordinary citizen, that we in Britain linger under the handicap of such a total intellectual paralysis in solving our underlying political problems.

2 – The poverty of new ideas

This paralysis is made evident not only by the failure to solve those problems, but more plainly by the dearth of new ideas emanating from the media or the world of learning, and even more so, by the lack of an effective forum for the expression of new or radical ideas, should any individuals or groups bother to create them in the first place. The first priority, therefore, in solving the major problems facing our country must be success in overcoming the intellectual paralysis blocking the road to progress and even blocking the process of creative thought itself.

It may be an invaluable consolation, therefore, to our loss of self-esteem, and indeed, in holding out a great hope for the future, if we can account the cause and solution of our major socio-economic problems purely to the lack of an effective rationale supported by willpower; rather than by accounting it to a belief in a miserable determinism which puts forward the argument that we exist in a condition of inevitable decline.   Unfortunately, it is the latter, compounded by an overwhelming apathy, which has sunk deeply into the hearts of the majority amongst all sections of our society.

3 – Comparison with the political creativity of the 19th century

There should be no doubt, however, about the existence of this intellectual paralysis of contemporary political life, but it has to be conceded that when an aspect of life is absent in a society, and possibly, has never been experienced by those living within it, it is not merely never missed but there may be no cognisance of its very existence.   The absence of constructive political thought in contemporary Britain may be best understood by making a comparison with the political intellectual life of 19th century Britain. That century produced such a huge number of original thinkers, and political pamphlets and journals with a wide circulation (bearing no comparison with the esoteric political journals of our own time with their very restricted specialised readership), as to make present-day Britain seem like an intellectual desert. The majority of those thinkers may not have held membership of the major political parties, even though they may have exerted a seminal influence on the future of political movements.   But even amongst leading party political statesmen of the 19th century there were great original and expansive thinkers by comparison with the tawdry tunnel-visioned party-men of the past or present century - statesmen more the victims of party machines and vested interests than inspired leaders in their own right. Is there any living statesman today, for example, whose literary output in terms of sheer quantity, can compare with those of Disraeli or Gladstone, or the even greater output of their contemporaries across the Channel, Thiers and Guizot?

4 – The eight causes for our intellectual paralysis

In attempting to solve our own political problems it therefore first becomes necessary to appreciate the wide ranging extent of this intellectual paralysis, and this can only be approached by analysing, what we have identified as their eight causes. Only after such an analysis can we then proceed firmly, on a step-by-step basis, to establish firm foundations for our political future. The eight causes are listed as under:-

1. The polarisation of political life;
2. The institutionalism of power bases;
3. The influence of philosophical pragmatism;
4. The general belief in historical materialism;
5. Repudiation of the methodology of constructive thought by modern British philosophy;
6. The undermining of the belief in reason by the revelations of psychology;
7. The advanced specialisation of knowledge into exclusive Departments; and
8. The general revolt against the power of reason.

5 - I- The polarisation of political life

The first, and by far the most obvious reason for the paralysis of our intellectual life, stems from the apparent polarisation of British politics. The qualifying term "apparent" must of necessity be used, since the polarisation of politics refers primarily to the intensity of conflict in terms of rhetoric as opposed to conflicts of interest with regard to the solution of substantive issues. Since this polarisation refers to differences between separate power groups they nonetheless remain *real* conflicts because of that fact. This polarisation has been exacerbated by the adversarial nature of our two-party system with its cross benches in our Parliament, when compared with the semi-circular and multi-party systems found in the great majority of other democracies. It is also exacerbated by the deeply ingrained class structured nature of British society, which again contrasts sharply with the far more democratic societies found throughout the industrialised West and even in the Far East. The true nature of our democracy has been discussed at length in Part III of this book.

6 – Group conflict buries truth

It need only be noted here that the two huge uncompromising adversarial political movements, reflecting an apparently immutable characteristic of our political life, at the same time react away and against one another on all major issues. This may be found on both the theoretical and practical levels, and irrespective of the objective value of any issue raised for discussion. This, of course, merely reflects the nature of confrontation itself. The nature of struggle makes this inevitable. A punch is always returned for a punch and no rationale is needed for pulling a punch or making it harder. Indeed, reason or disinterested integrity hardly enters into the matter, for party loyalty - and for the individual, party promotion - is the name of the game. As each adversary is obliged to deny any truth or underlying goodness that may be seen in its opponent, this compounds the falsity of both in their perception of the world.

7 – Multi-party systems tend to alleviate conflict intensity

In a healthy multi-party system, on the other hand, the powerful presence of other interests and opinions, usually brings to bear a sanity and natural balance which would otherwise be lacking. In such an environment, there is not simply a middle way but *other ways*, and in such a system no party can afford - or indeed would be tolerated - which took upon itself the exclusive claim to represent the true and only path ahead for its own people. The adversarial system in Britain is so deeply entrenched that even the highly successful - the six-year wonder of the SDP Liberal Alliance, was unable to exert any significant or long-term influence on the course of our polarised politics - and neither have their successors, the Liberal Democrats. The centre ground - the great hope of reasonable and well-intentioned people in the early eighties, proved in the end to be nothing more than a great bubble - a flash in the pan. The entrenched force of tradition, prejudice, ignorance and pig-headedness, was far too strong to allow for a sea change towards true enlightenment on anything more than a transient basis.

8 – SDP Liberal Alliance was unable to break the mould

The centre ground was not destroyed by any adversary from the Left or the Right, although it was loathed by both and held in contemptuous disdain. The centre ground was simply destroyed by itself. It never had a philosophy, and indeed, as we saw in Chapter 24, its leaders were opposed from the beginning to formulating any doctrine to give the movement coherence and lasting strength. It remained a fragile flower to the last. Consequently, with the first major personality split in 1987, the movement caved in on itself, for nothing permanent had been created to give it a lasting moral strength. It had no intellectual foundations; no great economic concepts; no categorical imperative; and no articles of faith - other than a total commitment to integration within the EU. As soon as the movement had shrunk into insignificance, in losing the support of the electorate, it was as if it had never existed in the first place. Its lack of any philosophy should have stood as a warning sign to New Labour but failed to do so.

The political life of Britain was once again as it had always been. The SDP never broke the mould of British politics or created anything new. It merely fell between two stools. It had the opportunity to create a synthesis between the demands of a competitive free enterprise society and those of social justice, but instead, it failed to grasp that opportunity and lost the chance of the century. Because of the failure to formulate an apt philosophical doctrine that might have broken the mould of British politics, it never succeeded in creating a genuine Centrist ideology, and consequently, its active members remained either marginally to the left or to the right of the centre, and this inevitably remained a source of simmering conflict which eventually was to boil over.

9 – Britain's system different from other dual party systems

Clearly, the polarised politics of Britain is quite different from that found in other Western democracies with two-party systems, as for example, as found in West Germany or Sweden. The differences are so great, in fact, that attempts to identify similarities would be absurd. The democracy of the Federal Republic of Germany is a recent creation, consciously created in view of the socio-economic needs of a modern industrialised state. Sweden, on the other hand, has almost become a one-party Social Democratic state, firstly on the grounds of a long cultural tradition promoting the ideals of an egalitarian but free community, and secondly, on the grounds of an almost fifty year continuous rule by the Social Democratic party - only recently broken by a short spell of government by a Conservative opposition.

In Britain, on the other hand, both the structure of society and the path of politics have become so intensified in their polarisation, that both parties have foregone sight of reality. Consequently, both parties attach to themselves and their opponents qualities which either simply do not exist, or are in themselves, false. They have become conservative and doctrinaire in the bad sense in which these terms are understood. Out of the intensity of conflict between them, empty rhetoric has taken on a reality displacing consideration of the real and underlying issues facing the country today.

CHAPTER 27
The Institutionalism of Power

"The members of a privileged class must, if they are to remain a privileged class, carefully resist the encroachments of wider conceptions of the public good."

L.T. Hobhouse, *Morals In Evolution*, Henry Holt, NY, 1915 ed., pp. 16-17.

1 – Politicians divide into the self-deceived and those with vested interests

The outcome of this political unreality is that those actually engaged in the struggle of political life can be divided into two groups, or combinations of those groups. On the one hand there are those motivated by self-deception, i.e. hopelessly lost in the delusions of party rhetoric taking on reality in their mind's eye; and on the other hand, those motivated by subjective vested interests, i.e. class and economic benefits, or simply the attractions of party or trades union promotion.

In contemporary Britain, hard-line Old Socialists, no less than wealthy Tory bankers, have their eye on a coronet and an ermine shoulder wrap, and party leaders of both factions ensure that these awards are kept readily available not merely for their own party people but also for those of the opposition. Nothing is so corrupting as the glory of a peerage and its multifarious financial spin-offs. Even the most pugnacious revolutionaries are turned into performing poodles by the attractions of these sweetmeats, and no country in the industrialised West has been so corrupted by the dazzling gifts of government patronage.

2 – British democracy upheld by a negative will

The emptiness of British political life; its deceit and self-deceit; its vulgar rhetoric; its poverty of ideas, and its imprisonment within the corrupting constraints of vested interests, are facts well recognised by the general population - even by the least educated - and this has led to a universal cynicism towards all political parties. Furthermore, over the past few decades (as we have already observed), research has demonstrated that large sections of the electorate do not vote to keep a political grouping in power but to keep the worst of the alternatives out of power. Nothing could be a sadder reflection of the purpose of democratic government than this, for if the exerted power of an electorate is only in a negative direction, this clearly means that there is no representative body promoting its positive will.

3 – Parties not experiencing any meaningful evolution

All this is not to suggest that the two great political movements in Britain are static or fail to change. They are constantly changing and compromising in the face of pressures from many directions, but they are not evolving in any meaningful sense in best serving the greater needs of the community. No great design can be perceived in their progress. They are merely muddling through on short-term objectives so that elections may be fought and won against all other odds. Above all, the intensity of their polarised conflict ensures that rigid ideologies are faithfully upheld, and this acts as a barrier against creative thinking.

4 – II The institutionalism of power bases

The second reason for the intellectual paralysis of British political life stems from the institutionalism of existing power bases. This, in turn, gives rise to the popular conviction that there are no conceivable alternatives to the existing political choices on the national menu, or at least, that such a hope would be futile as a practical expectation. Of more sinister significance, however, is the conviction that institutions are immovable monoliths with a will of their own, impervious to the will of individual or collective entities. The omnipotent and crushing power of institutions is distinctly a 20th century phenomenon, casting a shadow of pessimism over attempts to effect changes in public life.

5 – This has diminished the power of elected representatives

As institutional power has gathered momentum over the past century, in so many departments of life, the power of representative bodies, and of elected representatives as individuals, have diminished. There has been a horrific inevitability about the growth of public institutions, together with their statutory regulations, controls and restrictions. As members of Parliament have become increasingly frustrated by feelings of impotence, locally elected representatives have in fact simply surrendered their powers to the polite dictates of town hall officials. It is no accident that elected representatives, both national and local, have increasingly come to feel that they are the victims of forces beyond their own control, as they are buffeted by a combination of civil servants and vested interests: property developers; bankers; public sector accountants Treasury people, and others, who insist they are doing nothing more than pointing out the line of the law or accepted custom.

6 – And their energy and good intentions

In this kind of environment, not only are elected representatives confused by a mass of material thrust upon them on which they cannot hope to claim anything more than a cursory understanding, but they are easily inveigled into serving vested interests (not of their own choosing) or even into corrupt practices, often without being aware of the fact. The consequences of this is that our elected representatives eventually (and quietly) fall into the rut of conformism, i.e. conformism with the party line, with the requirements of town hall or ministry officials, or with the demands of specific vested interests in whose pay they happen to be. They have no energy for anything more. The demands of the job are such that they can no longer afford to be individuals. As for standing back and viewing an issue from an objective perspective, or in guarding the principles of a high ideal, these are the last qualities that would be expected of them. The worst outcome of these influences is a general aimlessness and loss of direction, eventually leading to anomie and total inner cynicism.

7 – The voter made cynical by institutionalism

On turning to the ordinary voter, his feelings are those of the futility of all parliamentary groupings. When he is spurred to act in casting a vote, he is more often motivated out of anger to expel a government than out of hope to effect some positive good. Most of all, however, he feels the insignificance of his power to effect change by any means at his disposal. He, too, recognises the omnipotence of institutional power, and since he sees this in neutral terms as a force for good or evil, he sees it as immovable and permanent. There is no point in attacking institutional power *per se*, howsoever oppressive it may feel. One may only attack its specific identifiable abuses.

The long tradition of the dual party system over a three hundred year period, has therefore instilled into the ordinary citizen a conviction that radical change is not to be, and that to hope for such change is merely utopian. He or she is not only left with the conviction that his only way of effecting political will is through utilising the existing parliamentary parties, either through the ballot box or active membership (and possibly through the formation or co-operation of pressure groups *within* the parliamentary parties); but more significantly, he is actually left with the intellectual impression that there is no conceivable potential alternative than those parties already represented in Parliament.

8 – Feels there can be no new alternative

This means that he is often locked into the belief that if a person is not a Conservative then he must be a Socialist, and if not a Socialist, then he must be a Liberal Democrat or a Green. If he denies a sympathy with any of these, then - shocking thought - he must either be a Communist or a Fascist. If he is neither of these, too, then he is simply a "crank," and best left to his own devices. This fixed pattern of political thinking reflects a static view of the world, unimaginative and averse to the formulation and serious consideration of any new concepts. It is an attitude encouraged by all our political parties in their striving for simplicity and in their obsession with holding onto power; and also by the national press, on whose sufferance they are allowed to flourish.

CHAPTER 28
The Sterility of Pragmatism

"Subjectivism is perhaps the most distinctive belief of our age, or more precisely, it is the philosophical attitude which underlies a number of its distinctive beliefs."

C.F.M. Joad, *Decadence*. Faber & Faber, 1948, p. 104.

1 – III Philosophical Pragmatism

The third reason for our intellectual paralysis stems from the all-pervasive influence of Philosophical Pragmatism in our public life. Pragmatism as a school of philosophy arose in America through the writings of Peirce, Dewey, Dr. Schiller and William James at the end of the 19th and start of the 20th centuries. Its character is pervasively American but its influence has been hardly less overwhelming in Britain as also elsewhere in the Anglo-Saxon world. It has not made a similar headway, it should be noted, in Continental Europe, primarily because of the existence of other schools of thought which more easily grabbed the imagination of those in power.

2 – Definition of this

The respected American scholar and civil liberties defender, George Novack, has perhaps most succinctly defined the nature of philosophical pragmatism, when he wrote, "pragmatism is what pragmatism does. It is the habit of acting in disregard of solidly-based scientific rules and tested principles. In everyday life, pragmatism is activity which proceeds from the premise (either explicit or unexpressed) that nature and society are essentially indeterminate. Pragmatic people rely not upon laws, rules, and principles which reflect the determinate features and determining factors of objective reality, but principally upon make-shifts, rule-of-thumb methods, and improvisations based on what they believe might be immediately advantageous.[129]... The pragmatists set up two criteria of truth other than correspondence with the real state of affairs. One is what people come to believe; the other is the advantages such beliefs bring. Both are subjective standards."[130]

Philosophical pragmatism arose in America most significantly in the light of two sets of contrasting socio-economic conditions: firstly, in the pioneering environment of a new society where inventions and business projects were developed and tested solely on the grounds of their immediate utility, and without regard to their long-term effects or the experience and judgement of tradition (since there was none); and secondly, in the shadow of new and mighty institutions, viz. Commercial conglomerates, and the bureaucratic power of separate States and Federal government.

3 – Its promotion of expediency and trial and error methods

Philosophical pragmatism which has penetrated the world of business and academia, as well as politics, is not embodied in the thoughts of any consciously formulated system. Its central belief is that Action (or *pragma* the meaning of its Greek derivation) should be judged solely on the successful outcome of any line of action to be undertaken. General principles or theory for the pursuit of Action are eschewed as irrelevant, as are also arguments based on the power of tradition or custom. Actions should therefore be undertaken on a purely trial and error basis: those found unsuccessful rejected, and those found successful, repeated as a basis for further development. There is a transparent simplicity in philosophical pragmatism giving it a wide popular appeal. It would seem to point to a common sense attitude that must be an effective guide to success in all departments of life. It is no surprise, then, that it attracted a universal appeal in a country with little respect for tradition and a strong bent for inventiveness and entrepreneurial flair. Also, the writings of the original pragmatists, amongst them being eminent psychologists and critics of a dated idealism, display a clarity of thinking and an apparent faultlessness which does not easily invite ready criticism.

---

[129] George Novack, *Pragmatism Versus Marxism*, Pathfinder Press Inc., NY, 1972, p. 17.

[130] Ibid., p. 177.

Despite this, however, even the first pragmatists were aware that their students looked askance at them in the face of such a startling philosophy. In an early lecture on the topic, William James covers over his embarrassment in the following words: "I am well aware how odd it must seem to some of you to hear me say that an idea is 'true' so long as to believe it is profitable to our lives."[131] A little later in the same lecture, he elaborates on the extraordinary breadth of criteria permitted in evaluating what is either desirable or true. "Pragmatism," he says, "is willing to take anything, to follow either logic or the senses and to count the humblest and most personal experiences. She will count mystical experiences if they have practical consequences."[132] This is carrying the theory of empiricism to its most absurd extreme.

4 – Over-emphasis on money values

The faults of philosophical pragmatism, however, are not so much to be found in the intrinsic nature of its ideas - despite their vagueness and superficiality - but in its general influence or outcome when applied in the real world. It is primarily from the standpoint of historical hindsight that philosophical pragmatism must stand the accusation of having wrought an overwhelming havoc in many spheres of life. It is hardly an exaggeration to contend that it must stand the criticism of bearing a significant responsibility for the decline of Anglo-Saxon civilisation in the 20th century. Its initial impression conveys a tendency of having promoted a crass materialism but this is the least of its faults. The criteria for the successful outcome of Action in the abstract naturally lays an emphasis on monetary success, or pure money profits. This is because the *final* outcome of most activities in public or business life tend to demand a monetary result - and almost certainly so if other values have to be eschewed in achieving this one and final outcome. Consequently the achievement of money values have been over-emphasised by those succumbing to the influence of pragmatism.

---

[131] William James, "What Pragmatism Means," in *Selected Papers On Philosophy*, Everyman Library, 1961 ed., p. 214.

[132] Ibid., p. 217.

5 – Clashes with the demands of education and modern business

Short-termism is inevitably the most distinctive characteristic of pragmatism. In practice it is always immediate ends which are sought. An over-emphasis is laid on subjectivity and the senses as criteria in using trial and error methods. This allows no room for appreciating the long-term view and so politicians have limited interest in pursuing the best needs for the future. As Dean Inge has so nicely expressed it, "although the welfare of the people of England a hundred years hence is as important, and as much our concern, as the comfort of our contemporaries, the practical politician knows that he may safely ignore the rights of those who, being unborn, have no votes."[133]Such alleged "practicality" stems only from the narrowness of pure subjectivity.

Knowledge is given a low priority and the benefits of past experience acquired through tradition is often simply dismissed as irrelevant or dated. Such extreme subjectivity not only turns its back on the objective world, but even has the myopic effrontery to deny that the objective world exists. This not only leads to an extreme individualism but to atomism in society. Co-operation and harmony are undermined as all are encouraged to "do their own thing." In education this had led to a drastic dropping of standards, or at least to a revision of standards whereby actual knowledge is given a much lower priority in place of abilities involving pure "doing."

The urge to "do" without "knowing" put the rising generation in a state of limbo. As they are not taught that things have Causes and Purposes, they are inevitably left with an agnostic view of the world. Nothing seems to possess a value unless it gives an immediate sensory satisfaction. This leads to a general hopelessness and cynicism, and consequently, the widespread drug addiction of contemporary American youth should be no surprise to their pragmatic elders who are the real culprits for having destroyed the natural human capacity and need for idealism. The technical deficiency of pragmatism in the sphere of education is that it has destroyed the capacity of the group to listen effectively in a classroom environment. This has partly been caused by the relinquishment of the lecture-style mode of teaching in

---

[133] Dean Inge, *Lay Thoughts of A Dean*, Putnams, 1926, p. 358.

favour of dividing up classes to undertake group project work. Inevitably this has led to a decline amongst the rising generation of language ability and comprehension.

In business this has led to individualistic attitudes, effecting the management of major conglomerates no less than smaller enterprises. The influence of the pragmatic approach has been so widespread that it has made it increasingly difficult for Anglo-Saxon countries to compete effectively with those nations still dominated by Hegelian patterns of thought, viz., Japan and most of Western Europe from Finland down to Italy. Success in managing the infrastructure of modern industrialised states has now been proven objectively to be dependent on a high degree of organisation and directed leadership, and this clashes sharply with the demands of pragmatic individualism.

6 – Sets a low value on creative theory

The most damning criticism of philosophical pragmatism, however, is to be found in the low value it puts on abstract ideas or constructive theory, since the worth of these things cannot readily be measured by their outcome. Indeed, measuring the value of many ideas by their probable outcome alone is an impossibility. This, of course, in no way necessarily undervalues the intrinsic worth of any particular idea. Almost all inventions and creativity in the modern world stems from the genius of some great abstract idea, as seen for example in the physics or mathematics of a Newton, a Leibnitz, or an Einstein, and it may be apt to remark in this context, that although America has been the most fecund country in the world in the production of inventions, all the great seminal scientific ideas enabling the development of those inventions were formulated in the Old world. Rudolf Eucken interestingly maintained that, "pragmatism disintegrates truth by reducing it to a crowd of separate truths, and even claims credit for doing so."[134]

7 – Consequences of the anti-intellectualism of pragmatism

The low value placed on ideas or theory by philosophical pragmatism becomes far more obvious, however, in the realm of philosophical or political thought than in those of science. It is here

---

[134] Rudolf Eucken, *Main Currents of Modern Thought*, Fisher Unwin, 1912, p. 78.

that pragmatism is shown up in its raw anti-intellectualism, and curiously, as an influence buttressing the foundations of conservatism. Since it is in the nature of philosophical pragmatism to see the world in an "as is" as opposed to an "ought" situation, there is no incentive to explore into the causes or general principles governing a situation. Institutions and situations are taken at their face value, with no attempt to fathom any deeper interpretation. To enquire into the goodness or badness of a thing is not so much regarded as irrelevant as futile. May Sinclair takes the argument a step further when she asserts that, "it did not and it could not occur to (the Pragmatists) that in this clean sweep of non-moralities, Morality itself must go."[135]

Consequently, in the face of pressing problems, these are dealt with in a piecemeal strictly utilitarian fashion. The inevitable outcome of this is that whilst superficial or cosmetic reforms may be achieved, the underlying weaknesses of basic structures are never even noticed. Consequently, with the passing of time, great institutions, political parties, etc., take on a characterless or even an apparently meaningless existence, as they become huge amorphous bureaucratic bodies responding to change in totally unpredictable ways. Eventually they can only relate to the public through a "show front," dreamt up and created by a public relations and advertising agency. The American political parties are an example of this extraordinary process.

8 – Contra theory equals intellectual paralysis

In Britain over the past thirty years, the influence of philosophical pragmatism in the realm of politics is most clearly seen in the attitude of accepting institutions and political parties for what they are without any attempt to question their underlying *raison d'être*. General ideas and theories are dismissed as impractical or irrelevant. The "age of general theorising ended with J.S. Mill," is a common but ridiculous notion held by great numbers of intellectuals. If, in assuming this, they refer to the situation as it exists in Britain - and it is a false assumption - they forget entirely the huge amount of political theorising which has taken place on the Continent in the 20th century. The attitude of these pragmatists - and it is an attitude enforced by our great institutions of learning - is that the business of politics should

---

[135] May Sinclair, *A Defence of Idealism*, Macmillan, 1917, p. 171.

strictly confine itself to the immediate and practical application of solving specific problems, each to be treated separately on its own merits without reference to any holistic theory for the direction or character of society. But these people do not seem to understand that eschewing constructive theory must eventually lead to the sterility of intellectual paralysis.

9 – Practical problems are compounded and divisions maintained

The outcome of this approach when applied to the entire realm of politics, which we witness, leads to the compounding of problems rather than to their solution. A confused and contradictory mass of statutes and regulations are piled one on top of the other, without the consideration of any underlying directional purpose for the good of the community. Consequently, we experience a process which fails to unite the community towards a feeling of common purpose, and on the contrary we see divisions in the community senselessly maintained. This pouring of new wine into old bottles, the instinct of pragmatism, not only leads to intellectual confusion in the public mind, but to a cynicism in political life. The anti-intellectualism of contemporary political life is everywhere evident, and although philosophical pragmatism is only partly responsible for this, nonetheless, the blame lies very deep.

All the short-sightedness and ills of rentier capitalism, as we experience it in contemporary Britain, can be put down in great part to the pragmatic instinct. May Sinclair's comments on the philosophical core of pragmatism are damning in their criticism, when she writes, "it is a method and not a philosophy. It is not even a philosophic method.[136]... The backbone of philosophy is logic. Pragmatism has no logic; it is spineless."[137] In conclusion it has to be noted that pragmatism has exerted a quiet but subtle influence, since those under its direct spell are often unaware of the movement or even its name, whilst even fewer have read the writings of its long-forgotten proponents.

---

[136] Ibid., p. x.

[137] Ibid., p. xiii.

CHAPTER 29
The End of Constructive Thought

"If we were not always trying to reduce diversity to identity, we should find it almost impossible to think at all."

Aldous Huxley, *Ends & Means*, Chatto & Windus, 1937, p. 12.

1 - IV: General belief in historical materialism   2 - Used as a basis for arrogance   3 - Or to justify determinism   4 - Points to the futility of intellectualising   5 - V: Negative approach of British modern philosophy to constructive thought   6 - But this is not a criticism of the integrity of British philosophers   7 - Their revolt against idealism   8 - Irony of Russell's failure to formulate a political philosophy   9 - The "impossibility" of constructive thought   10 - The tragic trivialising of philosophy

1 – IV General belief in historical materialism

The fourth reason for our intellectual paralysis in facing political problems, stems from the belief in historical materialism. This, of course originates from a fundamental doctrine of Marxism, but its influence has gone far beyond the purpose first envisaged by its creator.

Historical materialism embodies a theory of society laying down the law that ideas and attitudes are imprinted on the minds of individuals and classes according to their origin and status in society. The theory or "pseudo-science" argues that, in general, the individual is incapable of transcending the subjectivity of his class background. He is incapable of understanding the world in any other light than that of the environment in which he is nurtured. Taken in isolation, this sociological theory may seem to convey a pessimistic view of society, but Marx merely used it as the basis for his theory of the inevitable class war with its eventual outcome of the victory of the proletariat. Taken in that context, historical materialism conveys a millennial idealism.

2 – Used as a basis for arrogance

Stripped of its final analysis, historical materialism as understood as the subjectivity of individuals and classes locked into their own prejudices, carries a conviction that has caught the imagination of activists across the political spectrum. Conservatives no less than socialists use, or at least, comprehend this theory as a factor of life in stubbornly upholding their own particular cause. It may seem strange to some to contend that Conservatives, and others, have adopted Marxist attitudes, but as Ludwig von Mises has keenly observed, "not Marxists alone, but most of those who emphatically declare themselves anti-Marxists, think entirely on Marxist lines and have adopted Marx's arbitrary, unconfirmed and easily refutable dogmas."[138]

Non-Marxists interpret or at least perceive the theory of historical materialism in several ways. Firstly, from the standpoint of upholding the rightness of their own views they merely contend that it is they who have an objective understanding of the true ends of society, as against the unenlightened, ignorant, or subjective views of their opponents.

3 – Or to justify determinism

Secondly, less crudely but of far more sinister significance, they give full credence to the Marxist contention of subjective imprisonment within the class environment, and justify rather than merely explain all their attitudes and actions as the influence of determinism alone. This, of course, is cynicism carried to its furthest limits. It implicitly justifies Might as Right and absolves the need for any objective system of morality or even the need for a social conscience, on the grounds of determinism alone. What will be will be, and nothing can change the situation! It implies a more historically advanced Calvinistic theory of predestination, whereby the fortunate are blessed by fate whilst the luckless are doomed to a misfortune from which they can never be saved by any means.

4 – Points to the futility of intellectualising

Historical materialism, taken in its broadest sense and stripped of its last Marxist trappings, therefore creates an attitude of thinking which tends to argue that all political intellectualising is either futile or hypocritical. As subjective beings we are merely what we are, and nothing can change the most deeply rooted nature of our past environment. As we have no freewill, in any meaningful sense there is no point in hoping for a more objective basis on which to guide our actions.

---

[138] Ludwig von Mises, *Socialism*, J. Cape, 1953 ed., p. 17.

5 – V Negative approach of British modern philosophy to constructive thought

The fifth reason for our intellectual paralysis stems from the failure of modern British philosophy to accept any methodology for constructive thought. It has to be said in this context that British philosophy in the 20th century was a misfortune to itself. It entered an embarrassing cul-de-sac from which apparently it was impossible to re-emerge. In the first place there is something uneasy in having to consider a "British Philosophy," as if it was something quite separate from world philosophy, for the world of thought - as also of science - is essentially international. Of course we talk about a "German Philosophy," but not even Kant or Hegel could or would have ever existed without their precursors in Britain and France, against whose empirical or type of rational philosophy they reacted in building up their own great systems. In earlier periods, Descartes and Spinoza, and indeed all the greatest thinkers, worked within an international context. Modern British philosophy, on the other hand (which includes, of course, the Austrian and Cambridge scholar, Wittgenstein) became increasingly parochial and narrow during the 20th century in the methods and questions it considered. There is something unique about the isolation in which it found itself. As a positive force in serving the social sciences it had long ago surrendered any such responsibility.

6 – But this is not a criticism of the integrity of British philosophers

None of these remarks, however, should be taken as a criticism of British philosophy *per se*, and neither should they be taken as criticism of the integrity or high intellectual standing of the leading contributors to that philosophy. The criticism is nothing more than an expression of regret at the *outcome* of the path that modern British philosophy has chosen. The revolt against reason in English philosophy as a basis for constructive thought could, of course, be traced back to the empiricism of Hume, or even earlier, to the cutting criticism of the medieval scholar Occam. It was Hume's conclusion that sensory perception alone forms the basis of reality. It was Hume who argued that "reason should be the slave of passion," and possibly, the greatest aspects of his thinking may be seen in the opposition it subsequently aroused on the Continent culminating in the formulation of Idealism.

Indeed, the rise of Idealism may be seen as the inevitable counterpart of Hume's extreme form of sensory empiricism, which outraged the sensibilities of a later generation of thinkers. In the words of Lewis Mumford, "in analysing cause and effect, he broke down the rational connection between human events to a bald sequence of abstract sensations in time."[139]In response to Hume's contention that, "it is not contrary to reason to prefer the destruction of the whole world to the scratching of my finger," Mumford comments, "one could not caricature this doctrine if one wanted to. ... It stands self-condemned. But if one pursues the implications of this philosophy, one sees that this imperturbable philosopher has arrived at a position of absolute nihilism."[140]In another work, the same author remarks that, "when David Hume reduced value to whatever served impulse, he took the first intellectual step towards the nihilism that threatens to engulf our age."[141]How sad that we nevertheless have to maintain that this thinker is regarded as one of the greatest intellects these islands have produced.

7 – Their revolt against idealism

But it is not with 18th century empiricism we are now concerned. Modern British philosophy, as it is known, begins with the stupendous analytical work of Bertrand Russell and G.E. Moore, at the turn of the previous century. Russell's first book of lasting importance was a study of the mathematician and philosopher, Leibnitz, published in 1900. This was followed in 1903 by *The Principles of Mathematics*, and in 1910 appeared the first of the huge volumes of *Principia Mathematica*, written in collaboration with A.N. Whitehead. Moore, who was born in 1873, a year after Russell, owes his lasting fame to four works: *Principia Ethica*, published in 1903, *Ethics*, in 1912, *Philosophical Studies*, in 1922, and *Some Main Problems of Philosophy*, in 1953. It was G.E. Moore who led the reaction against

---

[139] Lewis Mumford, *The Condition of Man*, Secker & Warburg, 1944, p. 269.

[140] Ibid., p. 270.

[141] Lewis Mumford, *The Conduct of Life,* Secker & Warburg, 1952, p. 129.

Idealist philosophy, and his influence on Russell has been described by the latter in, *My Philosophical Development*, in the following words: "It was towards the end of 1898 that Moore and I rebelled against both Kant and Hegel. Moore led the way, and I followed closely in his footsteps." Their researches led them to demolish Idealistic philosophy, as it then existed, and eventually, their logic led them unhappily into a situation whereby philosophy could no longer hope to fulfil a constructive role in serving the life of the community.

8 – Irony of Russell's failure to formulate a political philosophy

There is a great irony in this fact as regards the thought and many political commitments of Bertrand Russell. Bryan Magee, in conversation with Prof. Stuart Hampshire, has expressed this in the following words: "One of the surprising things about Russell is what he did *not* do. For example, for most of his adult life he was active in politics (he even stood for Parliament twice) and he probably wrote more books about politics than he did about philosophy; and yet he never made any original contribution to political philosophy. Or, to take another example, history: his knowledge of history was vast. I think he knew more history than any non-professional historian I've ever met ... And yet he never made any contribution to the philosophy of history. And so one could go on: nothing original in morals or ethics, nothing in aesthetics."[142]

9 – The "impossibility" of constructive thought

Inevitably, British philosophy with Russell, Moore and Wittgenstein, and their numerous successors and variants, up until the present time, took on an exclusively analytical or critical role. Logical Positivism, and later, Linguistic Philosophy, were the great British philosophical movements of the 20th century. But the limitations of this philosophy as a positive social influence, or even as a guide to individual behaviour, are clear to perceive. G.E. Moore, for example, early in the century, came to the unfortunate conclusion that "the Good," was indefinable, and British philosophy in the latter part of the century has typically never even bothered to grapple with such grandiose (albeit abstract) notions of moral theory. Instead, it has

---

[142] Bryan Magee, *Modern British Philosophy*, Secker & Warburg, 1971, p. 28.

become far more concerned with the abstract problems of language and definition and meaning.

Meanwhile, central to "Wittgenstein's theory of factual propositions is that the so-called propositions of morality, religion, aesthetics and indeed philosophy itself lie outside the boundary of factual discourse."[143]Prof. Joad's criticism of modern British philosophy was damning when he wrote that, "emboldened by their successful use of the surgeon's knife upon the excrescences, (logical) positivists have proceeded to cut away healthy tissue and to present us with a theory of knowledge which denies substantive existence ... to the traditional objects of human aspiration and pursuit such as values and ideals. Dominated by an extreme empiricism which demands of every meaningful statement that it should be verifiable by experience conceived in sensory terms, they proceed to point out that judged by this standard of values and ideals are without meaning, and, therefore, without existence."[144]All this not only places theory in an extraordinarily difficult position but makes constructive philosophical thought impossible.

10 – The tragic trivialising of philosophy

It might be thought that the concentration of British modern philosophers on such "safe" issues as the abstract problems of language and definition and meaning, discussed in the sheltered environment of our older universities, well away from the stormy domains of public life, would at least contribute to unanimity of feeling. Far from it! The outcome of these philosophies on the meaning of meaning, have led to splinter groups and even quarrels of a very acrimonious and even childish nature, e.g. to instances when older men have refused to respond even to the criticism of their more eminent students. All this acrimony, of course, has taken place in the confined environment of the academic world, and to the wider public may be interpreted as little more than "storms in a teacup."

Worse, possibly, than these inter-academic squabbles amongst the philosophers, has been their inability even to agree with *themselves*.

---

[143] David Pears in conversation with Bryan Magee, *Modern British Philosophy*, op. cit., p. 37.

[144] C.E.M. Joad, *Decadence*, Faber & Faber, 1948, p. 23.

Wittgenstein, for example, totally repudiated his earlier philosophy, as elaborated in the *Tractatus Logico-Philosophicus* (by many regarded as his greatest work), in his *Philosophical Investigations*, published thirty years later in 1953. It is difficult to discover which of the Wittgensteins, the earlier or the later (if either), is the greater, or at least, presents the more valid thesis. Bertrand Russell applauded the earlier Wittgenstein as a genius whilst denouncing the later for his trivialisation. Sir Karl Popper, on the other hand, had a very low regard for both Wittgensteins. The latter's eventual repudiation of his own philosophy, many years later, might have been foretold by a discerning reader of the *Tractatus*, for as Anthony Quinton has observed, "right towards the end he says, in effect: 'Anyone who understands my propositions will eventually recognise that they are senseless.'"[145]This could hardly be a plainer example of self-condemnation.

Meanwhile, A.J. Ayer, the most distinguished of the British Logical Positivists, also turned against the philosophy of his earlier life in middle age. Not many years before his death, when asked what were the main defects of Logical Positivism, he replied that, "nearly all of it was false," adding, "first ... the verification principle never got itself properly formulated. ... Then the reductionism doesn't work. You can't reduce even ordinary simple statements about cigarette cases and glasses and ashtrays to statements about sense data - let alone the more abstract statements of science."[146]

Clearly these frail and ephemeral philosophies are a poor substitute for the great and powerful systems of earlier thinkers who exerted a positive force in advancing the cause of Western civilisation. Despite all the criticism of the great Idealists of the past, we are still forced to return to take note of their philosophies, simply because they dealt with issues which remain relevant and all-important for our time. To argue that an issue is un-discussable or unresolvable, as modern British philosophers have done, is merely to leave it as it was without it going away. Nothing is achieved except silence and the voluntary decision not to think. Modern British philosophy has merely

---

[145] Anthony Quinton in conversation with Bryan Magee, *Men of Ideas*, OUP, 1982, p. 81.

[146] In conversation with Bryan Magee, *Men of Ideas*, op. cit., p. 107.

vandalised constructive methodology, or decided to sacrifice it on the altar of an inferior intellectual truth of limited utility.

The tragedy of the British modern philosophers is that their purely critical and negative method has only culminated in trivialising the greatest branch of theoretical knowledge. Furthermore, possibly unbeknown to themselves, modern British philosophers have devalued the power of thought for social good, simply through creating an intellectual environment which seems to say that all constructive thought is futile. Despite our earlier reference to the possible irrelevance of modern British philosophy to the "wider public," its general influence as a critical and negative force amongst educated laymen should not be underestimated. The influence of modern British philosophy in academic circles has extended far beyond the reach of those philosophers themselves. It has not merely induced a profound scepticism (which of course is a healthy characteristic in any society) but has gone on to raise an insuperable barrier against the possibility of constructing any positive vision for the future on which to build a better and more just society.

It is the philosophers, more than any other sector in the world of learning, who have been most responsible, albeit in a kind of innocence, for the paralysis of constructive thought in Britain. We shall return to additional reasons for this contention, later in these chapters, in considering the vital role of philosophy in effecting changed attitudes in society.

CHAPTER 30
The End of Freewill

"The loose anti-intellectualism which now threatens to take the place of the old intellectualism may prove to be infinitely more dangerous in the twentieth century."

Graham Wallas, *The Great Society*, Macmillan, 1925, p. 43.

1 - VI: Psychology's undermining of the belief in reason   2 - Gives a scientific basis to determinism   3 - Perceived invalidity of speculative thought   4 - Man's alleged incapacity for objectivity   5 - This has devastated our intellectual life

1 – VI Psychology's undermining of the belief in reason

The sixth reason for our intellectual paralysis stems from the role that psychology has played in undermining the belief in reason as a reliable guide to the good life.

However, in this context, it has to be noted that although philosophers must bear some shadow of blame for the dearth of constructive thought, the same blame cannot be cast on the great investigative psychologists, even though the latter have been far more influential in undermining the faith in reason and all the benefits of reasoning. This exoneration is because philosophers are pure theorists constrained only by the limits of reason and known science, whilst psychologists are systematic researchers on the periphery of pure science. It is not - and (barring exceptional circumstances) cannot be - the function of investigative psychologists to philosophise or construct systems for the political guidance of society. Psychologists are pure discoverers and can only publish the results of those discoveries - although that is not to deny that they may upset society with their revelations when, on the odd occasion, they happen to be "politically incorrect." But it is not their function to promote pre-conceived ideas, and therefore, in maintaining their integrity, they cannot be held responsible for the publication of what appear to them to be purely disinterested facts. Nonetheless, the publication of their findings has often called upon their courage, for this disinterested scientific approach has not protected them from the ire and controversy of groups in society, who in the past, would have chosen to suppress their writings had they had the power.

2 – Gives a scientific basis to determinism

The role that psychology has played in undermining reason as *de facto* a criterion for action, stems from the inescapability of determinism, fundamental to most schools of psychology. We are what we are because of our environment, and all our actions are a response to deep-seated unconscious psychological stimuli of which we are unaware. To the psychologist the notion of freewill is of negligible or no significance. His findings give a definitive scientific basis to determinism. All the knowledge of his profession would seem to point to the fact that freewill is a fiction - a convenient invention of lawyers and churchmen - so that the criminal might be hanged on grounds of justice and morality.

Whilst questions of right and wrong are fundamental to serious philosophers they are of limited or no concern to investigative psychologists. The principal function of the latter is the treatment and cure of souls by the revelation of truth through uncovering the unconscious. On these counts it is no wonder that psychologists, in the past, enraged those jealously guarding the frontiers of religion.

3 – Perceived invalidity of speculative thought

The truths of psychological determinism have revolutionised our outlook on the world, and thereby humanity has been faced by a major problem with regard to the validity of all speculative thought. Consequently, the nature of the unconscious mind and its influence on all our actions would seem to reduce reason and all attempts at rationalising to futile, vain, or hypocritical attempts to push through our most selfish personal ends. Such efforts would seem a mere gloss over our most primitive and irrational psychic motivations. It is implied - and indeed, understood - amongst opinion formers and academics, that no individual is capable of transcending the pure subjectivity of his being.

4 – Man's alleged incapacity for objectivity

Hence, in public life, in the modern world, the habit has arisen that no argument (howsoever sound or seemingly disinterested) should be taken at its face value to be judged on its own merits. Instead, it is more customary for the respondent to enquire into the motivations of the speaker in stating the argument, and more often, the perceived motivations frequently take on a greater significance in the mind's eye of the respondent than the argument itself taken in isolation. This attitude is disastrous to all attempts at constructive or creative thought for the welfare of the community. The communication of all ideas are poisoned through unsubstantiated suspicion in the process. No line of argument is accepted *per se* for what it is, but only within the shattering framework of some ulterior motivation which cannot but destroy or, at least devalue, the pure objectivity of the argument as something approaching a thing in itself.

5 – This has devastated our intellectual life

All this has exerted a devastating effect on intellectual life in Britain since the latter half of the 20th century, for if no argument may be accepted seriously and judged on its own merits, then what intelligent thinker is going to have the courage or expend the energy in formulating and expressing his own notions for the public good? There has never been such a dearth in the expression of disinterested political speculation as we find in Britain today. Instead, we only witness the political speculation of vested interest groups or of individuals in the pay of powerful bodies.

It should be noted here that our argument is not that the perception of consciously biassed or one-sided reasoning is a totally new phenomenon due to the emergence of modern psychology (for one-sided political reasoning may be traced back to the times of Plato or Cicero) but that the influence of modern psychology has given rise to an irrational scepticism which is destructive of reasoning itself.

When the Reasoner rather than the Reason is the prime object of attention all argumentation becomes pointless. This, in turn, leads to a special kind of prejudice, viz., to a prejudice aimed against the outward forms of a personality. In this situation, the voice, gestures and mannerisms of a speaker become the main focus of attention, whilst the content of his speech is either ignored or considered of secondary importance. In such a society the ground is well prepared for the destruction of all rational communication in place of confusion, violence, anarchy and tyranny.

CHAPTER 31
The Failure of The Academics

"Our capacity for effective physical organisation has enormously increased; but our ability to create external linkages by means of co-operative and civic associations on both a regional and world-wide basis ... has not kept pace with these mechanical triumphs."

Lewis Mumford, *The Culture of Cities*, Secker & Warburg, 1944 ed., p. 7.

1 - VII: Exclusive specialisation of knowledge   2 - The fear of the esoteric   3 - Jealously guarded knowledge has led to academic myopia   4 - Specialists becoming guardians of "priestly" knowledge   5 - They are called upon to resolve untenable issues   6 - But their practical knowledge fails them in this   7 - They are often not qualified to pontificate on socio-economic issues   8 - Interconnecting knowledge creates new knowledge   9 - Examples of this   10 - Above conclusions drawn from personal experience   11 - Sense of status overrides sense of curiosity

1 – VII Exclusive specialisation of knowledge

The seventh reason for the intellectual paralysis of our political life stems from the advanced specialisation of most spheres of knowledge into exclusive watertight departments. The sciences as well as other spheres of knowledge splintered into a huge number of specialisms during the 20th century, and there is no sign that the tendency is abating.

The phenomenon has clearly arisen due to the vast increase in available knowledge, and if this extreme specialisation has to be accepted as inevitable, it has brought in its wake unique problems with which our civilisation was never before confronted. Expressed in the briefest terms, it reflects the problem of the inability to assimilate usefully or understand this knowledge in the context of its meaning to our culture or civilisation.

2 – The fear of the esoteric

In becoming highly specialised and exclusive, knowledge has lost the nature of its *universality* in becoming esoteric. In concrete terms, this can be best understood when comparing the educated man or woman of the 18th or 19th centuries, with his or her equivalent in the latter part of the 20th century. Our forebears had the ability and confidence to discuss scientific and cultural topics with a breadth and depth that can rarely be found today. They had, in fact, an appreciation and understanding of universal knowledge which was valued and cherished as part of their existing culture. We are talking here, of course, of the educated - and usually self-educated - minority, and not of the tavern-talkers, representing the common majority, who may be found in every land and age. In contemporary Britain, on the other hand, we find the extraordinary situation whereby the higher on the ladder of academic achievement an individual may be found, then the greater is his fear of those spheres of knowledge not falling within his restricted speciality. The dangers of this to our future welfare, and indeed, to civilisation itself, can well be imagined.

3 – Jealously guarded knowledge has led to academic myopia

This process has led to a new kind of stupidity and bungling in academic circles which was not apparent to any significant degree in earlier centuries. This stupidity has arisen from two causes: firstly, from the refusal, fear, or inability to appreciate the need for the interconnectedness of different spheres of knowledge, so that each discipline has become so inward looking and narrow as to almost become an isolated thing-in-itself. In this kind of environment, academics not only come to nurture the esoteric nature of their speciality, but in defending that speciality - or rather, the status of their own knowledge - they adopt a sniffy attitude towards all contiguous disciplines. This, of course, is a prime symptom of cultural decadence - and nothing new in this world of ours.

4 – Specialists becoming guardians of "priestly" knowledge

It is a situation when the vested interests of existing knowledge are promoted, and the expansion of true knowledge (through the acceptance of changing circumstances) is abandoned. The truth no longer counts - for the rejection or fear of contiguous or interconnecting spheres of knowledge can have no other meaning than that. Such academics continue to promote the vested interests of their narrow speciality in terms of increased quantity, i.e. the accumulation of evermore data for measurement, but not in terms of quality, i.e. intelligent speculation, constructive scepticism, and most significantly, the consideration of their particular speciality in the context of the wider world and interconnecting spheres of knowledge. These kinds of attitudes were prevalent in academic and priestly circles during the long decline and static centuries of Egyptian civilisation, as also in Greece during the third and fourth centuries of our own era.

5 – They are called upon to resolve untenable issues

The second cause for the stupidity and bungling of many academics has arisen when circumstances have forced them to face the hard world of reality. This is a direction in which they are not averse to move, for they are often inveigled into compromise by flattery and the financially rewarding inducements of powerful patrons. Many academics are called upon to be the great high priests of our time and few decline the honour and the limelight which this brings. When the economy is in crisis or politicians fall out or know not what to do, or when major industrialists are faced by an untenable situation, then it is always the academics who are pulled out of their cloistered halls to provide the magic cure. They are called upon as a last resort because all else has failed, and because they are a last resort, they virtually hold the status of high priests. That is, their every word is unquestioned and their answers are seized upon as final since there are no others on the horizon. Of course, like high priests, they are intent on serving their new employers (even though they adopt a disinterested guise), but imperceptibly, they serve the vested interests of their paymasters.

6 – But their practical knowledge fails them in this

This, however, is only the start of their awkward dilemma. As academics emerging from the environment of a narrow albeit respected speciality, they are forced within a short while to extend their knowledge to other contiguous disciplines. But unhappily, their academic speciality is not relevant to solving the problems they are called upon to cure - even though it may seem the closest at hand. This, however, is not good enough! In calling upon this government department and that, or in interviewing an eminent banker followed by a trades union leader, they are soon involved in questions of a socio-economic or political nature that might fall into a dozen or more recognised academic specialities. Consequently, such academics, who previous to their latest calling would never have dared whisper a pronouncement on any matter not falling within their narrow and specific discipline, are then found to be pontificating on all manner of matters for which they have no practical qualifications. Overnight they are found to have a confidence which they lacked before. Seemingly, they are transformed persons.

7 – They are often not qualified to pontificate on socio-ecnomic issues

The reality is that often they are dishing out instructions or advice on which they have no more claim to authority than a loquacious tippler. In this role it is not knowledge which clothes them with authority but the mantle of their academic status. The validity of such a statement, of course, must be tested by the outcome, and it is clear that all the knowledge of the numerous academics called upon to solve the crises of the past decades have been abysmal judged in the light of their anticipated long-term outcome. Although in fairness it has to be said that government departments have sometimes placed one academic against another - like cocks in a pit - the failure of our academics to shine as paragons of wisdom in the sphere of political life is principally accountable to *ignorance.*

8 – Interconnecting knowledge creates new knowledge

Such ignorance is solely due to the failure to create new spheres of knowledge through interconnecting contiguous academic disciplines. This is the greatest need of our age! It has to be understood - difficult as this may be to comprehend - that by systematically connecting related spheres of knowledge, new knowledge is thereby created. The difficulty, however, is that this can only be achieved through the medium of constructive speculation. Another difficulty is that we cannot easily draw on a paradigm illustrating such new spheres of knowledge - at least not from the recent past.

9 – Examples of this

To those with a somewhat longer historical perspective, however, it may be recollected that August Comte invented something which he called *Sociology*, drawn from a variety of academic disciplines. This has served a most useful function in society since that time in the mid-19th century. More recently, it may be contended that Freud developed psychoanalysis by bringing together medicine, psychology and a certain function of religion. Conversely, what used to be referred to as "Natural Philosophy" in the 18th century now divides into innumerable separate sciences. To contend, therefore, that the bringing together of different specialities in creating new knowledge is merely an empty abstraction, is therefore a nonsense. It is indeed the type of knowledge most needed today.

10 – Above conclusions drawn from personal experience

It was through the hard path of personal experience that I first came to learn of the dismal limitations of our leading academics. Some years ago, whilst organising the Campaign For Industry, I called on and had long discussions with many professors qualified in closely related fields. There was one particular institution that I called upon on a number of occasions over a period of months. In such a great rabbit warren, housing hundreds of academics, each in his own cubicle, side by side, in endless corridors with more doors than wall space, it might be thought that such cheek by jowl contiguity would at least have engendered a liberal sympathy - or at least a curiosity - between the proponents of one speciality and another. Far from it! Each professor was as remote from the other as if divided by a mountain range or the expanse of an ocean.

11 – Sense of status overrides sense of curiosity

But my major difficulty, as the founder of the Campaign For Industry, in discussing socio-economic topics with these alleged scholars of distinction, was coming up against the constant barrier of blind gaps in their knowledge. No single topic from the perspective of Social Capitalist Values could be discussed in any depth because these values crossed the barriers of existing academic disciplines. Consequently, there always came a point in the discussion, when my respondent exclaimed, "I'm afraid I know nothing about that - you'll have to see Professor So-and-so down the corridor. That's his speciality and I'ld never touch it." The conversation would be drawn to a sharp halt, and on each occasion I would be left dumbfounded, not merely by the limited knowledge of my respondent, but more so by his lack of an enquiring mind.

Increasingly, I was left with the impression that these academics did not value their knowledge for its use to society - as otherwise their curiosity would have got the better of their ignorance - but purely for the status it conferred on their professional role. Another factor I encountered in all these meetings, was the lack of balance of these academics in their perspective of the world - an imbalance due solely, I believe, to the cramped nature of the their restricted disciplines.

CHAPTER 32
The Revolt Against Reason

"Not less but more reason and an unabating search for the truth can correct the errors of a one-sided rationalism - not a pseudo-religious obscurantism."

Erich Fromm, *Man For Himself,* Routledge & Kegan Paul, 1949, p. ix.

1 – Current problems can only be solved by creating new knowledge

To anyone viewing objectively the major socio-economic problems facing Britain today, it must easily be perceived that those problems cannot be equated with deficiencies in existing specific academic disciplines. If indeed the problems are broken down into separate elements for consideration by different bodies of learning, then those problems can no longer be considered as they really are.

If they are broken into different elements they are no longer what they were in their whole state. To make a concrete comparison: if a car is malfunctioning it is not taken apart to be examined by a dozen mechanics each with a different expertise. It is simply examined by an expert who has an understanding of the mechanism in total. It should likewise be so in the realm of politics, but in fact, it never is. The body politic can either be conceived as a living organism or as a complex piece of machinery, but in either case, its treatment only calls for understanding, and as we have said, that understanding needs the creation of new spheres of knowledge. It is to the discredit of the academic world that it has stood aside and failed to create this new knowledge for the political future.

2 – Academics seek safety in their ivory towers

This returns us to the acute problems generated by extreme specialisation itself. It should be understood that we are not criticising the process of advanced specialisation - for it is both inevitable and necessary - but rather the ills which have sprung from the process. Most notably it has resulted in making mice out of men and women -

i.e. men made timid and over-awed by the vastness of knowledge by which we are confronted. As each speciality has become more professionalised, more organised, more demanding and more esoteric in its nature, so correspondingly it has become more frightening and threatening to academics in contiguous disciplines. Hence, it is only natural that many academics should seek safety for themselves, and such safety can only be found by locking themselves into their own separate ivory towers.

This fear of knowledge by academics, and even greater fear of theorising, is further exacerbated by the increased instability of all spheres of knowledge. In this context Bryan Magee in summarising the views of Prof. Ernest Gellner has stated that, "our knowledge has become so extensive, so complex, so technical and so specialised that it has to be formulated in language which is decreasingly related to that of ordinary life and interpersonal relationships. This in turns makes it ever less available to us as a basis for a view of the world that we can actually live with, in an everyday sense. The upshot of this is that we come very powerfully to feel that there is something dehumanising, depersonalising, about the consequences of the growth of our own knowledge."[143] In this way, all the problems in the world of learning, and the perception of the world in human terms, are merely compounded. We are in greatest need for the integration of sociology with economics, and then with philosophy, for with the achievement of that we would see the creation of a genuine social science.

3 – The fear of constructive theorising

The most damaging outcome of the advanced specialisation of knowledge in the 20th and 21st centuries is the fear of constructive theorising as found amongst the educated sectors of the population, for without serious efforts to theorise, no major ideas for the change or improvement of society can be properly developed. The most visible outcome of this advanced specialisation is the dearth of thought-provoking literature with a constructive purpose. Such literature seemingly came to an abrupt halt with the close of the 1950s, and this cannot be entirely put down to the revolution in the world of publishing which took place in the subsequent decades. Although hundreds of publishing enterprises have gone into liquidation since

---

143 Bryan Magee, *Men of Letters*, op. cit., p. 257.

that time, and despite the fact that publishing has now become the monopoly concern of a handful of financiers employing highly sophisticated marketing techniques in pushing their wares, this cannot entirely explain the dearth of respected and controversial thinkers who were still so numerous during the first half of the last century.

These were thinkers with irrepressible self-confidence, many who dared to be outrageous, and all who courageously stood by their convictions. Some were eccentrics or "cranky" but all had a positive contribution of some kind to make to British intellectual life on the popular front. If one looks to those in the forefront of their time, there are few today who can compare in stature with the Huxleys, Shaw, H.G. Wells, Walter Lippmann, H.L. Mencken, C.E.D. Joad, etc., etc. These were men who captured the popular imagination. In their place, today, are a handful of esoteric unknowns (some of whom are worthy in their own right) sponsored and published by various universities. This, however, can be no substitute for the popular knowledge directly communicated to the masses by some of the greatest minds of their age.

The extreme specialisation of knowledge has therefore not merely led to the fear of theoretical knowledge but to its demise. The academics, meanwhile, from whom one might expect some kind of intellectual leadership, merely exist - contemptibly - in fear and jealousy of one another.

4 – VIII The revolt against reason

The eighth reason for the intellectual paralysis of our political life stems from most of the seven points cited above. It is attributable to the general decline in the faith in the power of reason and rational decision-making. It is a characteristic which most distinguished the nature of the 20th century and was responsible for the major tragedies and destruction witnessed over the past eighty years. For this reason the revolt against the power of reason has to be placed in a separate category from those points previously considered.

Despite all the material improvements which have taken place since 1900, our descendants are likely to conclude that the late century is to be listed as amongst the worst during the past two millennia. Its apparent nastiness, with wars and human destruction on an unprecedented scale, is made to seem all the worse in view of the great intellectual and moral advances, and the spirit of optimism, felt towards the close of the 19th century. To such thinkers as J.S. Mill or T.H. Green, and indeed to the majority of our informed Victorian ancestors, the sheer horror of the 20th century would have been inconceivable. It would have defied the law of progress. Such hate and conflict and destruction was supposedly well behind them by two hundred years - i.e. with the terrible religious wars of the 17th century. Since the Victorian age, of course, we have learnt a great deal more about the nature of humankind and society - and indeed, about the nature of progress.

5 – Has penetrated all political parties

The revolt against reason in the sphere of politics simply reflects the call to exploit unthinkingly our most selfish feelings in achieving political ends. Thought is to be expunged in the place of passion and subjective vested interests. The Nazis expressed it in terms of the call "to think with one's blood." The Communists expressed it in terms of the call for class war and class aspirations as the criteria for achieving political truth. It is also implicit in the irrationality of determinism for as Isaiah Berlin has argued in criticising the false "scientific" pretensions of Marxism, "central theoretical issues can be solved only by rational thought - mathematical, philosophical, legal, philological, biological, physical, chemical, working often at high levels of abstraction, as each case demands."[144] It is in this sense that the authority of Reason must transcend that of science, for science is in itself self-limiting.

But Fascists and Old Socialists have not been alone in the battle against reason. The attitude, in some degree, has penetrated all political groups in the Western democracies. Just as Tories have insisted on the need for maximising short term rentier profits as their criteria for the good society (even though entire industries may be destroyed in the process), so Liberal Democrats have opted out of any attempt at serious social thinking by accepting a futile mish-mash of benevolent intentions to salve their middle class consciences. It is no wonder, therefore, that the previous century was marked by wars and social strife in their most malignant forms. There is no question that the paralysis of our intellectual life through the overthrow of reason has meant the abdication of progress.

------

144   Isaiah Berlin in *Men of Ideas*, op. cit., pp. 23-24.

6 – Unreason and the revolt against culture

But the 20th century revolt against reason goes far beyond the sphere of politics. It has been especially reflected in literature and the arts, where blind emotionalism, irrationality and violence have been glorified in contradistinction to form, harmony and the search for order. As Prof. Joad commented more than sixty years ago, "most post-war literature ... seems to me to be definitely retrogressive; it makes not for but against civilisation, and emphasises the forces of unreason in human nature. ... The world, I believe, is less reasonable than it was, or rather it is more disposed to use its reason to belittle reason and exalt emotion."[145]

During the past three decades the revolt against reason has been reflected in the upsurge of interest in the occult and witchcraft, astrology and fortune telling. As the influence of pragmatism has made its way in education, literary attributes and language comprehension have been devalued, so that each individual might "do his own thing." Spelling and grammar are no longer regarded as serious subjects for training, and with the general decline of language ability, the rising generation inevitably experience a difficulty in reasoning, and so in distinguishing reality from fantasy. Consequently, the occult, mysticism and witchcraft develop an appeal in society they could never have held in an earlier and more rational era. This tendency has moved so far that even bookshops and libraries have the effrontery to lump works on occultism and witchcraft together with philosophy - the latter usually being very much in the minority.

In this way, the most important discipline of contemplative learning is mixed up with superstitious verbiage which can only confuse the search for truth. But worse than that is the consequential revolt against any constructive use of the intellect. As a leading contemporary thinker has remarked, "what characterises our time is less the struggle of one set of ideas against another than the mounting wave of hostility to all ideas as such."[146]

---

145   C.E.M. Joad, *The Book of Joad*, Faber & Faber, 1935, p. 100.
146   Isaiah Berlin, *Four Essays On Liberty*, OUP, 1969, p. 32.

CHAPTER 33
The Nature of Reason

"All conflict is the result solely of the clash of reason with the imperfectly rational or irrational."

Melvin Richter, *The Politics of Conscience,* Weidenfeld & Nicolson, 1964, p. 210.

1 – Faith in reason: a first step towards safeguarding civilisation

If our most urgent and endemic political problems are to be resolved - indeed, if our planet and humanity are to be spared the Armageddon of some final catastrophe - the first step to be taken in the right direction must be a return to the belief in the power of reason. But this is *only* a first step. The *belief* in reason alone - as belief of any kind - vital as this is, is not sufficient to save humanity. Reason must in itself, as an objective entity, be made a tool sufficient to serve the greater purpose of the human race.

There is no other path we can choose to follow. This is because, in the words of Mannheim, "abstraction is a tool of enquiry,"[147] and so necessary for any intelligent achievement. The unthinking pragmatism of the Western world, with all its short-termism and implicit selfishness, is just a recipe for disaster in compounding present problems. Meanwhile, the historical materialism, everywhere essential to the doctrine of Old Socialism, is bankrupt, as Old Socialism itself is in intellectual ruin, as we stand at the frontier of a new era. In a world carried forward by technology, and moving faster than our ability to understand its changes, Conservatism in all its forms can only act as a regressive influence, or else attempt to create an anodyne illusive facade suggesting that all is as it always was. Liberals, meanwhile, can create nothing new but repeat the platitudes of their 19th century forebears - only in a modern dress.

---

147   Karl Mannheim, *Essays On The Sociology of Culture,* Routledge & Kegan Paul, 1956, p. 55.

2 – Reason is not sophistry but disinterested necessity

The instrument of reason, as an objective entity, therefore becomes a moral as well as a political imperative, since there is nothing else to fulfil the function of serving the true political needs of humanity. But the nature of this reason calls for clearer definition. It does not mean mere sophistry or the arbitrary subjectivity of individuals or groups. That would only perpetuate conflict or reflect the pursuit of egotistical vested interests. In paraphrasing the words of a major thinker, "it is the essence of reason that its entire process is necessary. Nothing in it can be arbitrary or accidental. It does not begin and end nowhere. Its progress is fixed by its own rational principles and cannot be altered by our individual whims. ... The essential character of reason is necessity. ... The process of reason is no doing of ours. We can neither create nor alter it. We can only discover it."148

Reason has to be at once disinterested, definitive, universal and constructive. Its objectivity must be such as to show an equal regard for all persons and groups within the context of social justice. Its certainty must be such as all its conclusions are no less definitive than the statement that two and two make four. Its universality must be of a kind that its conclusions appeal to the hearts and minds of all well-intentioned people in their better frame of mind. The constructive function of reason must embrace a logic stimulating a creative practical function, the outcome of which must fall within the system of that greater logic. This means that everything emanating from the system of logic, proceeds as a natural and inevitable process, belonging intrinsically to the whole. The purpose of such a logic and such a system is to ensure both compatibility and direction, as otherwise such reason could not maintain its universality. Only in this way can reason as a constructive method be established.

3 – And this must stem from sociological demands

But reason on such foundations cannot exist in a vacuum. It can only be constructed in the light of current knowledge and science, and the understanding of man in the light of his principal needs. These things must be considered with cool objectivity, both in their isolation and in interaction, and also in view of current custom and law. In considering the political issues facing a community, a sociological

---

148   W.T. Stace, *The Philosophy of Hegel*, Macmillan, NY, 1924, p. 257.

analysis must first be undertaken which succeeds in uncovering all the overt and hidden or subconscious vested interests of the different sectors of the community, and these must be revealed in a political context aiming to achieve disinterested social justice. The mirror thus held up to the community must then inspire the need for political change through its moral appeal.

4 – Constructive reasoning must be the method

Reason must then be utilised in constructing new forms for replacing those to be demolished in a society which is changed by the conscious efforts of those intent on the well-being of society. In such a society the rational as well as the General Will predominates, and greater long-term benefits are more easily achieved than in those societies where a greater emphasis is laid on the process of continuing conflict between economic or class groups. It has to be emphasised, however, that the outcome of this reason as a constructive method - even when most successful in its purpose - does not entail the achievement of perfection. It does not reach something permanent or static - something for all time - because knowledge as science is ever expanding, and the interaction of humankind with the environment not only changes *it* but *him* and *her*. Change, in a free world, it has to be understood, is the only permanence. But reason, as a constructive method, is the one hope for achieving change with least pain, in maintaining the demands for a just and democratic society.

CHAPTER 34
The Reality of Ideas

"Science is competent to tell us something about everything; but it cannot tell us the whole truth about anything."

C.E.M. Joad, *Guide To Modern Thought*, Faber & Faber, 1933, p. 106.

1 – Recognition of the ultimate reality of ideas is necessary for this

This argument for the belief in the need to utilise reason as a constructive method means that we uphold the ultimate reality of Ideas. This is because without Ideas, no constructive method or constructive theories can be formulated for interlinking the different spheres of specialised knowledge.   Without ideas no sensible or radical proposals could be made for changes in society.

But there is a more important reason for upholding the notion of the ultimate reality of ideas.   This stems from the necessity of humankind taking his fate into his own hands rather than accepting a determinism laid down by science (i.e. philosophical conclusions commonly drawn from the theories of evolution or psychology), or a determinism laid down by political doctrines (i.e. the conclusions of historical materialism of one kind or another).   If humankind is to take his fate into his own hands, then he will find no consolation (as we have already found) by turning to any contemporary school of British philosophy - and for that matter, he will find little hope by turning to any other school of modern philosophy, on the Continent or elsewhere. As for Pragmatism, the ruling school of philosophy in the contemporary industrialised West, as we have already explained, this merely entails the negation of thought in a call to follow our instinctual hunches and appetites.

2 – Deterministic attitudes both immoral and impractical

Whilst the experience of Pragmatism has demonstrated clearly its futility, since the short-sightedness of its method merely compounds problems one on top of another; there is something immoral in accepting fatalism or a deterministic philosophy. If our future is pre-ordained, which is the underlying message of evolutionists and many social psychologists, then there is little point in trying to change things. In this frame of mind, it soon becomes easy to slip into intellectually lazy or apathetic attitudes, for the stimulus towards constructive thought is taken away, and this is exactly what occurred during the 20th century. Furthermore, as we have already noted, it also becomes too easy to slip into a purely subjective frame of mind (indeed, implicit in determinism is the senselessness of objectivity) whereby we nurture selfish or narrow interests maintaining conflict in society. The Judaeo-Christian and Islamic traditions, of course, have always pointed to the immorality of deterministic attitudes by underlining the nature of humankind as a free agent - free and morally responsible for choosing the right or the wrong path.

3 – Freewill properly understood necessitates objectivity

Hence we are arguing that reason as a constructive method can only exist for humankind if he exists within a cosmos allowing for freewill. Freewill, however, must be understood in its true meaning. It does not simply mean the ability of an animal to follow its instincts in sniffing out a trail, or choosing this hollow rather than that in building its nest. In that sense freewill would be meaningless, for by that definition, even artificially constructed beetles with in-built magnetic repulsion and attraction sensitivity, interweaving amongst one another on a tray, may be said to have freewill. Furthermore, freewill does not simply mean the ability of a person to choose this dish rather than that, or to follow one sensuous desire rather than another. Freewill in its true meaning calls for the objectivity of a higher understanding, i.e. of the nature of the individual's relationship with his external environment; viz., a conscious appreciation of the need for an ordering of the universe so that he might integrate his being as a co-operative unit within the whole. Freewill necessitates the need to think about thought, for objectivity is impossible without this, and a consideration of the ordering of the universe and one's relationship within it is impossible without objectivity.

4 – Need for speculation transcending personal experience

In arguing for the ultimate reality of ideas, we are therefore emphasising the necessity that humankind must have the ability to ponder his existence intelligently as a social being (as well as in other more abstract contexts) independently of his experience or the empiricism of science.   There are two reasons for this necessity. Firstly, without the ability to formulate abstract principles and strive for objectivity, he remains imprisoned by the subjectivity of his being and immediate experience. He cannot develop his imaginative or creative potential.   Secondly, he cannot develop a moral sense of the universe. He may develop a sense of right and wrong in relationship to his own actions - but that is not enough, for even a dog has such a sense. But what he cannot develop is an ability to judge situations and others, not affecting his immediate welfare, in a disinterested ethical context.   In either of these two circumstances, without the capacity to think objectively, a mature person remains spiritually dead or empty, or retains a simplistic childish attitude to life. In the latter instance, if these grown people retain a naive moral sense, then such rare beings are mere innocents or "Idiots" as they were onetime described by Dostoevsky. As for the rest, and the great majority, they remain morally deficient, and are usually marked by those characteristics described as "degenerate" - "the spoilt things" in our society.

5 – And the individual achieves this through maturity

The efforts of the individual to objectify his relationship with the environment is not a complex process. It comes with maturity. The individual will stand by his contention that the objectivity of his Ideas are *real*, and that those Ideas do in themselves reflect reality. If, on the contrary, he is told that those ideas may be traced back to the stimulus of a psychological experience, he will merely reply that that fact is irrelevant. He may accept the contention of the psychoanalyst or deny it, but in either case, he will maintain both the *reality* and the objectivity of the ideas internally expressed.   This is because such ideas and such objectivity, uncovered by his own consciousness (and admittedly, in all possibility arising from psychological stimuli) take on a reality which is totally independent of his own existence. In contending the real existence of such objectivity, and the reality of such ideas, as they belong to the individual, is not to arouse controversy.

6 – Denying the reality of ideas has led to our intellectual paralysis

It is in the realm of discussing the social sciences, or politics, ethics, aesthetics, and other major topics not lending themselves to the exactitude of a scientific method, that the ultimate reality of Ideas is denied in our contemporary age by academics and power wielders. Of course the reality of any Idea must stand up to the rigorous scrutiny of examination - for one idea is not as valid as the next, and no credence can be given to pure whim or fancy - but unfortunately such questions are not even looked at in our contemporary age. The notion of the reality of ideas is simply rejected out of hand prior to any separate consideration of cited examples. This reflects a crazy situation and fully explains the intellectual paralysis of our age. We have already elaborated how this situation came about in earlier chapters, and although the causes may be explained they can never be excused. In an intellectually healthy environment, there is no more reason why ideas should be denied their reality in the world of respected public expression, than they should be in the world of the sane man or woman's private consciousness.

7 – Promoting the reality of ideas for political problem solving is a revolutionary approach

The formulation and use of Ideas as a basis for constructive theory, and the discriminating insistence on both the objectivity and reality of those Ideas, is a startling if not revolutionary method in approaching the intellectual problems of our age. It is, however, a vitally necessary approach - for there is no other - in unlocking the intellectual paralysis of our age. As a method it will not only succeed in formulating an imaginative and creative approach in solving our great social and environmental problems, but act as a social dynamic in both unifying communities and driving them forward towards a course of desired action.

CHAPTER 35
The New Idealism

"A philosophy of life, in harmony with the noblest feelings and
cleared of superstition, is the great want of these times."

J.S. Mill, *Letters*, Elliott (ed.), Vol. II, p. 363 (Diary extract of 23rd
January 1854).

1 - This entails the call for a new Idealistic philosophy   2 - Justified as a methodology for constructive thought   3 - Failure of mathematics as a basis for constructive philosophy   4 - Materialism versus Anti-materialism debate invalidated by 20th century physics   5 - The greater realism of such a philosophy   6 - Benefits of the constructive or idealistic method   7 - Characteristics of the New Idealism

1 – This entails the call for a new Idealistic philosophy

The advocacy of Ideas as a methodology for constructive thought entails nothing less than the call for the creation of a new Idealistic philosophy - a philosophy we have not seen flourish in this country since the age of T.H. Green, Bradley, Nettleship and Bernard Bosanquet at the start of the previous century. But a new Idealistic philosophy would be markedly different from that of previous eras, as indeed implicit in progress, is the fact that there can be no exact duplication of previous patterns of thought.

A new idealistic philosophy would be more intellectually rigorous than that of past eras, embodying a greater clarity of expression and appealing to a far larger proportion of the population. As with any idealistic philosophy, it would be imbued with a spirit of optimism, not only holding out hope for the future but offering a source of inspiration. Truth, according to the strictest criteria, must remain the ultimate test for any new idealistic philosophy.

2 - Justified as a methodology for constructive thought

The justification for idealism must lie in its efficacy as a methodology for constructive thought in the analysis and solution of problems, from their abstract or theoretical stage until they are carried through to their practical completion. The most valued schools of philosophy are all measured according to their positive and practical effects on the societies in which they flourish. If the New Idealism, now being advanced, fails to turn the wheels in our factories and mines in giving full employment to our people, it is of little value to the community or to itself.

The methodology of the New Idealism, on the most abstract level, entails the pursuit of monism as opposed to pluralism, since this demands the thinking through of problems to their ultimate conclusion. Pluralistic philosophies, on the contrary, are those of the intellectually weak or the lazy or the hypocritical. In the words of the eminent contemporary British Hegelian philosopher, G.R.G. Mure, "pluralism is the failure to philosophise; it is ultimately not thinkable."149 It should be noted, however, that the advocacy of a monistic as opposed to a pluralistic methodology has nothing whatsoever to do with the description of a desired state of society. That is, we live today in a multi-cultural and pluralistic society which is at the same time both acceptable and desirable.

The second aspect of its methodology is its *universalisation*, i.e., the consideration of problems on the individual, the communal and the cosmic levels, as with all the most significant schools of philosophy.

This, in turn, will lead to its third aspect, viz., the foundation of moral imperatives, drawing their authority from the concept of the Supreme Good, since ultimate and objective authority on ethical matters can only be drawn from such a source. The criticism which has been aimed at Utilitarianism has long since demolished any claims of this materialistic philosophy as a force for interpreting the supreme good.

The fourth aspect is the recognition, within its dialectic, of what is currently described as "water logic" in contradistinction to "rock logic" in solving the community's most intransigent problems. Implicit in this is the avoidance of senseless social conflict (e.g. costly and protracted strikes), and may be described as the Confucian aspect of the New Idealism.

The fifth aspect of its methodology is the construction of sound foundations for certitude, so that actions by and for the community may be carried out with decisiveness, free of hesitation or lingering doubt.

The sixth and overriding aspect is the recognition of the ultimate reality and power of ideas and thought as a desirable basis for individual and social action, in recognition of the fact that historically, all counterblasts against philosophical idealism, howsoever well-

---

149 G.R.G. Mure, *Idealist Epilogue*, OUP, 1978, p. 15.

founded as intellectual constructs in themselves, have fallen on the stony ground of their own nihilism.

3 – Failure of mathematics as a basis for constructive thought

The existence or cause of this nihilism is intellectually explicable through the limitations of mathematics and science employed as a useful basis for philosophical analysis or logic. Since the start of the last century, the fallibility of mathematics and science as a source for rock-hard authority in the sphere of speculation has long been recognised. A long time span has occurred since Moore and Russell published their findings at the start of the 20th century. We can now with confidence assert that philosophical concepts based on the theory of ideas stand on much sounder foundations than philosophical concepts based on the shifting theories of mathematics and science. Since 1900 the wheel has turned full circle, and May Sinclair's rearguard defensive action has at last been fully vindicated in the light of her contention that, "all idealisms, constructive or destructive, are based on the ultimate inability of mathematics to defend its own position. And it is claimed that with the reform of Symbolic Logic, the perfecting of the formal machinery, the bottom is knocked out of idealism."[150]

And now in the real world it is found that mathematics can have no validity as a basis for constructive speculation. And because of this, it will not be a threat to the New Idealism of the future. The conclusions of mathematics, in the context of philosophy, are simply irrelevant. But put the other way round, as G.R.G. Mure has argued, "mathematics has always been poison to philosophy,"[151] or at least, has left falsely that intellectual impression. Hence there is seemingly no substitute for philosophical idealism in helping to solve the contemporary world situation.

---

150 May Sinclair, *A Defence of Idealism*, Macmillan, 1917, p. 176. Interesting as this book may be, written as it was in the shadow of Moore and Russell, it cannot unreservedly be cited as a defence for Social Capitalism. The chapters on psychology and psychoanalysis, for example, entirely misrepresent the then new science.

151 G.R.G. Mure, op. cit., p. 11.

4 – Materialism versus anti-materialism debate invalidated by 20th century physics

Discussions of the New Idealism will not revolve around the futile age-old debate of Materialism versus Anti-materialism, for 20th century physics has destroyed the entire hypothesis on which 19th century materialism and materialistic philosophy was based. And neither will it revolve around the debate of mind versus matter, for as Bertrand Russell has argued, "the stuff of which the world of our experience is composed is, in my belief, neither mind nor matter, but something more primitive than either. Both mind and matter seem to be composite, and the stuff of which they are compounded lies in a sense between the two, in a sense above them both, like a common ancestor."[152] And this stuff has been called, by the American Realists, "Neutral stuff" or "Neutral entities." The New Idealism, whilst accepting the latest conclusions of physics, will adopt the theory of Ideas (for achieving the highest truths of constructive thought) as a hypothesis or methodology, in a similar way that thinkers from Hobbes to Rawls have adopted the Original Position for their Social Contract theories as hypotheses for revealing their own philosophical truths.

5 – The greater realism of such a philosophy

The realism of the Idealistic approach can be clearly understood in the light of the following two factors: firstly, on the insistence of achieving long-term solutions, being total and all-encompassing in their purpose. This contrasts sharply with the short-termism of the pragmatic method, usually the outcome of vested interests or the messy compromises arising from conflict. Secondly, Idealism calls for a much broader consensus than the pragmatic approach, since the solution of problems needs to be rationally justified on an objective and monistic basis, and the arguments presented with a deeper and more convincing clarity. This contrasts with the pluralistic superficiality of pragmatism as it now serves one master and then another in piling incompatible pieces of legislation one on top of the other. The idealistic approach inevitably carries a greater intellectual authority, and its conclusions tend more to be based on the

---

152 Bertrand Russell, *The Analysis of Mind*, Allen & Unwin, 1921, pp. 10-11.

conclusions of social justice and morality. Its practicality in solving problems in their entirety, from all aspects, can easily be perceived.

6 – Benefits of the constructive or idealistic method

The benefits of such a constructive or idealistic method in approaching our major political issues may be summarised as under:-
1. That issues are analysed and creatively resolved on an objective basis in the light of broadly based sociological criteria, as opposed to their biassed consideration by particular vested interest groups, economic, class, religious, or other.
 2. That issues are considered within an ethical framework related to the broader needs of the community, as opposed to the more common attitude of pure expediency, or the alleged demands of "neutral necessity" on the grounds that no other alternatives are practical.
3. That issues are soundly examined in the light of well-informed knowledge and science, intellectually in depth, and after open debate, as opposed to being pushed through by the well organised efforts of powerful cliques huddled together behind the closed doors of a committee room.
4. That issues are sensitively considered in the light of historical and cultural factors, supported by empirical evidence, as opposed to the hurried and careless intuitionism of contemporary pragmatists.

7 – Characteristics of the New Idealism

The technical definition of Idealistic philosophy, as we have said, means the recognition of the ultimate reality of Ideas, or the triumph of mind over matter, but there is another aspect of Idealism more commonly held by the majority. This entails the striving towards the Best, often with mystical or religious overtones. Whilst the New Idealism will repudiate mysticism or any kind of metaphysics (i.e. reasoning beyond physics) which cannot stand the test of some empirically based argument, it will nonetheless accept the possibility of religious overtones, in the sense of a belief in a moral presence transcending humanity. Belief in such a superhuman presence, however, will not necessarily give credence to any myths, superstitions or doctrines of existing religions or sects. This is because the reasoning behind the new politics or Social Capitalism must be universal in its appeal, in the sense of presenting a clarity worldwide that is no more complex than the assertion that two and two make four, whilst religions and sects (as history has amply demonstrated) are divisive and conflicting in maintaining doctrines and myths which fly in the face of truth, reason, ordinary commonsense, and sometimes, even practical morality. If the above four points lay emphasis on the constructive or immediately practical aspects of idealism, the following five points put emphasis on its underlying purpose:-

1. In identifying and promoting a set of policies within a framework expressing a common will.

2. In standing by the principle that the desirable is always possible or can be made so.

3. In the belief that the will for the best must be made to prevail in the end, and that that should be the prime motivation of government.

4. In the formulation of a general political philosophy, or theory embodying all major policies, and serving as a unifying and directional force within the community.

5. In pursuing the democratic will in achieving the above.

There is no question about the need for a New Idealistic philosophy, and it has to be emphasised that that need is practical in its purpose in the sense of achieving concrete political reform. As for the need of satisfying the intellect, an equally demanding requirement of our age, since we are dependent on this for effecting change, we might well heed the words of Albert Schweizer when he wrote that, "the collapse of philosophy and the rise and influence of scientific modes of thought made it impossible to arrive at an idealist theory which should satisfy thought."[153] It is our purpose, through developing the foundations of Social Capitalism, to establish a New Idealism which may fully satisfy the intellect for the new millennium.

---

153 Albert Schweizer, *The Decay & Restoration of Civilization*, A. & C. Black, 1950 ed., p. 84.

CHAPTER 36
A Warning For The Future

"I do not believe that a tolerable existence is possible for an individual or a society without some sense of duty. There is only one kind of duty that the modern man can acknowledge without superstition, and that is a duty to the community."

Bertrand Russell, *The Prospects of Industrial Civilization*, Allen & Unwin, 1959 ed., p. 157.

1 - Need to appreciate the reality of the "As is" situation   2 - Irrationality of beliefs held by the majority   3 - How the young mind is prepared for this   4 - Empty symbols have a stronger appeal than concrete truths   5 - The future: True democracy or an elective dictatorship?   6 - Vacuum in the sphere of reforming politics   7 - This portends great dangers ahead   8 - How an ideological vacuum may compound political ills

1 – Need to appreciate the reality of the "As is" situation

The above clearly implies the need for a system or doctrine to serve as the objective base for a politics serving the best good of the community. Idealists, however, must be Realists in every sense of the term: not only in appreciating the need that the best solutions must be made to succeed over the pragmatic approach of the sorry success of botched compromise, but in fully comprehending the nature of things as they exist at the present moment in time.

The "As is" situation cannot simply be dismissed in substituting it for the "ought" situation. Particular note has to be taken of the fact governing the overwhelming inertia or conservatism found amongst all sectors of the population against change of any kind. All change is painful or painfully inconvenient - including improvement - since it demands mental and physical exertion towards adaptation to new conditions. Even the darkened pig sty is sometimes preferable as opposed to the sheer effort of raising the body and strutting towards the warm sunlight and clean air.

2 – Irrationality of beliefs held by the majority

In this context, a full understanding must be had for the vast mass of humanity which prefers a no-change situation - and indeed, is often fearful even, of the talk of change of any kind. The mass of the populace have loyalties they may never forego. In the realm of politics, the majority hold beliefs that are false, irrational or even immoral by any objective criteria, and yet they stand by them with an unthinking trust.

They do this because they were "born into" those loyalties. They do not bother to question such allegedly held beliefs, simply because they are never "thought about," and if they were probed in depth by the Socratic method as to what they believed, it would often be found that such beliefs were superficial if not non-existent. This is because the majority, accepting unthinkingly, the beliefs of their forefathers, lay greater credence on labels, myths and superficial exterior appearances than on reality itself.

In fairness, it has to be said, that the sources of their beliefs (i.e. the character of political parties) change with the passing of time, but these changes go often unnoticed. Hence the beliefs of people are *not* really those of their forefathers (who might have been included amongst the early proponents of new political ideas and movements), since both social conditions change and political movements change. In the real world, everything is in a state of flux. Unfortunately, in the world of perceptions, on the contrary, things become fixed and outdated, and labels take on a reality in themselves - becoming totem poles.

In talking of the majority, it may be said that there is no more chance of a person changing his political allegiance, or his cherished prejudices, than there is of the leopard changing its spots. The greatest disasters of any government, either accidental or inevitable - even of an allegedly criminal nature - will have no more than a marginal influence in changing entrenched political loyalties - barring exceptions and occasions of an extraordinary kind. This is because the Opposition, or the emerging threat of the Opposition, is always perceived as worse, despite all the confusion and economic disasters of existing circumstances. Hence any attempt to change the loyalty of born Conservatives or born Old Socialists - or even born Liberal Democrats - if often futile.

3 – How the young mind is prepared for this

In illustrating the irrationality of the majority, this may be more clearly perceived by taking the sphere of religion. In religious questions, people take myths and explanations of occurrences as statements of truth, to which a seven year old child would give no credence, but laugh at as nonsense. In this context, solemnity is given by adults to matters to which they themselves could not uphold the truth in their more rational moments, and in so doing, they not only deceive themselves and the world, but profane the name of the Supreme Being who can only be known through reason and truth. The only mitigating circumstances for this sad situation, is the explanation that those indulging in such practices and beliefs, in all probability do so to enjoy an aesthetic or other sensory experience, but in the self-delusion or hidden hypocrisy of this, they clearly give a lower value to formal religion than to politics and practical life.

In facing the immediately practical problems of everyday life, these same people do not resort to magical or metaphysical formulas but call upon the cool reason of their intelligence as with the majority of the population. None of these arguments, however, should be construed as casting a shadow on the ultimate truth or value of religious verities. The arguments are merely taken to illustrate certain habits of mind, which when transferred to the realm of politics or purely rational thinking, reflect the sluggish and foolish nature of the human intellect. This example of the religious intellect in motion is only given since the vast majority of our population are exposed to religious teaching early in life, and thereby and unwittingly, sloppy and uncritical modes of thinking about the world are instilled into the developing mind. If such myths and doctrines are taught and accepted in early life, how much more truthful and readily acceptable in later life must seem the fabrications and ingenious lies of politicians. If religious leaders glorify stories about fantastic events defying ordinary commonsense, and insist that these are factual truths, how much more truthful must seem the most deceitful and cynical of our politicians when they merely repeat lies about normal and comprehensible happenings. In this way the superstition of religion is used to undermine the critical ability of men and women, so incapacitating them to judge the everyday events of the world.

4 – Empty symbols have a stronger appeal than concrete truths

The immovable conservatism of the vast majority, and that inertia allowing it to give credence to things which they cannot possibly believe as sane or healthy-minded beings, reflects a sad situation on the possibility of effecting socio-economic change by appealing to reason. There is only one way out of this dilemma. If the power of reason is to be made triumphant in allowing practical measures to be achieved, then the conversion to new ideas can only be attained by substituting new notions and policies within the framework of the old organisations.

It may sound an absurd exaggeration, but there is a greater possibility to successfully convert the majority to new formulas and ideas, by simply exchanging the terms Conservatism and Socialism, than by an overt attempt to change the way in which people actually think. This is because of the overwhelming, or more correctly, the magical power, of labels as things in themselves. The empty and abstract terms "Conservatism" and "Socialism" through the power of historical memory have more meaning to the majority, because of their emotionally charged political connotations, than any more concrete truths based on reality. To the majority of Conservatives, anything described as "Conservative," irrespective of its correlation with Conservatism will tend to appeal. Likewise, the same may be said of Socialists with respect to anything attributed to Socialism. This situation pertains simply because the majority do not want to *think*; they only want to *feel*. As for that thinking minority, the floating voter, it is so volatile and forms so small a part of the electorate (although it has grown in number over the past decade) as to have minimal influence on the culture of politics - even though it may (and does) destroy and create governments through the election box.

5 – The future: True democracy or an elective dictatorship?

All this may seem to cast a dark shadow of pessimism on our political life whilst conveying the impression that political activity has always remained the preserve of a small minority. Of course it is true that in the past political power has always been wielded by minority elites, and in democracies, these elites have cleverly manipulated the people immediately prior to elections. In modern representative democracies people power has gone no further than the casting of a vote - a momentary event taking place once in every several years. But now it is increasingly felt that in a true democracy, and not in an elective dictatorship (as we have noted an eminent former Lord Chancellor has described the British constitution) the majority in the future should play a much greater positive role in our political life. The call for this greater positive role is reflected in demands for co-determination in industrial enterprises; in employee share ownership; in demands for greater openness in many spheres of public life; in greater accountability to public opinion by government departments, financial institutions and conglomerates; in the higher profile of consumer associations and similar bodies protecting specific groups and the environment; and in all those aspects of the Social Charter as endorsed by the EU but vigorously resisted by previous British administrations.

6 – Vacuum in the sphere of reforming politics

If on the one hand there has been an increasing retrenchment of political feeling amongst the majority, loyal to the polarised groupings, on the other hand, there is occurring a growing vacuum in the sphere of reforming or radical politics - but a vacuum which is hardly visible to those still supporting the old ideals. This phenomenon has been brought about by the intellectual bankruptcy of Old Socialism in its failure to build a satisfactory workable society. In the East bloc, where this phenomenon is being demonstrated on a significant *practical* level, the realisation that it is Communism itself (and not merely a variation thereof) which is bankrupt has possibly not yet fully hit the consciousness of either the authorities or the people. This is partly because of the way in which Communism has been interpreted. The metamorphosis-type methodology of dialectical materialism in explaining the strangely unfolding process of history, has been cleverly used by Marxist theorists to conveniently mask the essential bankruptcy of Socialism.

If present changes in Eastern Europe are to progress along their existing path, the emergent societies and the emergent political systems will certainly not be Old Socialist despite any labels which may be applied in describing the eventual outcome. As to whether the eventual rulers in the East bloc will eventually repudiate Socialism is still an open question. What is clear is that any system of society permitting and encouraging competition, free enterprise, market forces, and production for profit as opposed to use, cannot possibly be described as Socialist, since all these things fly in the face of those beliefs lying at the very core of old-style Socialism. What will - or may emerge, is something entirely new, for which new labels and a new political language would be needed - and hopefully, this will be Social Capitalism as we advocate and define it in this book and the three successive volumes which appear under the general title of *Social Capitalism in Theory and Practice.*

7 – This portends great dangers ahead

In the meantime, however, an invisible and dangerous vacuum is in progress - the erosion of an intellectual ozone layer in the world of reforming politics. This phenomenon is of overwhelming significance to the future of the peoples of our planet. It portends great dangers ahead. A vacuum, of course, means an emptiness - a nothingness - and the intellectual ozone layer currently protecting our political environment, simply entails those hopes and deeply held beliefs entrenched in the socio-economic tradition of our past. What happens if the foundations of those hopes and beliefs are swept aside, or simply evaporate like a Scottish mist in the warm sunshine? The outcome is too painful to contemplate, for in the words of that foolish old British king, "Nothing can come of nothing!" Pure emptiness is merely a vision of Hell. Hence it is in human nature that long after the realities of a situation have perished, every attempt will be made to perpetuate the myths and illusions which once served as the intellectual constructs of those earlier realities.

8 – How an ideological vacuum may compound political ills

Meanwhile, as this situation takes shape, all manner of anarchic, reactionary, eccentric, extremist, and other mischievous influences may occur. In the absence of a unifying philosophy, all kinds of unanticipated, irrational and crazy conflicts will arise, astounding the rational half of humankind and destroying the other. This, in turn, will throw back humanity into the arms of the apparent safety of the old too-well-tried but bankrupt ideals of the past. And because of the bankruptcy of those ideals and their sheer unworkability on the practical level, they will be upheld by false perceptions alone and by the ruthless expediency of clever elites exploiting the credulity of the masses. In this way evils will be compounded and political life further polarised.

Such a scenario is likely to commence with the self-confident and damning indictment by the extreme right of any kind of reforming politics on the apparently credible grounds of the worldwide bankruptcy of Old Socialism. If Old Socialism is really discredited and nothing has taken its place, then surely that must mean that capitalism is exonerated in its leading aspects. The ground will appear clear for untrammelled rentier capitalism of the crassest sort, since there is nothing to fill the vacuum of reforming or creative politics. The increasing complacency and arrogance of the right will be horrifying in its force against reason and humanity. This in turn will be met by a savage opposition of any and every kind: nationalist, racialist, nihilist, religious, class and economic, etc., etc. Already we have witnessed the ugly rise of Neo-Nazi groups in East Germany, Romania, Russia, and elsewhere in response to the moral and practical bankruptcy of Communism in those countries. The unfortunate, underprivileged, or simply rebellious, will grasp onto any straw which offers to change the existing order of society.

But there is another vacuum to be filled. Men and women search for ideological windmills to destroy. With the demise of the world Communist threat, there will naturally develop on a certain level of consciousness, a unifying spirit amongst the European peoples of East and West, but already there is emerging the spectre of a world conflict between the Caucasian and Islamic peoples. Such a conflict, of course, would not necessarily take on the overt characteristics of racial struggle, for racialism is morally unacceptable (or "politically incorrect") in the contemporary age, but it could well take on the characteristics of a struggle between Christianity and Islamic fundamentalism, and it would nonetheless also represent a struggle between different races and language groups. The prospects of this are no less dreadful than they are real. Whilst the Islamic peoples of the Russian Confederation are in a ferment for independence (witness Chechnya), young British Moslems are developing a new consciousness against the liberal values of the West. They feel rejected in their new homeland by the alien values of the Occident, and yearn for the greater comfort and certainties of their cultural past. Recently, a young Moslem predicted on a BBC programme that the next generation might see gas chambers filled with Islamic believers during the conflicts of the future.

What unexpected repercussions might all this have on the peoples of the northern hemisphere? Conservative and fundamentalist Christians of all churches and sects, throughout the Anglo-Saxon world will be hardened in their attitude as they retreat into the narrow mysticism of their faith, locking out any desire to understand rationally the underlying sociological circumstances of the situation. Suddenly, a spark will ignite a blaze - some outrage calling for police or military action. At that point, the Christian will drop his meek and merciful mask, and in the spirit of the Crusades, will take up his Bible to justify revenge, bloodshed and genocide - for there is no book which more effectively exhorts its followers to annihilate the chosen damned - whoever and wherever they may be. When that fateful day arrives, millions of respectable and pious middle-aged and elderly churchgoers, throughout Britain, America, and elsewhere, will pray together and smile in quiet self-satisfaction, as the sword is brought down for the terrible slaughter.

How can the prospect of such a dreadful scenario be avoided? Only by erecting the cause of reason as an ideal for the future, and by condemning as evil all feelings which nurture nebulous enthusiasm of a crypto-religious nature! It has to be understood that those who cultivate the pleasurable feelings of mystical self-fulfilment, can only do so by placing a block against the development of their rational and intellectual selves, and in so doing, they are cultivating a mortal sin. This is because they ditch the objectivity of sound judgement, and when they are asked to commit wicked acts on the grounds that these are justified by "The Book," they then carry them out without thought or conscience.[147]

Hence fanaticism amongst Moslems as well as amongst Christians must be soundly condemned, and furthermore, theology itself must move ahead in helping create a more tolerant and morally better world. The previous Bishop of Durham, Dr. David Jenkins, for example, was apparently moved in this desired direction, in attempting to sweep away the superstitions and harmful myths of the past. Social Capitalism must therefore place itself in the vanguard of the struggle to create a philosophically sounder base for all our beliefs in the future.

****

---

[147] See my book, *Deism and Social Ethics*, which discusses these questions in greater depth, and attempts to formulate an answer.

Select Bibliography
and quoted texts

The following bibliography, divided into sectors as listed below, is necessarily limited by space due to the breadth and subject matter of the book, and so consequently, is mainly concentrated on quoted sources:-

1 - Culture and Egalitarianism 2 - The Politics of Property 3 - Democracy: Real and Illusory 4 - The Road To Constructive Politics

1 - CULTURE AND EGALITARIANISM

Arnold, Matthew, *Culture and Anarchy*, Macmillan, 3rd ed., 1882.
Arnold, Matthew, *Literature and Dogma*, Macmillan, 1873.
Baida, Peter, *Poor Richard's Legacy: American Business Values From Benjamin Franklin To Donald Trump*, William Morrow & Co., NY, 1990.
Carlyle, Thomas, *Essaays: J.P.J. Richter*.
Emerson, R.W., *Essays, Second Series: Experience*, 1844.
Goethe, J.W., *Faust, erster Teil*, Reclam Verlag, Stuttgart, 1986.
Juvenal, D.J. & Persius, A.F., *Satires*, William Gifford, 1817, 2 Vols.
Powys, J.C., *The Meaning of Culture*.
Renan, Ernest, *The Antichrist*, Walter Scott Ltd. (1876).
Santayana, George, *The Life of Reason*, Vol. II, iii, 1906.

2 - THE POLITICS OF PROPERTY

Acton, Lord, *History of Freedom and Other Essays,* Macmillan, 1907.
Atkinson, A.N. & Harrison, A.J., *Distribution of Personal Wealth In Britain,* Cambridge UP, 1978.
Becker, Lawrence C., *Property Rights*, Routledge & Kegan Paul, 1977.
Bellini, James, *Rule Britannia*, Jonathan Cape, 1981.
Coffield, James, *A Popular History of Taxation,* Longmans, 1970.
Cutler, Horace, *The Cutler Files*, Weidenfeld & Nicolson, 1982.
Frazer, Sir James, *The Golden Bough*, Macmillan, 1936, 13 Vols.
Friedman, Milton & Rose, *Free To Choose*, Harcourt Brace Javanovich, NY, 1980.
Fromm, Erich, *Man For Himself*, Routlege & Kegan Paul, 1949.
Galloway, David, *The Public Prodigals*, Temple Smith, 1976.
Goyder, George, *The Future of Private Enterprise*, Blackwell, 1951.
Goyder, George, *The Just Enterprise*, André Deutsch, 1987.
Green, Daniel, *The Politics of Food*, Gordon Cremonese, 1975.
Halévy, Elie, *England In 1815*, E. Benn, 1949.
Hannah, Leslie, *The Rise of The Corporate Economy*, Methuen, 1976.
Harris, Ralph & Seldon, Arthur, *Overruled On Welfare*, Institute of Economic Affairs, 1979.
Harrison, Fred, *The Power In The Land*, Shepheard-Walwyn, 1983.
Hegel, G.W.F., *Philosophy of Right*, trans. By T.M. Knox, OUP, 1942.

Honoré, A.M., essay on "Ownhership" published in the, *Oxford Essay In Jurisprudence.*Hudson Report, *The UK In 1980*, Associated Business Programmes Ltd., 1974.

Hume, David, *Treatise On Human Nature,* Clarendon Press, Oxford.

Joad, C.E.M., *Decadence*, Faber & Faber, 1948.

Johnson, Paul, *The Recovery of Britain*, Blackwell, Oxford, 1980.

Landtman, Gunnar, *The Origins of The Social Classes,*Kegan Paul, Trench, Trubner, 1938.

Leckachman, Robert, *Economists At Bay*, McGraw Hill, NY, 1976.

Likert, Rensis, *The Human Organisation: Its Management and Value,* McGraw Hill, NY.

Lippmann, Walter, *A Preface To Morals*, Allen & Unwin, 1931.

Lippmann, Walter, *The Public Philosophy*, Hamish Hamilton, 1955.

McEwan, John, *Who Owns Scotland*, Edinburgh University Publications Board, Edinburgh,1977.

Meade, J.F., *Efficiency, Equality and The Ownership of Property*, 1964.

Meade, J.F., "The Restoration of Full Employment" in *The Rebirth of Britain*, ed. Wayland Kennet, Weidenfeld & Nicolson, 1982.

Moss, Robert, *The Collapse of Democracy*, Temple Smith, 1975.

Northfield Report, Cmnd. 7599, HMSO, 1979.

Peikhoff, Dr. Leonard, *The Ominous Parallels*, Mentor Books, 1982.

Perkin, H.J., *The Social Causes of The British Industrial Revolution*, 1968.

Rand, Ayn, *Capitalism: The Unknown Ideal*, Signet Books, NY, 1967.

Regional Trends - 18, 1983 ed., published by HMSO & Open University Educational Enterprises Ltd.

Revells, J., *Changes In The Social Distribution of Property In Britain In The 20th Century,* 1965.

Rouseau, J.J., *Discourse On Inequality*, Everyman's Library, 1935 ed.

Salzman, L.F., *English Life In The Middle Ages*, OUP, 1920.

Schumacher, E.F., *Small Is Beautiful*, Blond & Briggs, 1973.

Schumpeter, Joseph A., *Capitalism, Socialism and Democracy*, Allen & Unwin, 1943.

Weber, Max, *Economy and Society*, Bedminster Press, NY, 1968.

Wells, H.G., *Anticipations*, Chapman & Hall, 7th ed., 1902.

3 - DEMOCRACY: REAL AND ILLUSORY

Acton, Lord, *Lectures On Modern History*, Macmillan, 1906.

Aristotle, *Nicomachean Ethics*, Welldon's trans., Macmillan, 1892.

Avineri, Shlomo, *Hegel's Theory of The Modern State,* Cambridge UP, 1972.

Barker, Sir Ernest, *Political Thought In England 1848-1914*, OUP, 1915.

Bellini, James, *Rule Britannia,* Jonathan Cape, 1981.

Beloff, Nora, *Freedom Under Foot,* Temple Smith, 1976.

Crozicr, J.B., *Civilization and Progress*, Longmans, 1888.

Dicey, A.V., *Law and Public Opinion In England*, Macmillan, 1905.

Engels, Friedrich, *The Condition of The Working Class In England* in *Karl Marx and Frederick Engels On Britain,* Foreign Language Publishing House, Moscow, 1953.

Goldthorpe, John, *Social Mobility and Class Structure In Modern Britain,* OUP, 1980.

Hailsham, Lord, *The Dilemma of Democracy,* Collins, 1978.

Halévy, Elie, *Imperialism and The Rise of Labour,* E. Benn, 1951.

Halsey, Heath & Ridge, *Origins and Destinations,* Clarendon Press, OUP, 1980.

Hayek, F.A., *The Constitution of Liberty,* Routledge & Kegan Paul, 1960.

Hegel, G.W.F., *Philosophy of History,* with Preface by Charles Hegel & trans. by J. Sibree, The Colonial Press, NY, 1900.

Hegel, G.W.F., *Political Writings,* trans. By T.M. Knox, OUP, 1964.

Lecky, W.E.H., *History of European Morals,* Longmans Green & Co., 1869.

Leigh, David, *The Frontiers of Secrecy,* Function Books, 1980.

Maine, Sir Henry, *Popular Government,* John Murray, 5th ed., 1897.

Margach, James, *The Anatomy of Power,* W.H. Allen, 1979.

Mencken, H.L., *Treatise On Right and Wrong,* Kegan Paul, Trench, Trubner & Co., 1934.

Mill, J.S., *Autobiography,* ed. By Helen Taylor, 1873.

Morley, John, *Life of Cobden,* 1881.

Orwell, George, *The Lion and The Unicorn,* 1941.

Owen, Dr. David, *A Future That Will Work,* Penguin, 1984.

Paine, Tom, *The Rights of Man,* Pelican ed.

Perkin, H.J., *The Social Causes of The British Industrial Revolution,* 1968.

Plamenatz, John, *Man and Society,* Longmans, 2 Vols., 1963.

Rawls, John, *A Theory of Justice,* OUP, 1972.

Rodgers, William, *The Politics of Change,* Secker & Warburg, 1982.

Russell, Bertrand, *Principles of Social Reconstruction,* Allen & Unwin, 1916.

Sabine, George H., *A History of Political Theory,* Harrup, 1937.

Sampson, Anthony, *The New Anatomy of Britain,* Hodder & Stoughton, 1971.

Seabrook, Jeremy, *What Went Wrong,?* Victor Gollancz, 1978.

Sedgemore, Brian, *The Secret Constitution,* Hodder & Stoughton, 1980.

Tawney, R.H., *Religion and The Rise of Capitalism,* Pelican, 1938.

Taylor, Charles, *Hegel,* Cambridge UP, 1975.

Tocqueville, Alexis de, *Democracy In America,* Vintage Books, NY, 2 Vols., 1945.

Toynbee, Arnold, *A Study of History,* OUP, 12 Vols., 1954.

Wallas, Graham, *Our Social Heritage,* Allen & Unwin, 1921.

Westermarck, Edward, *The Origin and Development of the Moral Ideas,* Macmillan, 2nd ed., 2 Vols., 1912.

Wiener, Martin J., *English Culture and The Decline of The Industrial Spirit,* Cambridge UP, 1980.

Wordsworth, William, *The Prelude,* 1805.

4 - THE ROAD TO CONSTRUCTIVE POLITICS

Berlin, Isaiah, *Four Essays On Liberty*, OUP, 1969.

Confucius, *Analects*, Jothill's trans., Yokohama, 2 Vols., 1910.

Eucken, Rudolf, *Main Current of Modern Thought,* Fisher Unwin, 1912.

Fromm, Erich, *Man For Himself*, Routledge & Kegan Paul, 1949.

Hobhouse, L.T., *Morals In Evolution*, Henry Holt, NY, 1915 ed.

Huxley, Aldous, *Ends and Means*, Chatto & Windus, 1937.

Inge, Dean, *Lay Thoughts of A Dean,* Putnams, 1926.

James, William, *Selected Essays On Philosophy*, Everyman's Library, 1961 ed.

Joad, C.E.M., *The Book of Joad*, Faber & Faber, 1935.

Joad, C.E.M., *Decadence*, Faber & Faber, 1948.

Joad, C.E.M., *Guide To Modern Thought*, Faber & Faber, 1933.

Keary, C.F., *The Pursuit of Reason,* Cambridge UP, 1910.

Magee, Bryan, *Men of Ideas,* OUP, 1982.

Magee, Bryan, *Modern British Philosophy*, Secker & Warburg, 1971.Mannheim, Karl, *Essays On The Sociology of Culture*, Routledge &
      Kegan Paul, 1956.

Mill, J.S., *Letters*, ed. By Elliott.

Mises, Ludwig von, *Socialism*, Jonathan Cape, 1953 ed.

Mumford, Lewis, *The Condition of Man,* Secker & Warburg, 1944.

Mumford, Lewis, *The Conduct of Life,* Secker & Warburg, 1952.

Mumford, Lewis, *The Culture of Cities*, Secker & Warburg, 1944 ed.

Mure, G.R.R., *Idealist Epilogue*, OUP, 1978.

Novack, George, *Pragmatism Versus Marxism*, Pathfinder Press Inc., NY, 1972.

Richter, Melvin, *The Politics of Conscience,* Weidenfeld & Nicolson, 1964.

Russell, Bertrand, *The Analysis of Mind*, Allen & Unwin, 1921.

Russell, Bertrand, *The Prospects of Industrial Civilization*, Allen & Unwin, 1928.

Russell, Bertrand, *Sceptical Essays,* Allen & Unwin, 1928.

Schweizer, Albert, *Civilization and Ethics,* A. & C. Black, 1929 ed.

Schweizer, Albert, *The Decay and Restoration of Civilization*, A. & C. Black,
      1950 ed.

Sinclair, May, *A Defence of Idealism*, Macmillan, 1917.

Stace, W.T., *The Philosophy of Hegel*, Macmillan, NY, 1924.

Wallas, Graham, *The Great Society,* Macmillan, 1925.

***

Lightning Source UK Ltd.
Milton Keynes UK
UKOW030751080513

210356UK00002B/16/P